Lecture Notes in Computer Science

Commenced Publication in 1973
Founding and Former Series Editors:
Gerhard Goos, Juris Hartmanis, and Jan van Leeuwen

Pablo Cesar   Konstantinos Chorianopoulos
Jens F. Jensen (Eds.)

Interactive TV:
A Shared Experience

5th European Conference, EuroITV 2007
Amsterdam, The Netherlands, May 24-25, 2007
Proceedings

 Springer

Volume Editors

Pablo Cesar
CWI, SEN5
P.O. Box 94079, 1090 GB Amsterdam, The Netherlands
E-mail: p.s.cesar@cwi.nl

Konstantinos Chorianopoulos
Bauhaus University of Weimar
Coudray-Str. 11, 99423 Weimar, Germany
E-mail: k.chorianopoulos@archit.uni-weimar.de

Jens F. Jensen
Aalborg University
Niels Jernes Vej, 14, rum 4-225, 9220 Aalborg Ost, Denmark
E-mail: jensf@vrmedialab.dk

Library of Congress Control Number: 2007926258

CR Subject Classification (1998): H.5, H.4, H.3, I.3, I.7, J.5

LNCS Sublibrary: SL 3 – Information Systems and Application, incl. Internet/Web and HCI

ISSN   0302-9743
ISBN-10   3-540-72558-X Springer Berlin Heidelberg New York
ISBN-13   978-3-540-72558-9 Springer Berlin Heidelberg New York

Springer is a part of Springer Science+Business Media

springer.com

© Springer-Verlag Berlin Heidelberg 2007

Typesetting: Camera-ready by author, data conversion by Scientific Publishing Services, Chennai, India
Printed on acid-free paper   SPIN: 12064861   06/3180   5 4 3 2 1 0

Preface

The fifth edition of the European Conference on Interactive Television (EuroITV) was organized by CWI (Centrum Voor Wiskunde en Informatica), Amsterdam. Previously, EuroITV was organized by Athens University of Economics and Business (2006), Aalborg University (2005), and Brighton University (2004 and 2003). EuroITV07 was held in cooperation with the Association for Computing Machinery (ACM) and co-sponsored by the International Federation for Information Processing (IFIP).

The aim of the conference is to bring together researchers from different regions and diverse disciplines. This volume includes contributions from Europe, America, Asia, and Oceania, with researchers representing disciplines such as media studies, audiovisual design, multimedia, human – computer interaction, and management. This way, the conference tries to develop a common framework for this multi-disciplinary (usability, multimedia, narrative) and new field, interactive television. Because of the multi-disciplinary nature of the field, the conference was held in cooperation with the ACM Special Interest Group on Multimedia (ACM SIGMM), ACM Special Interest Group on Computer – Human Interaction (ACM SIGCHI), and ACM Special Interest Group on Hypertext, Hypermedia and Web (ACM SIGWEB).

Interactive television is a new field born from the digitalization of the transmission medium. This field is still in its infancy and, we hope, the EuroITV conference series will promote the field and helps to identify the scientific challenges, while presenting the current innovations from both industry and academia. This volume is divided into five sections: Social TV Systems, User Studies, The Future of TV, Social TV Evaluation, Personalization, and Mobile TV. The reader will find relevant and current research that deals with:

- Applications and systems: infrastructure and applications that provide an enhanced experience to television viewers.
- Usability evaluation: user-centered research regarding innovative applications.
- Social interactive television: since watching television is a shared experience, research is needed in order to accommodate new technologies for sharing interactive media at home
- Content personalization: the amount of digital content available for users is constantly increasing, hence research on content personalization is mandatory.
- Mobility: Hand-held devices already provide audio-visual support. What is the expected user interaction for such devices?

In addition to academia, industry played an important role in this conference. For this reason, this volume combines papers from academia and industry. Just to mention a few, Motorola, Microsoft, Philips, Nokia, Alcatel-Lucent, and BT presented their work during the conference. This way, innovative ideas from industry were combined with theoretical studies from academia, providing the reader a complete overview of the current state of the art in the field.

Special thanks are due to Aalborg University (on behalf of EuroITV organization) for investing so much time and effort in providing a reliable and easy-to-use submission system. This year, without such a system, it would have been impossible to handle the 80 submissions for the conference.

Out of the 80 submissions, 24 articles (30% acceptance rate) were selected for this volume. Each of the papers was reviewed by at least three members of the Program Committee. In addition to this volume, the interested reader can consult the adjunct proceedings of the conference, in which work in progess papers, workshops, demos, tutorials, and doctoral consortium papers can be found.

Organizing a conference requires help from many people. In Amsterdam, much of the work was done by CWI's various support departments. Special thanks go to Dick Broekhuis (Treasurer), Wilmy van Ojik and Susanne van Dam (Local Arrangements Chairs), Tobias Baanders (Designer), Jan Kok (Web Support), Aad van de Klauw, and Henk Roose

Finally, thanks are due to all members of the Program Committee and external reviewers for their efforts in reviewing the contributions. The remaining pieces of the conference program were made possible by the efforts of Lyn Pemberton (Work in Progress Session Chair), Mark Howell and Ben Gammon (Demonstrations Chairs), Brunhild Bushoff and Chengyuan Peng (Tutorials Chairs), Liliana Ardissono and Artur Lugmayr (Workshops Chairs), and Judith Masthoff (Doctoral Consortium Chair).

We would like to express our gratitude to all the institutions that sponsored this conference. Special thanks go for UITV.INFO for acting as the communications sponsor and EuroITV organization for their effort in providing the submission system. Special thanks are due to the European Research Consortium for Informatics and Mathematics (ERCIM), the Royal Netherlands Academy of Arts and Sciences (KNAW), the Centre for Mathematics and Computer Science (CWI), and the New AMbient MUltimedia research group (Tampere) for their financial support.

March 2007   Pablo Cesar
                                          Konstantinos Chorianopoulos
                                                       Jens F. Jensen

Organization

EuroITV 2007 was organized by CWI - Centrum voor Wiskunde en Informatica (the Centre for Mathematics and Computer Science) in Amsterdam, The Netherlands.

Organizing Committee

General Chair	Pablo Cesar (CWI, The Netherlands)
Conference Chair	Konstantinos Chorianopoulos(Bauhaus University of Weimar, Germany)
Program Chair	Jens F. Jensen (Aalborg University, Denmark)
Work in Progress Chair	Lyn Pemberton (Brighton University, UK)
Doctoral Consortium Chair	Judith Masthoff (University of Aberdeen, UK)
Tutorials Chairs	Brunhild Bushoff (Sagasnet, Germany)
	Chenyuang Peng (VTT, Finland)
Workshops Chairs	Liliana Ardissono (University of Turin, Italy)
	Artur Lugmayr (Tampere University of Technology, Finland)
Demonstrations Chairs	Mark Howell (BBC Future Media and Technology, UK)
	Ben Gammon (BBC Future Media and Technology, UK)
Treasurer	Dick G.C. Broekhuis (CWI, The Netherlands)
Local Arrangements	Wilmy van Ojik (CWI, The Netherlands)
	Susanne J. van Dam (CWI, The Netherlands)
Technical Support	Aad van Klauw (CWI, The Netherlands)
	Henk Roose (CWI, The Netherlands)
Graphic Design	R.T. Baanders (CWI, The Netherlands)
Web Support	Jan Kok (CWI, The Netherlands)

Program Committee

S. Agamanolis, Distance Lab, UK
L. Ardissono, University of Turin, Italy
L. Aroyo, Free University, The Netherlands
L. Barkhuus, University of Glasgow, UK
A. Berglund, Linköping University, Sweden
M. Bove, MIT Media Lab, USA
B. Bushoff, Sagasnet, Germany
P. Cesar, CWI, The Netherlands

K. Chorianopoulos, Bauhaus University of Weimar, Germany
N. Ducheneaut, Palo Alto Research Center (PARC), USA
L. Eronen, Helsinki University of Technology, Finland
D. Geerts, Katholieke Universiteit Leuven, Belgium
D. Goren-Bar, Haifa University, Israel
T. Hujanen, University of Tampere, Finland
J. F. Jensen, Aalborg University, Denmark
J. Henriksson, Nokia, Finland
M. Howell, BBC Future Media and Technology, UK
C. Klimmt, Hanover University of Music and Drama, Germany
H. Knoche, UCL, UK
N. Lee, ACM Computers in Entertainment, USA
G. Lekakos, Athens University of Economics and Business, Greece
J. Lilius, Åbo Akademi University, Finland
A. Lugmayr, Tampere University of Technology, Finland
J. Masthoff, University of Aberdeen, UK
M. Pagani, Bocconi University, Italy
J. Pazos, University of Vigo, Spain
L. Pemberton, Brighton University, UK
C. Peng, VTT, Finland
J.A. Pouwelse, Delft University of Technology, The Netherlands
R.P. Picard, Jönköping International Business School, Sweden
R. Puijk, Lillehammer University College, Norway
C. Quico, TV Cabo, Portugal
T. Rasmussen, Aalborg University, Denmark
M. Rauterberg, Technical University Eindhoven, The Netherlands
B. Shen, HP Labs, USA
L.F.G. Soares, PUC-RIO, Brazil
J. Stewart, University of Edinburgh, UK
G. Uchyigit, Imperial College London, UK
P. Vuorimaa, Helsinki University of Technology, Finland
J. Yagnik, Google Research, USA
Z. Yu, Nagoya University, Japan

External Reviewers

Regina Bernhaupt	Carlos Herrero	Mark Rice
Jerker Bjoerkqvist	Jan Kallenbach	Rogerio Rodrigues
Dick Bulterman	Janne Kempe	Mohsin Saleemi
Songqing Chen	Tibor Kunert	Carlos Salles Soares
Romualdo Costa	Martín López Nores	Mark Springett
Michael Darnell	Marcelo Moreno	Tommy Strandvall
Pawel Garbacki	Kristian Nybom	Marian F Ursu
Vibeke Hansen	Marianna Obrist	Ishan Vaishnavi
Gunnar Harboe	Marta Rey López	Duane Varan

Conference Sponsored by:

CWI, the Centre for Mathematics and Computer Science, The Netherlands
KNAW, Royal Netherlands Academy of Arts and Sciences, The Netherlands
ERCIM, the European Research Consortium for Informatics and Mathematics
NAMU, New AMbient MUltimedia research group, Tampere, Finland
EuroITV Organization (http://www.euroitv.org/)
UITV.INFO, Understanding Interactive Television (http://uitv.info)

Conference in Cooperation with:

ACM, Association for Computing Machinery
ACM SIGMM, ACM Special Interest Group on Multimedia
ACM SIGCHI, ACM Special Interest Group on Computer – Human Interaction
ACM SIGWEB, ACM Special Interest Group on Hypertext,
    Hypermedia and Web

Conference Co-sponsored by:

IFIP, International Federation for Information Processing

Table of Contents

Social TV Systems

Awareness and Conversational Context Sharing to Enrich TV Based
Communication   1
    Bart Hemmeryckx-Deleersnijder and Jeremy M. Thorne

An Architecture for Non-intrusive User Interfaces for Interactive Digital
Television   11
    Pablo Cesar, Dick C.A. Bulterman, Zeljko Obrenovic,
    Julien Ducret, and Samuel Cruz-Lara

Model-Driven Creation of Staged Participatory Multimedia Events on
TV   21
    Jan Van den Bergh, Bert Bruynooghe, Jan Moons, Steven Huypens,
    Koen Handekyn, and Karin Coninx

EPG-Board a Social Application for the OmegaBox Media Center   31
    Arianna Iatrino and Sonia Modeo

User Studies

Human-Centered Design of Interactive TV Games with SMS
Backchannel   37
    Malte Reßin and Christoph Haffner

Acceptable System Response Times for TV and DVR   47
    Michael J. Darnell

Exploring the Effects of Interactivity in Television Drama   57
    Stacey Hand and Duane Varan

Focusing on Elderly: An iTV Usability Evaluation Study with
Eye-Tracking   66
    Marianna Obrist, Regina Bernhaupt, Elke Beck, and
    Manfred Tscheligi

The Future of TV

Accessibility of Interactive Television for Users with Low Vision:
Learning from the Web   76
    Mark V. Springett and Richard N. Griffiths

Will Broadcasters Survive in the Online and Digital Domain?   86
    Andra Leurdijk

Conceiving ShapeShifting TV: A Computational Language for
Truly-Interactive TV 96
  Marian F. Ursu, Jonathan J. Cook, Vilmos Zsombori,
  Robert Zimmer, Ian Kegel, Doug Williams, Maureen Thomas,
  John Wyver, and Harald Mayer

User Interfaces Based on 3D Avatars for Interactive Television 107
  Alex Ugarte, Igor García, Amalia Ortiz, and David Oyarzun

Social TV Evaluation

Perceptions of Value: The Uses of Social Television 116
  Gunnar Harboe, Noel Massey, Crysta Metcalf, David Wheatley, and
  Guy Romano

Sociable TV: Exploring User-Led Interaction Design for Older Adults... 126
  Mark Rice and Norman Alm

Psychological Backgrounds for Inducing Cooperation in Peer-to-Peer
Television 136
  Jenneke Fokker, Huib de Ridder, Piet Westendorp, and
  Johan Pouwelse

Trends in the Living Room and Beyond 146
  Regina Bernhaupt, Marianna Obrist, Astrid Weiss, Elke Beck, and
  Manfred Tscheligi

Personalisation

SenSee Framework for Personalized Access to TV Content 156
  Lora Aroyo, Pieter Bellekens, Martin Bjorkman, Geert-Jan Houben,
  Paul Akkermans, and Annelies Kaptein

AIMED- A Personalized TV Recommendation System 166
  Shang H. Hsu, Ming-Hui Wen, Hsin-Chieh Lin,
  Chun-Chia Lee, and Chia-Hoang Lee

Fuzzy Clustering Based Ad Recommendation for TV Programs 175
  Sudha Velusamy, Lakshmi Gopal, Sridhar Varatharajan, and
  Shalabh Bhatnagar

Towards Content-Aware Coding: User Study 185
  Nele Van den Ende, Huub de Hesselle, and Lydia Meesters

Mobile TV

Personal TV: A Qualitative Study of Mobile TV Users 195
  Yanqing Cui, Jan Chipchase, and Younghee Jung

"I Just Want to See the News" – Interactivity in Mobile
Environments 205
    Anne-Katrin Hübel, Johannes Theilmann, and Ulrich Theilmann

Mobile TV in Everyday Life Contexts – Individual Entertainment or
Shared Experiences?... 215
    Virpi Oksman, Elina Noppari, Antti Tammela, Maarit Mäkinen,
    and Ville Ollikainen

Semantic Modelling Using TV-Anytime Genre Metadata 226
    Andrius Butkus and Michael Petersen

Author Index 235

Awareness and Conversational Context Sharing to Enrich TV Based Communication

Bart Hemmeryckx-Deleersnijder[1] and Jeremy M. Thorne[2]

[1] ReNA, Alcatel-Lucent, Antwerpen, Belgium
bart.hemmeryckx-deleersnijder@alcatel-lucent.be
[2] BT Group CTO, Adastral Park, Ipswich, UK
jeremy.thorne@bt.com

Abstract. This paper discusses domestic video calling over the TV and how such an experience might be enhanced through Awareness and Context Sharing. Video based Awareness will provide a sense of visually being together outside the call, such that users feel more connected and the perceived barrier to entry into the call is lowered. Rich Context Sharing within the call allows conversations to flow more freely as callers throw items from each others' lives onto the 'table' for discussion. We also discuss some mechanisms for transition between awareness and a context enriched call and structure the paper around a family scenario.

1 Introduction

The failure of video conferencing to become a mainstream application since its introduction 50 years ago, has been much documented [1][2]. However the ubiquity of cheap broadband, the maturity of video codecs and the availability of webcams has heralded a resurgence of use over the internet. Where financial cost is no longer an issue, video based conversation is an attractive proposition for some consumers. Broadband enabled set-top boxes and games consoles also permit the transition of video communication off the PC and onto the TV. In many instances, however the current manifestation of video chat applications are engineering solutions whose key aim is the transmission of moving images across a network, with little account of the human issues [3][4][5].

Of particular interest to this paper are the digital on/off nature of current call based metaphors and the narrow fixed view point that a video call provides. Firstly, when people share a physical space such as a home or open plan office, they have a continual sense of visual awareness of each other. This provides the impression of shared activity that helps foster connectedness [6]. In contrast, communication is completely shut off when a video call comes to an end.

The second issue concerns activity within the explicit foreground parts of the conversation. A video call typically provides one fixed, narrow viewpoint onto the other. The eye is unable to wander and any clutter that is visible just detracts [7] from the conversation, this is in marked contrast to face to face conversations, where items in the environment can stimulate and shape the conversation.

P. Cesar et al. (Eds.): EuroITV 2007, LNCS 4471, pp. 1–10, 2007.

We will discuss solutions to these two areas later. A challenge remains as to how to bridge these two endpoints. How might users transition seamlessly from a state of background visual awareness to active context sharing and foreground communication on the TV?

Rather than attempt to solve this issue for all potential users and situations, we concentrate on a single domestic scenario.

2   Scenario

Our scenario concerns a family situation where one member works away from home during the week; in this case the father, Gary who works in Brussels (NATO employee), Belgium during the week and then returns to his family in Ipswich, UK at weekends. He has a wife Sue and three children Bart 5, Jez 9 and Rebecca 11. In the home in Ipswich all four share close awareness of each other, but Gary only joins them briefly and quite tired for a short couple of days each week [1].

How can Gary keep in touch with his family? How can he maintain his relationship with his wife and participate properly as a parent. Bart, the youngest is starting school soon and life is changing rapidly for him, how can Gary keep up with all these changes and provide the support that Bart needs?

Normally Gary tries to phone home one or two evenings a week, but catching up with everyone is hard; Bart is often on his way to bed and finds it difficult both to relate to this voice on the phone and remember coherently what he's done that day. Sue laments the difficulties of keeping the rabble under control, the lack of a father figure and the need for a hug at the end of a long day.

3   Related Work and Background

3.1   Awareness

Traditionally it has been thought that the goal of electronic communication is to provide very rich media - sight, stereo, sound, touch. However, as Nardi [6] notes, the single bit of information on an instant messenger client, that a friend is online, is sufficient to provoke feelings of warmth and closeness.

From her study of the ability of existing electronic media to support relationships, Nardi goes further to posit three underlying dimensions to connectedness - affinity, commitment and attention. The first dimension, Affinity, is not so much concerned with explicit information exchange as the implicit background trickle of non verbal behaviour that occurs when people spend time together or engage in shared activities. It is here that the instant messenger example above falls, the status icon providing information that the friend is online at the same time. We can term this background exchange as Awareness.

---

[1] As a reference, of the 300 thousand employees in Brussels, 1400 work abroad. Regarding our scenario, 91 of those work in the UK [8].

It is worth noting briefly that awareness can also affect the other dimensions - users might perform deliberate actions (expressing commitment) so that the other gains good awareness of them, it may also indicate that now is a good time to contact the other (capturing attention).

There has been a relatively long history of the provision of awareness in research institutions. Xerox PARC's original 'Media Space' (1986) allowed the flexible connection of always on audio-video connections between offices and common spaces [9]. It was not unusual to find that users had connected the monitor in their office to one of the common spaces. As people walked across this space or doors banged, the office dweller became aware of the shared activity. Portholes (1997) [10] formalised this usage by creating an awareness only medium. A virtual common space was created as a grid of images. Each image represented a user and was taken at regular intervals from a webcam in the user's office.

More recently there has been a focus on awareness systems in the home. Designing for the home is different to the workplace, and awareness systems have been developed to specifically address the differences. For example privacy in the home is highly valued and to respect this need some home awareness systems have sought to use only abstract measures of presence [13][11][12]. Howard [14] provides a good overview of a range of recent systems, and draws a distinction between systems that enable contact and those that allow the exchange of content. Howard notes that some designers feel exchanging content can actually be limiting to our ability to affectively communicate. Dey [13] suggests that abstract measures of contact such as instant messenger status can be sufficient to support connectedness.

3.2   Conversational Context Sharing

Consider visiting the home of a friend. As they disappear into the kitchen to fetch you a coffee, your eye wanders round their living room. You take in the books they have left artfully scattered on the table, the new items in their CD rack and the pictures on the walls. The trust and vulnerability they have displayed by leaving you alone amongst their private possessions allows you to build a greater understanding of them, provides topics of conversation, and strengthens the relationship. As CD and photo collections become digital, it becomes possible to restore this activity of sharing context, in a virtual sense, within a video call.

Bente Evjemo et al. reported in their paper, 'Supporting the distributed family: The need for a conversational context.' [15]: that in grandparent to grandchildren conversations the face-to-face conversation was tied to the concurrent activity and that phones do not have this type of communication support. Through focus group research they offered their target group a solution where the context of the children and grandparents was shared through introduced screens. Their conclusion was that context sharing in addition to the phone call conversation was perceived appealing, where if context was highlights of activities (like videos and picture snapshots), the appeal was at its highest.

On context and or content sharing in a remote collaboration environments, there has been a significant body of research. Most, however, within the field of

Computer Supported Collaborative Work (CSCW). Within this field videoconferencing is increasingly used as the communication layer. But more important for our scenario is the use of the virtual table (and desktop) metaphor in both two and three dimensional collaborative work spaces (collaborative virtual environments) e.g.: cAR/PE!, a 3D teleconferencing application [16] and others.

3.3   Negotiation

In face to face situations a negotiation occurs in which it is possible for a party to decline or postpone the conversation without seeming rude, and without shifting all their attention away from their current task. Is it possible to replicate this functionality for video communications? If a caller believes making a call will cause the recipient discomfort, they may be reluctant to call at all.

Negotiation and acceptance of video calls is currently done very badly. A recent domestic TV based video calling trial required three remote controls to answer a call (one to pause the satellite TV, one to switch channels, and one to accept the call). In contrast, Instant Message conversations often begin with a short query (e.g. 'Hello?') allowing the recipient to see who is interested in communicating without committing them to reply.

Of note in early video communications systems that deliberately tried to introduce a negotiation is Montage [17]. This was developed at SunSoft where a researcher wishing to talk to someone would peer in the door to their office. Montage attempted to replicate this system of glances at the office door on the computer screen. Clicking the desktop icon of someone you wanted to talk to caused a two way video window to fade in on both screens. No audio channel was established at this point to protect privacy at the remote end. Both parties could glance at each other and if the recipient was happy to talk she clicked on a button and a persistent 2-way audio video call was started. If no click was made, the windows would fade out again after a few seconds.

With the development of sensors that can detect eye contact, Queens University Canada [18] developed a system of negotiation that more closely mimics the use of eye gaze in face to face situations. Because direct eye-contact cannot be established, eye contact is made with a physical proxy that looks like a pair of eyeballs. At the recipient's end, a second proxy attempts to engage the recipient in eye contact, which they can acknowledge or refuse with a quick glance. On acceptance an audio channel is established.

4   Solution for Our Scenario

Returning to our scenario, awareness then might provide a continual sense of being together and sharing context might help frame the conversations Gary has with his family, but what specific forms might these take and how will he transition between them?

After work, Gary has a few beers with his work colleagues (many of whom face a lengthy commute) at a local bar, and then returns to his small rented flat in central Brussels. As he flicks on the lights and throws his keys down on the table he glances at the photo frame on the shelf and smiles. Displayed on the frame, are captured moments from the day of his family back in Ipswich. The most recent shot is empty, but in the image from 1-2 hours ago he sees his wife Sue, struggling in with shopping and kids from school. He feels reassured that life is going on as normal, and remembers the near disasters on the few days that he has been responsible for the school run. Gary turns to the kitchen and begins to make himself some dinner.

Quarter of an hour later Sue glances at her photo frame, she sees Gary has returned and keeps looking. After a few seconds of prolonged gazing, the photo frame recognises the explicit action and displays an icon to indicate this. Meanwhile Gary's frame begins to flash and an alert sounds. Gary however is having a crisis with his cooking and the pasta is boiling over. He glances hurriedly at his frame, and then returns to the stove. His frame spots this glance, silences the alert, and displays an icon on Sue's frame to indicate the call was declined. Sue is not worried, she knows Gary will call back when he's free.

Young Bart though is less easily placated and doesn't fully comprehend the subtleties of polite communication. He takes his teddy and places it deliberately down on the coffee table in front of the TV. In Brussels Gary's cooking is now finished. While watching TV Gary is notified of an incoming call. Gary and Bart engage in an animated discussion. Bart's teddy is no ordinary bear. It is used to capture images and as a trigger for a conversation.

As Bart carries his teddy around during the day he used it to capture the things he is doing through images, knowing that if teddy saw them then his dad will too. With this in mind young Bart took snapshots of his giant castle, he constructed that day. And later that day he and mum captured some of his drawings. During the call Gary picks out some of these images and throws them one at a time onto the 'table'. With each one he asks Bart to describe what is happening and Bart happily recalls the story of his day.

Later in the evening, after Bart has been put to bed, Sue gazes at the frame again. This time Gary returns her gaze and a video call is setup over the TV automatically. Sue immediately tells about her latest encounter with an old schoolfriend and the good times they had together. Sue remembers an old school picture, quickly she throws it on the 'table' and they both have a laugh at the nostalgic dressing code of the eighties. As usual the parents end up talking about the kids, a hard job for both. Bart misses Johnny, his pet yellow bird that died two weeks ago. Gary recalls his talk with Bart, and the reoccurring birds in his drawings. As he rethrows on the table they both talk on how they can make the loss a bit easier for the whole family.

5   Discussion

5.1   Awareness Aspects

In contrast to previous awareness systems, in the intimate situation of a family, it could be argued that participants will be sufficiently trusting of each other to allow the use of captured images to present awareness. This might have the following advantages: first, users would not need to learn a new skill to interpret the awareness information as we are all familiar with natural imagery and looking at photos. Second, because the users are already visually aware of each other, it should be easier to transition into a full rate video call over the TV. A common situation in existing video calling systems is that an audio call is made first to establish whether visual communications would be appropriate. If the participants already have sight of each other this might not be necessary.

The obvious method to display this visual awareness for Gary and Sue in the home is as a photo frame. Photo frames are typically hung or stood on a surface so that they are visible from some distance at all times (See Figure 1).

Fig. 1. Visual Awareness prototype photo frame and (Inset) Visual Awareness display with history of images and self view

A single camera in the home cannot give a good indication that the occupant is or isn't in the house. This is because homes have several rooms and occupants move between them frequently. So in walking past a frame and glancing at it, the chances are that the current image will be empty. This creates a need for either several cameras around the house or some sense of history.

To avoid introducing too many devices our solution is to provide history. The display shows three images arranged in a comic like layout (See Figure 1). The main image is the current 'best' image [2] from the camera updated every 10 seconds. The two smaller images show the 'best' image of the scene in the last 10-20 minutes and in the last 1-2 hours ago. The simple fixed layout should allow quick learning of what each image represents. The chances are, that even if the current image is empty, there will have been someone passing the remote camera at some point in the in the earlier periods.

Bart's teddy forms our second awareness device. Bart will also be captured on the awareness frame, but as Bart is small, taking the teddy around with him allows his father to join in his unique viewpoint. The teddy is very tangible giving Bart some of the emotional connection of physical touch. Photos are only taken by the teddy when explicitly requested; this allows Sue to help Bart deliberately capture useful items such as the drawings that can form a structure in their later conversation.

---

[2] As chosen by the system - images with something large and moving score highly.

5.2   Conversational Context Sharing Aspects

As introduced, in our every day conversations our line of sight is never limited to the face of our counterpart. If we are in another living room for example our view does not rest, it can also wonder around. Video communication as deployed on the telephone and TV does not comply with this freeflow of conversation.

The introduction of cheap webcams enabled a lot of communication applications on the PC to use this feed to communicate. Inspired by this new trend, video feeds are increasingly being introduced on interactive television (iTV) platforms. [19] [20]

Another, well studied aspect is 'multitaksing', which is a trend where young people are able to do multiple things at the same time (surfing, IM, TV watching, newspaper reading), but without going too deep or being able to concentrate for too long [3].

Both trends and the thought that during a conversation our line of sight is seldom that of our counterparty brought us to a 'context enriched communication' application. An application where video communication is enriched with the possibility to share each-others context via explicit and implicit actions (user initiated and generated actions).

The application as such is an iTV application with a viewing/conversational client on TV/STB combination and an authoring part on PC. TV/STB implies that the conversational part of the application is completely controlled via a classical iTV remote control. In our case a user can handle the application by using the 'arrow' and 'ok' keys (menu browsing and confirmation button).

How then is context shared? In our scenario two types of context evidence are collected. In the first twist of the story, you have Bart who is collecting both pictures of the drawings he made for his dad and his giant castle he build that day. As these pictures are automatically uploaded to the context vault, our application can introduce this as context into the application. The same is true for the pictures taken by the photoframe of both Gary and Sue.

Now if Bart contacts his dad with the application Gary can browse through (via the photo menu, see Figure 2) Bart's drawings and throw them on the table. Bart on his side sees the same drawing. This mental image of throwing a drawing on the table is literally translated into the iTV application. As a consequence when Gary decides to (presses the OK button) select a certain drawing it is graphically thrown onto the table (a table represented in the application). Both Gary and Bart can now talk about their common context. This 'throwing on the table' is done via an explicit context action. The context enriched conversation tool not only shows a table which displays actual conversational context, it also has some additional contextual window. That offers both users, Bart and Gary in our case with some more context on the current context topic (one of Bart's drawings). This context is activated through an implicit context action, which

---

[3] Today's youth are efficient multi-taskers - cramming 8 hours of media exposure into only 6 hours. The amount of time kids spend media multi-tasking rose from 16 percent in 1999 to 26 percent today, with one in four young people saying they 'often' or 'sometimes' multi-task [21].

can come from the shared context meta-data (meta-data on Bart's drawing: when it was created, an annotation by mum Sue, an actual or recorded webcam feed of the kids playroom where the drawing was made, etc.).

Fig. 2. Rich Context Sharing

5.3   Transition and Negotiation Aspects

In the solution to our scenario two probes, Bart's teddy and the photoframe, are introduced that have a double role. Bart's teddy at first a collection tool for his daily activities. Secondly that same teddy senses Bart's activity with it, which is translated and communicated towards Gary (at Gary's those are again translated in a awareness device).

In daily life we are aware of each-other and multiple verbal and non verbal actions can engage our awareness towards an actual conversation. The former two discussed topics, awareness and conversational context enriched communication, have their assets in our scenario. But what of the transition from one to the other? In the case of Bart's awareness teddy, the captured evidence can be stored into a context vault. So when Bart engages with Gary in conversation, Gary can access Bart's evidence (e.g. Bart's drawings). Here a context transition is made.

In addition the Teddy is Bart's connection with his dad. This is a result of Bart, Gary and Sue tagging the bear with an extra layer of intelligence. In the world of Tangible Interfaces real life objects often represent people. In our case we see the use of RFID enabled sticker which can be attached a physical object, giving it extra meaning (functionality). In our scenario Bart and his parents could easily have decided to attach the sticker onto Barts favourite toy car. When Bart feels like talking to his dad he places the labeled object (his teddy or the toy car) on to the smart area where the presence of the teddy is translated in a call setup to his dad. Here the bear functions as a token representing the call setup to his dad. Similar scenarios are described within the Smarttouch project [22], where VTT describes a RFID enriched business card, when read by a NFC (Near Field Commmunication) enabled mobile a call setup is made to the cards owner.

Similar aspects are true for the second probe, the awareness photoframe. Here the frame shoots continuous or at regular intervals pictures. Those are analysed for aware specific activities, again these pictures can be imported into the context vault. And they are again used as context in the conversation Sue and Gary have. This way the probe is used as an awareness device, a context collector and conversation engager (via the eye contact sensor).

6   Future Work

To build (cyclicly develop towards) our solution, we plan to test aspects of it through home trials, focus groups and simple experiments.

Planning for a small home trial of visual awareness is in progress. Pairs of households from geographically separated families will be given a picture frame like device with a camera. The frame will display images captured by the device in the paired household. They will be interviewed at monthly intervals to determine their attitudes to the affective benefits and costs [23] of visual awareness and how these change with time.

To further test the father son communication, we will perform a friendly environment test by selecting various families, with father and son present. The test will be set up as follows: First the son (5 year old) will be asked to draw some stuff that he wants to tell his father of what he did the day(s) before. After this stage, mother and son will be invited to photograph these drawings. These pictures will be introduced into the system. Later, the communication session between father and son will be set up, where both the interface and concept will be tested.

7   Conclusions/Summary

We have presented some extensions that turn video calling on the TV into a rich, extended and free flowing image based conversation. By introducing awareness, conversations can become both foreground and background activities, helping families feel more connected. Through the introduction of context sharing, callers have the ability to give their conversations focus, structure and a reason to be visual. By suggesting mechanisms for transition between awareness and active conversation, we hope to make the negotiation of intimate conversation more natural and also allow awareness to influence the context available for sharing.

References

1. Lewis, A.V., Cosier, G.: Whither video ? - pictorial culture and telepresence. BT Technology Journal Vol 15, Issue 4, (1997).
2. Lipartito K.: Picturephone and the information age: The social meaning of failure. - Technology and Culture, (2003)
3. Reeves B., Nass C.: The Media Equation: How People Treat Computers, Television, and New Media Like Real People and Places. Cambridge Univ. Press, (1996)
4. Chatting D. J. and Thorne J. M.: Faces as Content. HCI and the Face - CHI2006 Workshop (April 2006)

5. Bekkering E., Shim J.P.: Trust in videoconferencing. Communications of the ACM Volume 49, Issue 7 (July 2006)
6. Nardi B. A.: Beyond Bandwidth: Dimensions of Connection in Interpersonal Communication. CSCW (2005)
7. Chatting D. J., Galpin J. S. and Donath J. S.: Presence and Portrayal: video for casual home dialogues , ACM Multimedia (2006)
8. Algemene socio-economische enqute (2001), FOD Economie, KMO, Middenstand en Energie - Algemene Directie Statistiek en Economische Informatie
9. Bly S., Harrison S., and Irwin S.: Media spaces: bringing people together in a video, audio, and computing environment, ACM '93, (1993)
10. Lee A., Girgensohn A., Schlueter K.: NYNEX Portholes: Initial User Reactions and Redesign Implications. ACM GROUP '97 (1997)
11. Brown S., Hine N., Sixsmith A. and Garner P.: Care in the community. BT Technology Journal, Vol 22 No 3, July (2004)
12. Vallejo G.: ListenIN: Ambient Auditory Awareness at Remote Places. MIT (2003)
13. Dey A. K., De Guzman E. S.:From Awareness to Connectedness: The Design and Deployment of Presence Displays CHI '06 (2006) 899-907
14. Howard S., Kjeldskov J., Skov M. B., Garnoes K. and Grunberger O.: Negotiating Presence in Absence: Contact, Content and Context, CHI '06, (2006)
15. Evjemo B., Gunnvald B., Svendsen, Rinde E.& Johnsen J.-A. K.: Supporting the distributed family: The need for a conversational context. NordiCHI '04, (2004)
16. cAR/PE! http://www.igroup.org/projects/carpe/
17. Tang J. C. and Rua M., Montage: Providing teleproximity for distributed groups, CHI '94, (1994)
18. Jabarin B., Wu J., Vertegaal R. and Grigorov L.: Establishing Remote Conversations Through Eye Contact With Physical Awareness Proxies CHI '03 (2003)
19. Philips showcases advanced home entertainment and communications solutions at IBC 2006,
    http://www.newscenter.philips.com/About/News/press/article-15508.html (2006)
20. Siemens SURPASS Home Entertainment Licences Espial Escape Browser For IPTV Set-Top Boxes,
    http://www.espial.com/index.php?action=news,press_release&view=223 (2006)
21. Roberts D. F, Foehr U. G.,Rideout V.: Generation M: Media in the Lives of 8-18 Year-olds, The Henry J. Kaiser Family Foundation, March (2005)
22. SmartTouch - Browsing Through Smart Objects Around You,
    http://www.vtt.fi/proj/smarttouch/index.jsp?lang=en (05/12/2006)
23. van Baren, J., IJsselsteijn, W.A., Markopoulos, P., Romero, N., de Ruyter, B.: Measuring Affective Benefits and Costs of Awareness Systems Supporting Intimate Social Networks. In: Nijholt, A. & Nishida, T. (eds.), Proc. Social Intelligence Design. CTIT Workshop Proceedings Series WP04-02, 13-19. (2004)

An Architecture for Non-intrusive User Interfaces for Interactive Digital Television

Pablo Cesar[1], Dick C.A. Bulterman[1], Zeljko Obrenovic[1], Julien Ducret[2], and Samuel Cruz-Lara[2]

[1] CWI: Centrum voor Wiskunde en Informatica
Kruislaan 413, 1098 SJ Amsterdam, The Netherlands
p.s.cesar@cwi.nl, dick.bulterman@cwi.nl, zeljko.obrenovic@cwi.nl
[2] LORIA / INRIA Lorraine
Campus Scientifique - BP 239, 54506 Vandoeuvre-lès-Nancy, France
Samuel.Cruz-Lara@loria.fr, Julien.Ducret@loria.fr

Abstract. This paper presents an architecture for non-intrusive user interfaces in the interactive digital TV domain. The architecture is based on two concepts. First, the deployment of non-monolithic rendering for content consumption, which allows micro-level personalization of content delivery by utilizing different rendering components (e.g., sending video to the TV screen and extra information to a handheld device). Second, the definition of actions descriptions for user interaction, so that high-level user interaction intentions can be partitioned across a personalized collection of control components (e.g., handheld device). This paper introduces an over-all architecture to support micro-personalization and describes an implementation scenario developed to validate the architecture.

1 Introduction

Watching television is usually a shared experience: a family (or group of friends) watch a shared output device (the screen) and interact with that device using a single shared control object (the remote control). A social protocol exists that determines the content displayed on the output device. This protocol is required because there is no differentiation between common content for the group and optional information that may be of interest to only a sub-set of the group. In this paper, we propose a model in which personal devices and sensory enhanced everyday objects can be used to render and interact with television content. We refer to this model as a non-intrusive user interface because the selection and interaction with personal content streams do not disturb the television experience of other viewers.

Our research considers the last stage of the media distribution chain, when the user is actually consuming and interacting with TV content. In order to limit the scope of this paper, we constrain our interest to the interactions with an active content stream that is stored on a local home media server such as a Personal Digital Recorder (PDR).

P. Cesar et al. (Eds.): EuroITV 2007, LNCS 4471, pp. 11–20, 2007.
© Springer-Verlag Berlin Heidelberg 2007

2   Related Work

The main motivation of our research is to provide a user, or group of users, with advanced control over the content they are viewing. We share the view presented by Baker [1] that current intrusive interfaces are not the solution. We feel that a value-added experience must rely on non-intrusive user interfaces for content selection, navigation, rendering, and interaction.

Much of the research on content selection within a digital television environment has focused on the macro-level concerns of selecting an entire program among a wide range of content available to a user. This is often done by some form of recommender system [2]. While we agree that recommender systems will play an important role in the future, they provide little or no assistance in navigating through content once it arrives in the home. To add personal value to the viewing experience, we feel that micro-level content personalization is also required.

Macro-level content selection is supported by the TV-Anytime Forum[1]. Interesting research in this area includes the UP-TV project. The UP-TV project [3] presents a program guide that can be controlled and managed (e.g., delete programs) from personal handheld devices. Our work also studies navigation using personal devices, but focuses on a finer level of granularity: how fragments within a program can be managed and personalized, and then controlled using a variety of light-weight end-user devices.

In order for micro-level personalization to be effective, a structured content model is useful. Several approaches to content structuring have been proposed world-wide: Digital Video Broadcasting - HyperText Markup Language (DVB-HTML)[2] (Europe); Advanced Common Application Platform - X (ACAP-X)[3] USA; and Broadcast Markup Language (BML)[4] (Japan). These solutions are based on a number of World Wide Web Consortium (W3C) technologies, such as eXtensible Markup Language (XML), Cascading Style Sheets (CSS) and the Document Object Model (DOM).

Unfortunately, they also rely on a non-declarative framework for modeling the temporal relationship between media elements in the document, such as ECMAScript or Java. Because declarative data is easily converted to other formats, is more likely to be device-independent and tends to live longer than programs [4]; we use a complete declarative solution, SMIL.

Regarding content rendering and interaction, Jensen [5] defines three basic types of interactive television: enhanced (e.g., teletext) personalized (e.g., pause/play content stream using a PDR), and complete interactive (i.e., return channel). In this paper, we extend Jensen's categorization with a new television paradigm: viewer-side content enrichment. In this paradigm, the viewer is transformed into an active agent, exercising more direct control over content

---

[1] http://www.tv-anytime.org
[2] http://www.mhp.org/
[3] http://www.atsc.org/
[4] http://www.arib.or.jp/english/index.html

consumption, creation and sharing. A key element of our paradigm is that the television viewer remains essentially a content consumer who participates in an ambient process of incremental content editing. Similar results, but intended to broadcasters, has been presented by Costa [6].

Finally, Chorianopoulos argues that traditional metaphors cannot be applied to digital television [7]. He proposes a metaphor called the Virtual Channel: dynamic synthesis of discrete video, graphics, and data control at the consumer's digital set-top box. In this paper we extend that notion by providing a system that can retrieve enriched content from external web services.

3 Contribution

The main contribution of this paper is a model and an architecture that support an enhanced experience of the user in comparition to traditional interactive television services such as the red button or SMS voting solutions. We can divide this contribution into three different categories: content modeling, content consumption, and user interaction.

First, we propose modeling the content using rich-description standards such as SMIL in combination with TV-Anytime metadata descriptions [8]. The major benefit of this approach is that the content can be enriched by different parties at different times. For example, content creators can include enriched material at the creation stage, while individuals might further enhance the content at viewing time. Moreover, at viewing time, content enrichment can be obtained from different freely available resources such as Wikipedia.

Second, we study the differences between the private and the shared space. For example, the television in the living room is a shared space between family members, while a handheld device is a private space. This paper proposes as an innovation the development of a non-monolithic multimedia player that is capable of rendering parts of content into different output devices depending on the share/private nature of the content.

Finally, we propose a model for user interaction that focuses on more abstract concepts of actions instead on particular interfaces [9,10]. We define three types of components: actions, handlers, and activators. The action is the description of the user intention (e.g., pause content or add media), the handler is the implementation of the action, and the activator is the user interface for the action (e.g., play button, speech recognition engine, or gesture). The activators can be implemented in a variety of ways (e.g., gestures, voice, or sensory enhanced everyday objects). The major benefit of this solution is that the user is not limited to the remote control interaction, but can use his personal device or even enhanced everyday objects to interact with the content.

4 Architecture

This section introduces our architecture for providing non-intrusive user interfaces in the home environment. Figure 1 shows the architecture of our system, that includes the following components:

- an intelligent and flexible middleware component, called AMICO
- a non-monolithic SMIL rendering component, the Ambulant Player
- the actions handler called Ambulant Annotator.

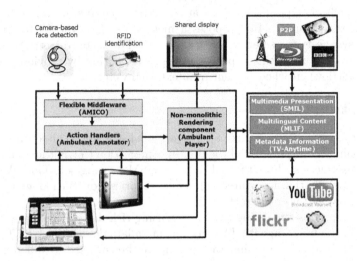

Fig. 1. System Software of the Proposed Architecture

4.1   Content Modeling

The television experience, we propose, uses an enriched description of the multimedia content that includes SMIL files linked to TV-Anytime metadata description and to Multi Lingual Information Framework (MLIF) [11] textual content. Our architecture is also open to external services such as BabelFish, Flickr, YouTube, and Wikipedia that might provide additional content. SMIL code is small, it is easily verifiable, it allows content associations to be defined, it provides a separation between logical and physical content, and it provides as base for license-free implementation on a wide range of platforms. MLIF provides a unified conceptual representation of multilingual content and its related segmentation (i.e. linguistic granularity). The advantage of MLIF is in its ability to deal with different hierarchies of textual segments: linguistic granularity (i.e. sentences, words, syllables), document structure (i.e. title, paragraph, section), or any other personalized textual segmentation which may allow, for example, to associate time and format to any specific segment.

4.2   The Brokering Infrastructure: AMICO

Supporting novel interaction modalities with TV requires usage of many heterogeneous software modules, such as sensors, reasoning tools, and web services. The desired functionality is often available in a form of open-source and free software, such as libraries for vision-based interaction modalities, lexical tools, and speech input and output for many languages. The main problem when using these components is that they are developed for other purposes, in diverse implementation environments, following standards and conventions often incompatible with multimedia and TV standards.

We have developed Adaptable Multi-Interface Communicator (AMICO)[5], an infrastructure that facilitates efficient reuse and integration of heterogeneous software components and services. The main contribution of AMICO is in enabling the syntactic and semantic interoperability between a variety of integration mechanisms used by heterogeneous components.

Our brokering infrastructure is based on the publish-subscribe design pattern. It is well suited for integration of loosely-coupled parties, often used in context-aware and collaborative computing. AMICO provides a unified view on different communication interfaces, based on a common space to interconnect them. It supports several widely used standard communication protocols. AMICO is extensible, and it is possible to add new communication interfaces.

4.3 Non-monolithic Rendering of Content and Actions Handlers: Ambulant

In previous work, we have described the first prototype implementations of the Ambulant Player [12] and Annotator [13]. The player is a multimedia rendering environment that supports SMIL 2.1, while the annotator is an extension of the player that is a bidirectional DOM-like interface to the player implemented in Python. Together, player and annotator, provides viewer-side enrichment of multimedia content functionality at viewing time.

In addition to those capabilities, this paper introduces two extensions to Ambulant:

- end-user actions handler: the Ambulant Annotator handles the user actions. These actions can come from personal activators (e.g., Nokia770) or from AMICO middleware. Some simple actions the annotator understands are *play/pause*; more complex actions include, for example, *provide me extra information in French about the movie I am watching now.*
- non-monolithic rendering: the Ambulant Player is responsible of targeting different parts of the presentation and content to different rendering devices. For example, the Ambulant Player can render extra information or commercials in my personal device.

4.4 Component Integration and Interfaces

In order to enable integration of components, our architecture support a variety of interfaces. Figure 2 shows the interfaces that the AMICO middleware uses in our studies. Through these interfaces, AMICO integrates a number of services that provide the following functionality:

---

[5] http://amico.sourceforge.net/

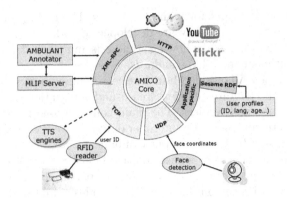

Fig. 2. AMICO Interfaces

- Non-intrusive activators: catches, handles, and interprets the input from non-intrusive activators (e.g., RFID reader).
- User Profile: retrieves and utilises the different user profiles encoded in Resource Description Framework (RDF) files.
- External Services: allows content integration from external services.
- Output Transformation: provides output transformation features.

Figure 3 shows the interfaces of the Ambulant Player and Annotator with the rest of the components of the architecture. It provides the following functionality

- Action Handling: the Ambulant Annotator handles user input coming from different activators.
- Content Retrieval: the Ambulant Player accesses different content resources, including broadcast, optical disk, P2P network, and local storage. The Ambulant Player can also request content from external services via AMICO.
- Non-monolithic Rendering: the Ambulant Player can divide and target the multimedia presentation to different rendering components. These components include the television set and other personal devices.

5 Implemented Example

In order to validate the ideas presented in this paper, this section presents an implemented example and an analysis of the benefits of our solution over traditional interactive digital television systems.

Non-Monolithic rendering: Dick (a US national) and his (Dutch) wife are watching TV. Dick uses a personal device (e.g., Nokia 770) as an extended remote control to navigate through media content based on his personal preferences, as shown in Figures 4(a) and 4(b). The personal devices can inform him when extra (personalized) fragments have been detected by the non-monolithic player. In both cases the content is rendered in the personal device and, thus, do not

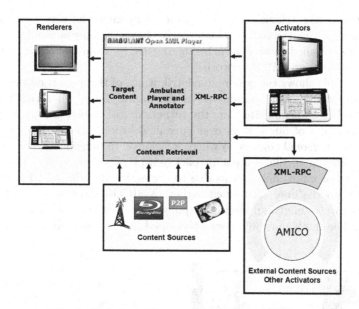

Fig. 3. Ambulant Player and Annotator Interfaces

disturb the television viewing experience of the rest of the family. The personal content might include, for example, instant translation of sentences he might not yet understand in Dutch, personalised commercials, or extra features extracted from web services.

Non-Intrusive input: We apply non-intrusive activators such as RFID readers and camera-based face detectors to assist in interaction with the television content. For example, the sensors detect the identity of Dick and his wife and their distance to the television set, and identify the language settings for subtitle language selection.

User Interaction Capabilities: our system provides as well a shared experience for connected people. For example, Figure 5(a) shows the content Dick

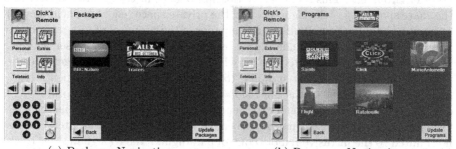

(a) Packages Navigation.   (b) Programs Navigation.

Fig. 4. Screenshots of Micro-Level Personalization in a Handheld Device

is watching on the television screen. At some moment, he uses the Ambulant Annotator to enrich the content. Figure 5(b) shows the interface in his handheld device. This enriched content is then shared with, for example, his brother living in the USA by using a P2P network.

This example shows the two main contributions of this paper: non-monolithic rendering of content and non-intrusive user input. Based on a rich television content model, we believe they are the cornerstone of valued group experiences. Clear advantages of our system over current solutions include the capacity of targeting the personal content to where it belongs: to personal devices; the possibility of linking media content in packages or experiences, and the support for a variety of input mechanisms due to the action descriptions. For example, in addition to the ones mentioned earlier, AMICO supports voice input and, even more interestingly, an intelligent pillow interface for controlling the media playback. The intelligent pillow was developed by the company V2_ [14].

(a) Content in the TV Screen.   (b) Enrichment Interface in a Handheld Device.

Fig. 5. Non-Intrusive Rendering

6   Conclusion and Future Work

This paper has presented an architecture for non-intrusive user interfaces in the home environment. This architecture takes into account the differences between the share space (e.g., television set) and the private space (e.g., handheld device) at home. The main contribution of this paper is the proposal of an architecture based on non-monolithic rendering of content and description of user actions. In the first case, the architecture provides the mechanisms to target specific parts of the digital content at home to different rendering components (e.g., high-definition content to the television set and personal material to handheld devices). This way, the personal experience of the user is enriched, while the television viewing experience is not disturbed. In the second case, user interaction is not limited to the intrusive remote control paradigm. Even though in some cases such interaction is desirable, we propose enriching the user potential impact on the content. Some examples include the use of personal devices for personal content interaction. In addition, other devices such as personal identifiers and a camera can register the identity and context of the user in a non-intrusive manner. Based on those variables, our system can derive actions on the multimedia content (e.g., to pause the show when there is nobody in front of the TV).

In addition to non-monolithic rendering of digital content and descriptions of the actions, this paper presents a solution for modeling interactive digital television content. The key question that this paper handles is how to model interactive television content in a rich and scalable manner. The solution provided is to use SMIL language linked to TV-Anytime metadata and to MLIF multilingual content. The major advantages of this solution is that the content can be annotated in a finer level of granularity, other resources can be included in the television packages, and further enrichments can be provided by professional and amateur users.

Finally, in order to validate the ideas presented in this paper we presented the implementation of an architecture and of a particular scenario. The implementation of the described examples required usage of diverse components, and consequently solving many software interoperability problems. Firstly, we had to support several integration interfaces. Components that we have used came from various (open-source) projects that use diverse integration interfaces, such as XML-RPC, OpenSound Control, HTTP, TCP, of which none is predominant. Adapting components to one common interface is not an easy task, and sometimes not possible, as components are developed in diverse implementation environments. Additional problem was that low-level components, such as sensors, and higher level components, such as web services, work with significantly different data structures and temporal constraints. For example, sensors, such as a face detector, can send dozens of UDP packages per second with simple data structures about detected events. Web services, on the other hand, use a more complex protocol (i.e., HTTP) and complex XML encoded data, with delay which is sometimes measured in seconds. To enable integration of components that work with significantly different data structures and temporal constraints, we had to abstract and map different data types and use temporal functions, such as frequency filtering.

Future work includes describing business models based on the ideas presented in this paper, and more importantly, carrying out a number of user studies for further validation. This studies will be performed in collaboration with other research laboratories with experience in usability.

Acknowledgements

This work was supported by the ITEA project Passepartout, by the NWO project BRICKS, and the IST-FP6 project SPICE. The development of Ambulant is supported by NLnet.

References

1. Baker, K.: Intrusive interactivity is not an ambient experience. IEEE Multimedia **13** (2006) 4–7
2. Blanco, Y., Pazos, J.J., Gil, A., Ramos, M., Fernández, A., Díaz, R.P., López, M., Barragáns, B.: AVATAR: an approach based on semantic reasoning to recommend personalized tv programs. In: Special interest tracks and posters of the 14th international conference on World Wide Web. (2005) 1078–1079 ISBN 1-59593-051-5.
3. Karanastasi, A., Kazasis, F.G., Christodoulakis, S.: A natural language model for managing TV-anytime information in mobile environments. Personal and Ubiquitous Computing **9** (2005) 262–272 ISSN 1617-4917.
4. Lie, H.W., Saarela, J.: Multipurpose web publishing using HTML, XML, and CSS. Commun. ACM **42**(10) (1999) 95–101
5. Jensen, J.F.: Interactive television: New genres, new format, new content. In: Second Australasian Conference on Interactive Entertainment. ACM International Conference Proceeding Series; Vol. 123, Sydney, Australia (2005) 89–96 ISBN 0-9751533-2-3.
6. Costa, R.M.R., Moreno, M.F., Rodrigues, R.F., Soares, L.F.G.: Live editing of hypermedia documents. In: Proceedings of the ACM Symposium on Document Engineering. (2006) 165–175
7. Chorianopoulos, K.: Virtual Television Channels: Conceptual Model, User Interface Design and Affective Usability Evaluation. PhD thesis, Athens University of Economic and Business (2004)
8. Cesar, P., Bulterman, D.C., Jansen, J.: Benefits of structured multimedia documents in iDTV: The end-user enrichment system. In: Proceedings of the ACM Symposium on Document Engineering. (2006) 176–178
9. Nichols, J., Myers, B., Higgins, M., Hughes, J., Harris, T., Rosenfeld, R., Pignol, M.: Generating remote control interfaces for complex appliances. In: Proceedings of the ACM Annual Symposium on User Interface Software and Technology. (2002) 161–170
10. Beaudoin-Lafon, M.: Designing interaction, not interfaces. In: Proceedings of the International Working Conference on Advanced Visual Interfaces. (2004) 15–22
11. ISO: Multi lingual information framework – multi lingual resource management. ISO/AWI 24616 (October 2006)
12. Bulterman, D.C., Jansen, J., Kleanthous, K., Blom, K., Benden, D.: Ambulant: A fast, multi-platform open source SMIL player. In: Proceedings of the 12th ACM International Conference on Multimedia, October 10-16, 2004, New York, NY, USA. (2004) 492–495 ISBN 1-58113-893-8.
13. Cesar, P., Bulterman, D.C., Jansen, J.: An architecture for end-user TV content enrichment. In: Proceedings of the European Interactive TV Conference. (2006) 39–47
14. Aroyo, L., Nack, F., Schiphorst, T., Schut, H., KauwATjoe, M.: Personalized ambient media experience: move.me case study. In: IUI '07: Proceedings of the 12th international conference on Intelligent user interfaces. (2007) 298–301

Model-Driven Creation of Staged Participatory Multimedia Events on TV

Jan Van den Bergh[1], Bert Bruynooghe[2], Jan Moons[2], Steven Huypens[1],
Koen Handekyn[2], and Karin Coninx[1]

[1] Hasselt University – transnationale Universiteit Limburg
Expertise Centre for Digital Media – Institute for BroadBand Technology
Wetenschapspark 2, 3590 Diepenbeek, Belgium
{jan.vandenbergh,steven.huypens,karin.coninx}@uhasselt.be
[2] Alcatel-Lucent
Copernicuslaan 50, 2018 Antwerp, Belgium
{bert.bruynooghe,jan.moons,koen.handekyn}@alcatel-lucent.be

Abstract. Broadcasted television shows are becoming more interactive. Some shows even let home viewers without professional equipment be part of a broadcasted television show. Staged Participatory Multimedia Events on TV take this approach another step further. In this type of television shows, viewers can not only participate in the show through interaction or videostreams, but also direct the show. In this paper we discuss this type of participation TV into more detail and discuss the models allowing quick and graphical creation of the structure of a format. The models can be serialized to a set of XML-files, which can be interpreted by the ParticipationTV runtime. Working proof-of-concept implementations for creating the models, generating the XML-files and the runtime that interprets the XML-files have been realized.

1 Introduction

The world of broadcast television is changing from analog to digital broadcasting and from a mostly passive towards a more interactive medium with increased viewer participation in the broadcasted shows. Many television shows also have related counterparts in other media such as websites offering additional capabilities.

Increasingly television streams are also transmitted over the Internet or traditional TV broadcasts are viewed on desktop computers, laptops or even mobile phones, offering new possibilities for interaction. Many of these devices are sold with cameras, built into the device or as accessories and have the possibility to send live video-streams over the Internet. At the same time the usage of set-top boxes, which have high-speed Internet access, built-in hard-disk and ample computing power increases.

Staged Participatory Multimedia Events on TV (SPMEs) will exploit these additional interaction and participation capabilities. SPMEs are events whose director and participants can all be television viewers. In this paper, we only discuss

P. Cesar et al. (Eds.): EuroITV 2007, LNCS 4471, pp. 21–30, 2007.
© Springer-Verlag Berlin Heidelberg 2007

the television-based viewers, although other devices such as PCs or smartphones will also be supported. Section 2 describes the structure and properties of such shows into more detail and introduces an example. Section 3 then discusses the ParticipationTV runtime infrastructure and the XML files used to configure the flow of the SPME. These XML files can be generated from graphical models. These models are discussed in section 4. The paper ends with a discussion of related work and the presentation of conclusions and future work.

2   Staged Participatory Multimedia Events

Staged Participatory Multimedia Events are broadcasted (for large audiences) or multicasted (for small communities) television events that actively engage TV viewers and turn them into true participants. They thus provide a stage for viewers to participate in interactive television applications that are not yet publicly or commercially available. The basic requirement for viewing a SPME is having a television. In order to participate, a viewer will have to have some means of communication with server such as a set-top box and appropriate remote control or a device that can send a SMS. For full participation, other devices such as webcams and microphones and a high-speed Internet connection will be necessary; live video and audio streams from selected participants of the show will be merged and integrated into the multimedia stream.

SPMEs belong to a *format* whose structure can be defined using the graphical modeling language discussed in section 4 or directly using the XML-language that is used as a blue print of the show (see section 3). Show participants can have different interaction capabilities based on their *role*. Some roles may have hardware requirements such as a webcam and microphone. Each format allows all participants to chat with one another.

A SPME is started when the first viewer activates a format. This first viewer will not only start the show but will also become its director, identified by the role *master*. All other viewers that join the active format will initially get the same role, *participant*. The show is driven by viewer interaction (and time-based events when desired). The format, however, determines the actions that can be performed by viewers based on their role and the actions that are already performed.

AuctionTV is an example of such a format. It is a format that allows one of the participants to offer an item for sale through an auction. The format is started by the auctioneer, who gets the role *master*. All other people that join the format afterwards, have the initial role *participant*. One of these participants can offer an item for sale and as such becomes the seller; the seller does no longer have the role *participant* but gets the role *seller* instead. Then the auctioneer initiates an interview with the seller, followed by the bidding process. Whenever a participant p bids, the auctioneer raises the price, confirming the bid. In doing so the role *winner* is added to the roles of p and removed from the previous bidder (if there was one). When an acceptable bid has been made and confirmed, the bidding process is ended by the auctioneer. The auctioneer finally does an interview with the winner of the highest bid. As long as no bid is made, the auction can

 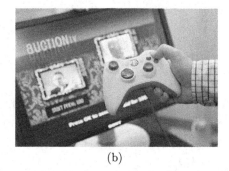

(a)   (b)

Fig. 1. AuctionTV application used with different interaction methods/devices (a) a TV remote control (b) a game controller

Fig. 2. Example structure of the screen contents of an SPME

be cancelled by the auctioneer, just as all other viewer actions, using a remote control (see Fig. 1).

The AuctionTV example illustrates some important properties of SPME:

1. SPME can be completely driven by viewer actions, although time-based events can be used.
2. Each person watching a SPME has one or more roles.
3. Fig. 2 illustrates that viewers with different roles can be part of the show through live video streams provided by webcams.
4. SPMEs have a script; the consequences of viewer actions have predefined (predictable) results.
5. In some situations, it is necessary that one action is to be performed before any other actions can take place. For example, when a bid is made the auctioneer has to accept it and raise the amount for the next bid.
6. Highly different interaction methods or devices can be used (see Fig. 1).

All SPME formats have a similar screen structure, which is illustrated in Fig. 2. The *background* consists of non-interactive content and is shared by all

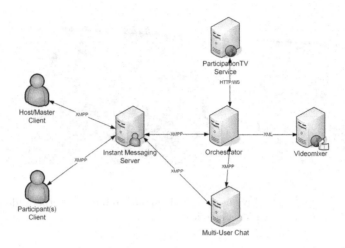

Fig. 3. Runtime infrastructure

viewers whatever their role is. All interactive content (including instructions) is shown in *interaction panels* or *popup dialogs*.

Each interaction panel allows the viewer to perform one task such as making a bid, setting the price of the item to be sold, start the interview with the winner (a transition to a new screen layout). The interaction panels are layered on top of each other in one designated area of the screen, the *interaction bar* (see Fig. 2). A *popup* allows its viewer to perform exactly one task, while temporarily disabling the performance of all other tasks (realizing property 5). A popup thus has behavior similar to that of a modal dialog box on a desktop computer.

3   The SPME Runtime Support

3.1   The Runtime Infrastructure

The ParticipationTV infrastructure (see Fig. 3) is build around an instant messaging (IM) server that is based on the eXtensible Messaging and Presence Protocol, short XMPP [4,5]. Although this is not a necessity it gives a lot of advantages. The protocol is based on XML, which means that it is easily extensible with ParticipationTVs own XML-based SPME language.

ParticipationTV clients or server-side components that need to send ParticipationTV specific messages to each other can simply do so by embedding them in an XMPP message and the IM server will make sure that they will arrive at the corresponding entity. Furthermore the presence part makes it easy to see which buddies are online and you can invite them to play a TV program that you made or host, although people can also join a ParticipationTV program if they know the format and host.

The actual core of ParticipationTV is the Orchestrator, a server-side XMPP component that plugs into the IM server. The Orchestrator has a variety of functions: keeping track of ParticipationTV format instances and sessions, making sure participants have the correct roles, handling workflow, sending the right interactive components to them and steering the videomixer.

When a user logs into ParticipationTV he will send an XMPP message to the Orchestrator component to ask for the available formats. The Orchestrator will make use of the ParticipationTV web service to retrieve the list of formats. After the user has selected a format and states that he wants to be the host, the Orchestrator will exercise the following steps: (1) Load the corresponding XML SPME files into its workflow engine. (2) Create the new session and informs the web service of the newly created session. (3) Attach the role *master* to this user. (4) Start an instance of the videomixer. (5) Create a room in the Multi-User chat component [2] of the IM server. (6) Send a message back to the user that everything is setup correctly and that he can join the Multi-User chat component. All participants of the same format instance will end up in the same Multi-User chat room.

All other users that subsequently log in will be able to join the format instance/session created by this first user. The workflow engine that is part of the Orchestrator will now start to process the XML SPME files and will act accordingly: (1) Steer the videomixer, which composes the correct video image for all users. (2) If there is interactivity, make sure the user with the correct role will receive it and can act upon it. (3) Go through the flow until the format has finished or stopped by the user who has the role *master*.

3.2   The Runtime SPME Description

The XML SPME description consists of two parts: the layout and the flow description. The layout consists of three major blocks: the *background* (which is the same for every user), the *interaction panels* that can be added to the interaction bar based on the actual roles of the user, and *popup* dialogs for modal dialogs to users, based on the roles. The description of the layout is based on MyXaml [1], an open source language and library to describe GUIs of Windows applications. This XML language, together with some custom controls for ParticipationTV, allows to position labels (**Label**), pictures (**PictureBox**), synchronized video (**Video**), presence (**Presence**: webcam, microphone input, avatar, ...) on the screen. Some of the XML for such controls is shown in Listing 1.1. Furthermore, some specific interactions were developed to allow interaction based on a standard set-top box remote control.

The flow description is a list of named *events* and the according event descriptions, which consist of a set of *commands* such as those shown in Listing 1.2. The first group of commands applies to runtime items known as *variables* and *roles*. Both variables and roles can be resolved to strings to be used in the layout files. Variables will typically be used for the dynamic behavior of the show as they support basic JScript [2] evaluation, while roles have to be considered as

---

[1] http://www.myxaml.org

[2] http://msdn.microsoft.com/library/default.asp?url=/library/en-us/jscript7/html/jsoriJScript.asp

Listing 1.1. SPME XML - control examples

```
<Label Location="75,400" Size="200,60" Text="Bid:_$RequestedBid$" />
<Presence Location="100,230" Size="160,_115" Source="#MASTER#"
    video="true" audio="true"/>
<PictureBox Location="0,_0" Size="720,_576">
 <Image>
  <Bitmap URL="http://participationtv/auctiontv/sellerinterview.png"/>
 </Image>
</PictureBox>
<Video Source="#MASTER#" Filename="ItemPresentation_SGI.avi"
    Location="400,150" Size="160,_115"/>
```

Listing 1.2. SPME XML - example commands

```
<AddToRole user="#INTERACTOR#" roleName="Seller" />
<RemoveFromRole user="#INTERACTOR#" roleName="PARTICIPANT" />
<SetVariable name="RequestedBid" value="100" />
<SetVariable name="RequestedBid" value="$RequestedBid$+100"/>

<SetBackground panelName="Intro" />
<AddInteraction user="#PARTICIPANT#" panelName="Sell"
    associatedEvent="BecomeSeller" />
<RemoveInteraction user="#MASTER#" panelName="Cancel" />
<ShowPopup user="#MASTER#" panelName="AckBid"
    associatedEvent="MasterAckBid"/>
```

dynamic groups of users, which are typically used for role dependent content and interactions (popup dialogs and interaction panels).

The second group of commands defines the layout of the screen of the different users: a new background can be assigned, interaction panels can be added and removed, and popup dialog can be displayed. Interaction panels and popup dialogs also have an associated event, which the user will spawn when he presses OK when the interaction panel or popup is active. These graphical items are designated by a panelName, which maps to a description in the corresponding layout files.

4   SpIeLan: Models for SPME

SpIeLan (*SPME interface language*) is a graphical modeling language created for the design of SPME. It consist of three models: the scenario, the scene stage and scene script. It is important to note that the names and the contents of these models have been slightly changed to better fit the updated requirements of the runtime infrastructure discussed in section 3 since earlier reports on SpIeLan [6,7]. The visual syntax has also been slightly updated, based upon an informal test with both programmers and non-programmers, people familiar with participation tv and people that were not familiar with it.

The first model describes the *scenario* of the SPME; it provides a high-level overview of what the show is about. Fig. 4 shows a part of the AuctionTV scenario. It shows all roles that are involved in the show in the header, including

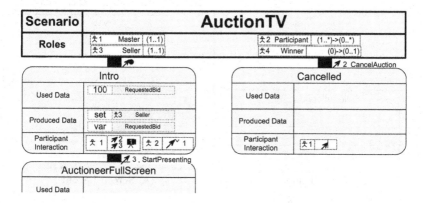

Fig. 4. Partial scenario of AuctionTV SPME

Icon	Semantics
⫞	Starts the SPME
⫞	Ends the SPME
⫞	Performs a simple action not defined by the other types
⫞	Selects a value from a predefined set (currently only strings)
⫞	Edits a value (currently only numbers)

Fig. 5. Types of user-generated events in a SPME

the maximum amount of viewers that can take this role initially (i.e. before the end of the first scene) and during the rest of the show. The rounded rectangles represent the *scenes*, a part of the show continuously showing a single *background*. The roles that are actively involved in a scene (providing live streaming of video or sound or able to interact) are represented in the rounded rectangle, as well as the data that is used or changed in a scene. Each of the scenes is activated by a user-generated event.

The different types of events that are currently supported by SPME are shown in Fig. 5. The symbols for these actions are taken from the Canonical Abstract Prototypes notation [1]. The semantics of these symbols is kept the same, although it is more restricted and more specific to SPME. Depending on the actions performed by the viewers, alternative sequences of scenes may be specified. E.g. in Fig. 4 action 2 and 3 trigger to alternative sequences of which the sequence triggered by action 2 is the "normal" sequence. Should this not be sufficient, control structures can be used. Discussion of the control structures is however out of the scope of this paper. The symbols for these actions are abstract because highly different remote controls could be used to interact with the SPME, even when only the TV is considered as a visual medium, as can be seen in Fig. 1.

The second model specifies the *scene stage*; the arrangement of the user interface controls on the television screen. The model consists of two required parts and two optional parts. The first required part is the scene header (see Fig. 6(a))

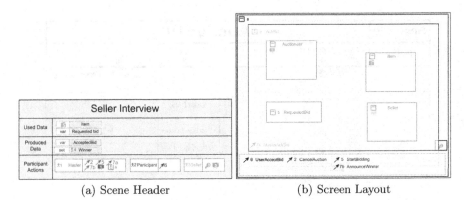

(a) Scene Header   (b) Screen Layout

Fig. 6. Scene stage specification

Icon	Semantics
	Passive user interface controls
▣	Displays media or text
▣	Displays media about a viewer
▣	Displays media about a group of viewers
	Interactive user interface controls
⏏	Allows selection of a value
⏏	Allows editing a value (currently only numbers)

Fig. 7. User interface controls for SPME

which contains the name of the scene, the roles actively involved in the scene, and the data used and produced during the scene.

The second part describes the screen layout. It completely specifies the *background* and specifies the regions where the *interaction bar* and the *popups* will be placed. Each part of the screen is identified by a rectangle with one or more icons and an explanatory text in it. The rectangle always contains an icon that identifies the purpose of the part (see Fig. 7) and optionally a source (such as recorded video, live video or live audio).

The location of the interaction bar is indicated by a dashed rectangle. All the contained interaction panels are represented by the corresponding events. A similar approach is taken for popups; only the area where the popup will be placed is indicated in the screen layout. The contents of both the interaction panels and the popups is shown seperately.

The third and last model specifies the scene script; it specifies which actions can be performed by the viewers in which order and what the consequences are. It has the same header as the scene stage (see Fig. 6(a)) but the rest of the model content differs. An example of this contents is shown in Fig. 8. It shows that in the scene *Seller Interview*, the *master* can initially see two interaction panels (with associated events 2 and 5). Event 2 cancels the auction and ends the scene while event 5 enables the *participants* to make a bid (event 6). When a bid is made,

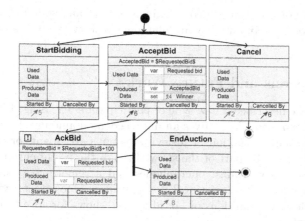

Fig. 8. Scene script corresponding to the header in Fig. 6(a)

the auction cannot longer be canceled. The *participant* that makes the bid gets the additional role *winner*. In addition to this, the value for *AcceptedBid* is set and a popup with associated event 7 is shown. When the *master* acknowledges the bid, RequestedBid is incremented. The auction can be ended (event 8) or a *participant* can make a new bid.

We have implemented a tool that can generate the SPME XML from the models. The information for the layout-related SMPE XML is (almost) entirely generated from the scene stage specifications, while the flow description is generated by combining the scenario and scene scripts.

5   Related Work

There is a body of work regarding participation TV besides the effort discussed in this paper. Some participation shows have already been broadcasted such as CultTV in France and Mattina in Italy. The latter uses the Mycast system from Digital Magics [3] to integrate live feedback from viewers from videophones and webcams into the daily morning show by Rai Uno, a national TV station in Italy [3].

OpenTV offers a tool and framework that allows creation of Participation TV [4] without coding. As far as the authors know the framework is focussed on enhancing existing television shows and formats with interactivity and extended statistics and does not allow the advanced viewer-driven shows which integrate live video-feeds as we presented in this paper.

TVML [5] has a different focus and allows to easily create 3D non-interactive TV shows using a simple scripting language. SoapShow [6] allows users to create

---

[3] http://www.digitalmagics.com
[4] http://www.opentvparticipate.com/
[5] http://www.nhk.or.jp/strl/tvml/
[6] http://www.soapshow.nl

their own soap online using video, still images, text and sound clips. Currently it is limited to the web, but they are planning to show the best soaps on Dutch television.

6   Conclusions and Future Work

In this paper we described a new type of participation TV: Staged Participatory Multimedia Events on TV. It gives an unprecedented amount of control to television viewers: they are no longer just viewers but participants or even the host of a show. They can be part of the show through the use of currently available technology such as webcams, microphones and a remote control.Examples of SPME formats can include existing TV shows adapted for greater viewer participation, AuctionTV, adaptions of board games, shows for specific communities or even a headbangers competition.

The runtime infrastructure is flexible and uses open specifications and protocols such as MyXaml and XMPP. The creation of a format can be done using the SPME XML or through graphical models, from which the SPME XML can be generated. The creation and evaluation (possibly in cooperation with a TV production company) of an end-user tool that allows to quickly and graphically model, generate and preview SPME is a major focus of current and future work.

Acknowledgements. This research was performed in the context of the IWT project Participate of Alcatel Bell. Part of the research at the Expertise Centre for Digital Media is funded by the ERDF (European Regional Development Fund), the Flemish Government and the Flemish Interdisciplinary institute for Broadband Technology (IBBT).

References

1. Larry L. Constantine. Canonical abstract prototypes for abstract visual and interaction design. In *Proceedings of DSV-IS 2003*, number 2844 in LNCS, pages 1 – 15, Funchal, Madeira Island, Portugal, June 11-13 2003. Springer.
2. Toon Coppens, Lieven Trappeniers, and Marc Godon. Amigotv : towards a social tv experience. In *Proceedings of EuroITV 2004*, 2004.
3. Monique Van Dusseldorp. Video-phone feeds getting into mainstream media. E-Media TidBits, http://www.poynter.org/column.asp?id=31\&aid=81683, 2005.
4. P. Saint-Andre. Extensible messaging and presence protocol (xmpp): Core. ftp://ftp.rfc-editor.org/in-notes/rfc3920.txt, 2004. ©The Internet Society.
5. P. Saint-Andre. Extensible messaging and presence protocol (xmpp): Instant messaging and presence. ftp://ftp.rfc-editor.org/in-notes/rfc3921.txt, 2004. ©The Internet Society.
6. Jan Van den Bergh, Steven Huypens, and Karin Coninx. Towards Model-Driven Development of Staged Participatory Multimedia Events. In *Proceedings of DSV-IS 2006*, LNCS, Dublin, Ireland, July 2006. Springer. To be published.
7. Jan Van den Bergh, Kris Luyten, and Karin Coninx. High-Level Modeling of Multi-User Interactive applications. In *Proceedings of TaMoDia 2006*, Diepenbeek, Belgium, October 2006. To be published.

EPG-Board a Social Application for the OmegaBox Media Center

Arianna Iatrino and Sonia Modeo

CSP – Innovazione nelle ICT
Via Livorno 60, 10144 Turin, Italy
{arianna.iatrino,sonia.modeo}@csp.it

Abstract. The goal of this research project is to investigate the use of technology in supporting social relationships to help users throughout the decisional process ("What program could I watch this evening?"). In order to do that, we are developing an innovative social EPG, called EPG-Board, that integrates a to-watch planner, a message board, a rating and a tagging system. We are testing these functionalities in OmegaBox, a Linux based media center.

Keywords: social media, media center, television, EPG.

1 Introduction

Home environment is a relevant issue in HCI (Human Computer Interaction) field since *"information and communication technologies have moved out of the office into the living room"* [1]. Home environment is changing because of digitalization of information, ubiquitous computing and media convergence. In particular, media convergence can be considered as the decoupling and re-modulation of functionalities, technology and content of different media types [7]. In the past, the core of home environment was the traditional television. Now, media convergence enhances the traditional TV with new functionalities and creates a novel form of hybrid media: the media center. A media center is a computer adapted for playing multimedia content stored on a local hard drive or in a network. They are often operated with a remote control, connected to a television set for video output. Interacting with this new media, users have access to a wide number of functionalities and content. For example, they can watch TV, play music and manage photos and videos using a single interface. So, the media center becomes the most important gateway from the home environment to the world. This unified content environment is based on: broadcast content, the Internet and the home network [5]. For the Internet the search is based on engines and directory services, while for locally stored digital content (music libraries, stored videos, documents, photos and so on) there is a PC-like file system interface. Instead, for broadcasting, the search is based on the Electronic Program Guide (EPG), a tool that helps people to easily find programs that match their interests. But, considering the increasing number of available channels and programs of analogical, satellite and digital terrestrial TV, traditional EPGs are not suited to support users in the decisional process ("What

P. Cesar et al. (Eds.): EuroITV 2007, LNCS 4471, pp. 31–36, 2007.

program could I watch this evening?"). In order to overcome the information overload caused by the growing number of programs, many research projects developed personalized EPGs (PPG) based on predictions or recommendations [12] [14]. But, considering that the decisional process is driven not only by personal preferences but also by social relationships, these PPGs are not adequate to support users. In fact, as ethnographic studies demonstrate, *"TV and other mass media, rarely mentioned as vital forces in the construction or maintenance of interpersonal relations, can now be seen to play central roles in the method which families and other social units employ to interact normatively"* [8]. In particular TV supports two kinds of sociability: direct (i.e. when you talk to your mother about a TV program while watching it) and indirect (i.e. when you talk to your colleagues about the program you saw the day before) [10].

Our goal is to investigate the use of technology in supporting social relationships to help users throughout the decisional process. In order to do that, we are developing an innovative social EPG, called EPG-Board, that integrates a message board, a rating and a tagging system. We are testing the EPG-Board in OmegaBox[1], a Linux based media center. The paper is organized as follows: in chapter 2 we describe the OmegaBox project, while in chapter 3 we present some related works. In chapter 4 we detail the idea of the EPG-Board and in chapter 5 we underline conclusion and future works.

2   The OmegaBox Project

OmegaBox is a Linux based media center that enables the convergence of entertainment and communication devices like Voice over IP and IPTV (Internet Television). It is an open environment for both entertainment and content management applications. Like other media centers [9] [18], OmegaBox provides access, use and management of services and multimedia content by integrating several functions such as Digital Terrestrial Television, Satellite Television, IPTV, PVR (Personal Video Recorder), Video, Audio and Image Management, Internet access, GPRS/UMTS connectivity and MHP (Multimedia Home Platform).

The OmegaBox project is very similar to the TiVo box[2]. As OmegaBox, TiVo offers a home entertainment experience, including *i*) an automatic recording of favorite shows; *ii*) a search engine to find and automatically record the shows that match user interests; *iii*) a network access to online services (such as weather forecast and movies' trailer). Moreover, the EPG-Board, described in this paper, adds to an advanced PVR some social features in order to support user in the decisional process. In particular, the EPG-Board collects four modules: the To-Watch Planner, the Message Board, the Program Rating and the Content Tagging (see Section 4).

---

[1] ΩBox is developed by CSP research centre (http://www.csp.it/en/view?set_language=en). The technical details of ΩBox are: Intel® Pentium IV 3GHz, 800 MHz FSB, ATI® Radeon Xpress 200 Chipset, 512MB DDR2, 250GB of Hard Disk capability, DVD-ROM DL Burner, Infrared Remote Control and Wireless keyboard/mouse.

[2] http://www.tivo.com

3 Related Works

The main goal of an EPG is to help users to easily find programs. It is an on-screen guide to schedule broadcast TV programs that allows a viewer to navigate and select content by time, title, channel, genre, etc. The information is typically displayed on a grid with the option to select more information on each program, such as program titles, synopsis, actors, directors, year of production, the channel name and so on. In order to better support users in the decisional process, many research projects developed the so called Personal Program Guides. The PPGs are adaptive EPGs according to user preferences and as a consequence, they improve traditional EPGs. But, as well as adaptive systems, PPGs have some problems, for example the well known cold start problem [13].

Since TV is a social experience and the decisional process is based on sociability, the research trend is the integration of social network in television context. An example of this trend is the **Mass Personalization** project [5]. It is a framework for combining television with a personalized web based experience. It puts together four applications: personalized content layers (that is an additional layer with information related to the TV program), *ad hoc* social communities (that is a chat for users who are watching the same TV program), real-time popularity ratings and virtual media library services (that is a video bookmarks). Like our project, the Mass Personalization offers a chat and a rating system but these services are web based. So user has to interact with a computer and not with a TV screen. We think that this way of interaction could be a problem because users have to split their attention between television and computer.

Even the **Tribler** project [16] describes a social network for TV. It presents a novel scheme – called BuddyCast – that builds a social network for a user by exchanging user interest profile. The profile information can either be based on ratings or on log-archives regarding zapping behavior. The ratings and loggin-information are used to suggest user personalized content. Instead, our EPG-Board uses user's behavior as a rating system to communicate user's preferences to her community. Our choice is due to assume an indirect sociability [10].

The importance of communication in TV context is also underlined by the project **AmigoTV** [4]. It enables a real voice communication over television. In particular, user can speak with her friends using an avatar. This project uses an innovative approach because it assumes the direct sociability [10] as we tried to do with our message board. We chose a text message board because this communication modality allows the messages to overstay on the screen even if the user is not in front of the TV.

Finally, an interesting idea comes from Tom Coates who spins out a vision of the future television that incorporates social software into the experience [3]. In his vision he describes the future social TV: a *buddy-list* to see what a friend is watching, a *presence alerts* to remind you that there are other people in your social circle watching TV at the same time as you, a *watch with your friends* - a webcam above the television to see how your friends is responding to what is on screen - and *chatting and planning* that allows you to chat about the programme you've just been watching.

4 The EPG-Board

In the following we describe the four modules of our EPG-Board.

To-Watch Planner
In order to describe this application, we start with a brief scenario.

It is Monday night, Jakob is watching TV and, during the advertising, he decides to have a look to the OmegaBox EPG. He notices that during the week there will be some programs he would like to watch (for example the football match of his favorite team) and so he selects them in order to fill in his personal program planner. The following night, while he is watching a TV quiz, an alert on the screen reminds Jakob that the football match is starting on channel 5. Because the football match is not so exciting, Jakob decides to chose another TV program but he is hesitant between two movies. In order to choose, Jakob refers to the shared OmegaBox EPG, showing the watching preference of his friends. He notices that "Saw" is the preferred one and so he starts to watch it.

The To-Watch Planner is composed of two main features: a remainder and an innovative shared EPG. The remainder works like a planner in which user takes a note about programs she would like to watch. Instead, the shared EPG shows the most interesting program for the user's buddy-list. In particular, the shared EPG changes the background saturation color of each program according to i) the number of friends that are watching the program and ii) the number of friends that took a note of it in their remainder. We decide to use the background saturation color as rating indicator being inspired by the e-learning project Knowledge Sea [2]. Knowledge Sea is a system that provides a social adaptive navigation support in a Open Corpus context. The system is called Knowledge Sea because the content was background colored using several shades of blue, similar to real ocean maps, deeper color saturation indicate that the information under the cell was deeper (more users selected that content). The idea at the base of this suggestion method is that people tend to follows the "footprint" of other people [17]. We done an heuristic evaluation with experts on the To-Watch Planner prototype interface. Moreover, we planned other usability evaluations with real users in order to understand if they comprehend the meaning of different background colors (saturation).

Message Board
The Message Board application allows user to communicate both in real time and in asynchronous way. In our system, users can assign a comment to each TV program. If a friend of Jakob posts a comment about the movie "Sliding Doors", Jakob can read it immediately or, for example, he can read it two months later, when the movie is broadcasted again. Moreover, users can resolve to visualize messages grouped by her buddy-list rather than by TV program or TV series. We know that it is not easy to enter text using a remote control [6] so users can interact with OmegaBox both using a remote control and a wireless keyboard.

Program Rating
The Program Rating application allows the user to say her opinion about a TV program ("I like it"/"I don't like it"). This explicit feedback the user gave is used by

the To-Watch Planner application in order to evaluate the popularity of each program and to determine the level of background saturation.

In order to simplify the user interface and the interaction, we decided to implement the rating system using just two rating options. In particular, we decided to dedicate two buttons of the remote control (the red and the green ones) to that function even if we are still studying new rating strategies.

Content Tagging

By the Content Tagging application user can semantically enrich the EPG. Consequently, users can search for a program browsing tags from the EPG or from a Tags Cloud. For example, you can imagine that Jakob wants to enrich the OmegaBox EPG by adding some tags to the "Saw" movie ("Thriller", "James Wan"). Agata, a friend of Jakob, is looking the OmegaBox EPG and she reads the tag added to the movie and, being a fan of thrillers, she decides to watch it.

5 Conclusions and Future Works

The goal of this research is to investigate the use of technology in supporting social relationships to help users throughout the decisional process. In order to do that, we are developing an innovative social EPG, called EPG-Board, that integrates a message board, a rating and a tagging system. As future work we plan to close the development of this ongoing project and to test the prototype in a real context of use with a real user group. Moreover, we are studying how to support the use of the EPG-Board by people of the same household.

Acknowledgment

We thank the CSP staff for their participation in the project and their support. A special thank to five anonymous reviewers for their fruitful suggestions and comments.

References

1. Blythe, M. A., Overbeeke, K., Monk, A. F., Wright, P. C.: Funology From Usability to Enjoyment. Dordrecht: Kluwer Academic Publishers (2004).
2. Brusilowsky, P., Chavan, G., Farzan, R.: Social Adaptive Navigation Support for Open Corpus Electronic Textbooks. Proceedings of the conference AH 2004 (2004) 24-33
3. Coates T.: PlasticBag.org - A weblog by Tom Coates at the URL: http://www.plasticbag.org/archives/2005/03/social_software_for_settop_boxes/
4. Coppens, T., Trappeniers, L., Godon, M. AmigoTV: towards a social TV experience. In J. Masthoff, R. Griffiths, L. Pemberton (Eds.), Proceedings from the Second European Conference on Interactive Television "Enhancing the experience", University of Brighton (2004).

5. Fink, M., Covell, M., Baluja, S.: Social- and Interactive-Television Applications Based on Real-Time Ambient-Audio Identification. Proceedings of the 4th Euro iTV conference, Athens, Greece (2006) 138-146
6. Iatrino, A., Modeo, S.: Text Editing in Digital Terrestrial Television: a comparison of three interfaces. EuroITV'06 Athens Greece, May (2006) 198-204
7. Lugmayr, A., Pohl, A., Muehhaeuser, M., Olimpiu, M., Kallenbach, J., Köbler, F., Niiranen S.: Ambient Media and Home Entertainment (Workshop Review). Proceedings of the 4th Euro iTV conference, Athens, Greece (2006) 477- 481
8. Lull, J.: Inside family viewing: Ethnographic research on television's audiences. London: Routledge (1990)
9. MediaPortal, at the URL: http://www.team-mediaportal.com/
10. Oehlberg, L., Ducheneaut, N., Thornton, J. D., Moore, R. J., Nickell, E.: Social TV: Designing for Distributed, Sociable Television Viewing. Proceedings of the 4th Euro iTV conference, Athens, Greece (2006) 251-259
11. Severin, W. J., Tankard, J. W. Jr.: Communcation Theories, 5 ed. University of Texas at
12. Smyth, B., Cotter, P.: A personalised TV listings service for the digital TV age. Knowledge-Based Systems, vol. 13 (2000) 53-59
13. Tang, T., McCalla, G.: Utilizing Artificial Learners to Help Overcome the Cold-Start Problem in a Pedagogically-Oriented Paper Recommendation System. Adaptive Hypermedia and Adaptive Web. Lecture Notes in Computer Science, Springer Berlin / Heidelberg, vol 3137/2004 (2004) 245-254
14. van Setten, M., Veenstra, M., Nijholt, A., van Dijk, B.: Prediction Strategies in a TV Recommender System: Framework and Experiments. Proceedings of IADIS WWW/Internet 2003, Faro, Portugal (2003) 203-210
15. van Setten: Designing Personalized Information Systems – A Personal Media Center. In: Personalisation in Future TV. User Modeling Sonthofen, Germany (2001)
16. Wang J, Pouwelse J, Fokker J, Reinders MJT: Personalization of a Peer-to-Peer Television System EuroITV Athens Greece, May (2006) 147-155
17. Wexelblat, A., Mayes, P.: Footprints: history-rich tools for information foraging. In: proc. of ACM Conference on Human Computer Interaction (CHI'99), Pittsburg, PA (1999) 270-277
18. Windows Media Center, at the URL: http://www.microsoft.com/windowsxp/mediacenter/default.mspx

Human-Centered Design of Interactive TV Games with SMS Backchannel

Malte Reßin and Christoph Haffner

Multimedia Campus Kiel
Boschstr. 5
24105 Kiel
malte.ressin@gmail.com, c.haffner@hci-research.de

Abstract. This paper determines key success factors for interactive TV games with SMS as a return channel. User requirements are determined by survey, a game application is developed and subjected to usability tests, examining the connection between game usability, gameplay concept and entertainment. Particular attention is paid to the leap between the two separate mass media by performing eye-tracking analysis of players.

Keywords: games, usability, eye-tracking, iTV, interactive Television, SMS backchannel.

1 Introduction

Computer games have made the jump from a niche product to a mass media phenomenon rivaling turnover, revenue and reach of both movie and music industry. In order to tap into new target groups, developers of software and hardware alike are aspiring to adapt to users previously deterred from electronic entertainment. Innovative game concepts based on group activity and social interaction are deployed to overcome the inhibition barrier. New input concepts based on intuitive control schemes like touchscreens or spatial motion are supposed to overcome the technological barrier.

Both tasks have already been achieved very well by mobile phones. Most users are not aware that they are actually handling a small computer and quickly adapt to handling their device in a very uncomplicated way [1].

Hence the idea of combining interactive TV games with mobile phones. The game is brought to potential players by TV, a well-known medium, and controlled by the mobile phone, an accustomed device. We will call such games iTV-SMS games.

This paper considers different aspects of the development, deployment and success measurement of iTV-SMS games. We look at the formative criteria that make up casual games in iTV and determine requirements, expectations and demands from potential users of iTV-SMS games. Based on the results, we design a game and conduct a usability study using eye tracking. We finish the paper by analysing our results, summing up our conclusions and giving an outlook on open questions and possible further research for the future.

P. Cesar et al. (Eds.): EuroITV 2007, LNCS 4471, pp. 37–46, 2007.
© Springer-Verlag Berlin Heidelberg 2007

2 ITV-SMS Games

ITV-SMS games are games in which mobile phones serve as input device for game moves issued by SMS, while TV sets serve as display device for the game states.

Essentially, iTV-SMS-games are pay-per-play games with SMS serving both as method for player input and billing. Pay-per-play itself is a challenging approach: players must be motivated to spend more money on another move, a concept similar to arcade games where players need to be motivated to spend more money on another game. Like episodic gaming, the price for both concepts falls well within the impulse buy range [2].

Due to their nature, iTV-SMS games belong to the casual games market. Casual games distinguish themselves by simplicity and forgiving gameplay. They are usually inexpensive to produce and often distributed by "try before you buy"-models. For an exhaustive treatment of casual games, see [3].

Possible concepts for iTV-SMS games must consider several requirements mostly caused by technical prerequisites:

1) possibility to describe a game move within an SMS
2) achievement rating, e.g. by counting points
3) information sharing between all players
4) possibility to issue game moves in any order at any arbitrary point in time
5) no limitation regarding amount of simultaneous players and moves
6) visible and encouraging result for any move
7) rule acquisition by observation
8) interface suited for low TV resolution
9) game theme tailored to target group
10) entertainment value for passive participants (viewers)

3 User-Centered Design

For iTV games, the same questions as for any iTV application apply: what are the specific wants that can be fulfilled by iTV-SMS games, what might potential users consider attractive and which interactivity makes a difference?

To allow for user-centered design for future iTV-SMS games, we designed a simple questionnaire with three main goals:

1) Have test persons evaluate screenshots of actual iTV-SMS games in order to get their feedback regarding appealing and unappealing layouts.
2) Learn about ideas, motivations and expectations of test persons unfamiliar with the technical restrictions of iTV-SMS games.
3) Gather opinions how test persons feel about playing iTV-SMS games.

The questionnaire consisted of 9 multiple-choice questions and 24 Likert scale questions and an additional 2 free text questions. Two multiple choice questions enabled the test person to specify an individual answer in case it felt none of the given answers applied. Completion time was approximated to be 15 to 20 minutes.

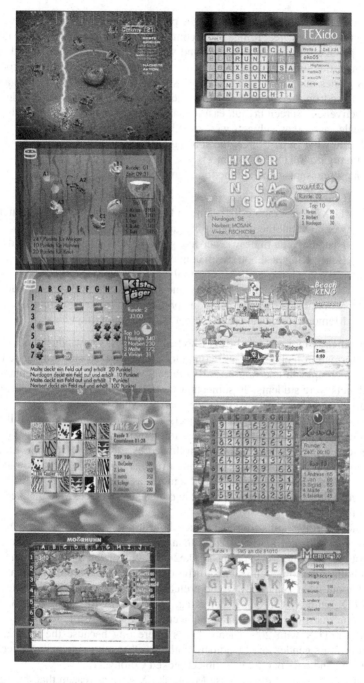

Fig. 1. Survey Screenshots: from top left: Colony 21, TEXido, fake screenshot, worTEX, Kistenjäger, Beach King, Take 2, Xu-Do-Qu, Moorhuhn X and Memorix

The questionnaire was divided into three parts. In part one, the subjects were asked about statistical data regarding age, computer/mobile phone usage and television/videogame consumption to understand what kind of entertainment and electronics consumer the subjects are. In part two, the subjects were briefly introduced to iTV-SMS games and shown ten screenshots: nine from actual iTV-SMS games and one fake. Based on the screenshot, the subjects were asked to evaluate rule conveyance, attractiveness, screen layout, easiness and entertainment value for each game on a Likert scale. After that, subjects were asked to choose the game they would prefer to play, and state why. In part three, the subjects were asked about motivations and inhibitions with regard to iTV-SMS games.

The nine screenshots depicted the following games (see Fig. 1):

1) Colony 21, a science fiction-themed shooter game
2) TEXido, a scrabble-like game to find words in a collection of letters
3) worTEX, another scrabble-like game to find words
4) Kistenjäger, a minesweeper-like game developed during this study
5) Beach King, a shooter with comic-style graphics
6) Take 2, a mind-game similar to the card-game Memory
7) Xu-Do-Qu, a number puzzle game much like the well-known Sudoku
8) Moorhuhn X, a shooter and the only game to use an existing IP
9) Memorix, identical to Take 2 but with different graphics

We specifically looked for subjects who had little to no knowledge about iTV-SMS games, information technology and computer games. Of 26 surveys handed out, 24 copies were completed and returned. 10 subjects were male, 14 were female. 62.5% of the subjects were students. 20 subjects were from Germany, 1 each was from Italy, India, Turkey and China. The average age was 29.3 years.

In the screenshot rating, female subjects rated Moorhuhn X best, followed by Memorix as second, Sudoku third, Beach King fourth and worTEX fifth. Women disliked the screenshot of Colony 21 most, followed by the fake screenshot. The screenshot of Moorhuhn X received also the highest ratings from male subjects, followed by Sudoku as second, Beach King as third, Memorix as fourth and TEXido as fifth. Colony 21 received the same rating as Take2 and made sixth place. Men disliked the fake screenshot most, followed by worTEX.

Other noteworthy results from the screenshot ratings were that games with abstract gameplay generally got a worse rating than non-abstract games. The fake made-up screenshot received the worst ratings. Take2 got rated distinctly worse than Memorix although both games are identical and differ only in graphical representation.

Asked about what game they would prefer to play, 35,7% of female subjects chose Moorhuhn X, with Xu-Do-Qu, Beach King, and worTEX following with 8,3% each. On the same question, 40% of male subjects chose Colony 21, followed by Beach King and worTEX with 20% each. This is interesting because the most appealing screenshot of one gender fared mediocre with the other: only one male subject picked Moorhuhn X, and only one female subject picked Colony 21.

80% of female subjects who chose Moorhuhn X gave as reason that they knew the Moorhuhn-franchise already, suggesting that franchise recognition might play an important role in the success of iTV-SMS games. 75% of male subjects who chose Colony 21 stated that they were attracted by the technological science fiction theme.

When comparing this with the screenshot ratings, it is striking that the choice of female subjects matches closely with the screenshot ratings, while it doesn't for male subjects. This might be a hint that assumed difficulty and entertainment, layout and game concept recognition play an important role for women when they decide about game appeal. For men, the setting or graphic theme appears to play a major role.

Regarding motivation to play iTV-SMS games, achievement was rated lowest and entertainment highest. Female subjects rated diversion as strongest incentive to play, for male subjects it was brain training. Regarding reasons not to play iTV-SMS games, both genders stated the cost of SMS as primary concern (at the time this questionnaire, SMS in Germany cost around 20 cents depending on the provider), followed by the statement that such games are uncommunicative. Women were not concerned about iTV-SMS games being unchallenging, playing games in public or being second in making a specific move. Men were undecided about such games being challenging and on average did worry a bit about being slower at others when making a move.

Women were rather interested in single player versions of the games, in storyline and had a slight interest for achievement display on the internet, prizes, tournaments and team functionality. Men, on the other hand, strongly liked the idea of achievement display, storyline and team functionality, some interest for prizes and tournaments and slight interest for a chat function. Accompanyment by a real-life moderator was not of interest for any gender.

Due to the small number of subjects, the results must be considered carefully. The survey results suggest different preconceptions and preferences by men and women. Further, the results of the survey suggest that it is not just the game concept, but also the representation which influences the appeal of a game to a viewer.

4 Creating an iTV-SMS Game

The game idea for "Kistenjäger" evolved from the well-known game "Minesweeper" which has been supplied with every copy of the operating system Microsoft Windows since Windows 3.1 in 1992.

To adapt Minesweeper to the requirements of iTV-SMS games, a minor modification to the original game concept was made: Mines are replaced with treasures, which are not to be avoided, but to be found. Task of the game is no longer for a single player to uncover all untrapped squares, but for multiple players to collect as many points as possible, where different amounts of points are awarded depending on how many treasures are adjacent to the uncovered square. A maximum of points is gained by uncovering a treasure square.

The layout was designed according to predefined provider specifications: the game area uses most of the screen, an information bar at the bottom informs players about in-game events, a vertical bar on the right shows a preliminary high score and remaining game time both as text counter and clock-like icon.

After a pen-and-paper prototype testing of the game concept led to minor modifications of the concept, the game was implemented with a treasure island-theme. Treasures are represented by a half-opened chest. The numbers indicating the amount of adjacent treasure squares are represented by an according amount of coins: one coin would represent one adjacent treasure, two coins would represent two adjacent treasures and so on. The game obtained the title "Kistenjäger" (german for "chest hunter"). The playing field is a rectangular matrix of equal-sized squares. Rows and columns are labeled with letters and numbers, thus each square can be designated by a 2-tuple consisting of letter and number. An uncovered treasure square is worth 100 points, any other square is worth 10 points for each adjacent square containing a treasure. Exception is when there are no treasure squares adjacent, in which case 1 point is awarded. When a player uncovers a field with no adjacent treasure squares, all of the not yet uncovered eight surrounding squares are uncovered as well. No points are awarded for the uncovering of those surrounding squares. A game ends when all treasures have been uncovered.

We considered a Minesweeper-like game a good choice for implementation because it is comparatively simple to implement and, due to the product bundling mentioned above, likely one of the most widely-known game concepts.

5 Usability Testing

Usability of a software application is very closely connected to the task the software is supposed to serve. A central part of usability measurement is finding out what exactly usability means in a respective situation [5]. Since a game is supposed to entertain the player, effectiveness and efficiency are difficult to measure and might be inapplicable indicators for its usability. Whether a task presented within the scope of the game can be effectively or efficiently executed must depend on the player's abilities. The measures available within a game might intentionally be ineffective and inefficient to increase the challenge for certain tasks and thus entertainment value.

Obviously, there are many ways how games differ from work applications. For an exhaustive list, see Pagulayan et al. [4]. Games and work applications share a design principle, though: inconsistent user interfaces as well as confusing layouts are detrimental to both. But since usability of a game is closely connected to its entertainment value, improving game usability must not end in removing fun and entertainment.

The question what makes fun in games is still unresolved. An exhaustive answer would go far beyond the scale of this paper. According to Klimmt [9], the three core mechanisms identified by research are self-efficacy, suspense cycles and role model identification. Not all of these mechanisms have to be present in a game at all times. For example, role model identification can be applied better to narrative or immersive games, while casual games profit most from suspense cycles.

The usability testing was conducted at the MMC in Kiel. Test setup and procedure were shaped according to "discount" usability evaluations using a small number of subjects (Kjeldskov et al. [11]). The usability test and eye tracking experiment was conducted with 3 men and 2 women. 4 of them were students, 4 of them had previously taken part in the questionnaire. The average age was 27.2. None of them had played games based on SMS before. All of them knew the game Minesweeper, but just one of them considered itself proficient at it.

The subjects were sitting in front of a laptop with a 15.1 inch TFT-display with 1400 x 1024 pixels, running at an extrapolated resolution of 768 x 576. Since the game ran in PAL resolution, a horizontal strip at the right side of the display remained white. A Nokia N-Gage QD mobile phone was supplied to the subjects for game control by SMS. The experiment controller was sitting to their left controlling the eye tracking device.

The procedure was as follows: First, the subjects were introduced to the experiment and the game. Then, the subjects were asked to familiarize themselves with the mobile phone, the game, the rules and the command syntax. A five-point calibration was conducted for the eye tracking system and the subjects were then asked to play at least one round of Kistenjäger, lasting four minutes. If they wished to, they were allowed to continue playing for as many rounds as they wanted.

After they finished, the subjects were asked to rate the hedonic aspects of the game according to a semantic differential (after Hassenzahl et al. [10]). Following that, the usability interview was conducted. While the subjects could relate their experience of playing the game, the experiment controller worked off a set of questions.

For identification during the game, the subjects were designated the screen name "DoraMMC". The SMS format for sending commands was "ki (column) (row)". Along with the players, seven computer players with different screen names would make moves, revealing yet unrevealed fields at random.

On average, each subject played for 2 rounds and sent 2,1 SMS per round. The subjects did not pay for their moves and were encouraged not to worry about cost. Despite that, four of five subjects were visibly reluctant to send game moves at random, suggesting a subconscious concern about SMS cost. It does resemble real-life behavior.

The eye tracking worked well. Unfortunately, it didn't give exact information when the subjects were writing and sending SMS. During the examination, it showed that subject behavior differed in this regard: one would look back on the screen immediately after sending a command, another would wait for the mobile phone to announce successful sending of the SMS. One subject sent several SMS without looking at the screen in between.

Differences could be observed in the eye movements: the proficient subject's movements were much faster, the eyes remained a much shorter time on the same spot. Also, eye fixations went much straighter to the revealed squares with the most amount of coins, that is the most adjacent treasures. In contrast, two of the other subjects were mainly looking at unrevealed squares, which indicates that they were not trying so much to gain information from the revealed squares.

Another major difference was that after sending an SMS, the unproficient subjects were mostly focusing on the square they intended to reveal, waiting for the revealing animation. The proficient subject did not wait for this, but usually concentrated on the revealing animations of the computer players or the unrevealed fields.

It was not measured how long it took from sending an SMS until a reaction on the screen occurred. Test runs and the experience relayed by the subjects show that reaction time is mostly between one and three seconds. However, singular delays of 15 seconds and more were observed. As long as a reaction occurred eventually, the subjects generally did not mind the delay. When an SMS failed to produce a result, the users assumed a technical problem and never considered an input mistake. Apparently, users expect the system to be forgiving in this regard, and also to message both syntactic and semantic errors. Each subject made at least one formatting mistake preventing game move procession.

Fig. 2. Sample eye tracks for an unproficient (left) and a proficient player (right)

In the semantic differential, the game received a bad rating: it was considered second rate, nondescript, dull and boring and judged as unexciting, difficult to play and uninspiring. Only one subject, the one who considered itself proficient with Minesweeper, actually stated to have enjoyed the game.

All subjects commented that it was not apparent to them at what time the game actually started and when they could start making moves. Although none of the seven computer players ever made a move until 25 seconds into the game and the game start is clearly designated by a text "new round" floating over the screen, no subject made a move before a computer player did. Apparently, an empty playing field discourages users from making moves. Similarly, all subjects were surprised by round endings despite text and graphical representations of remaining game time.

Two subjects stated they had no firm idea about iTV-SMS games before playing. Two said that prior to playing, the idea of iTV-SMS appeared games funny and weird, but afterwards they considered it unsuitable in practice. One subject commented that the experience would likely have been different and more positive if the game had actually been played on TV on a public channel. In this configuration, however, it just appeared as computer game with strange control input. In general, all subjects stated they were struggling with the mobile phone which they were unused to. Four subjects stated they would have done better with their own mobile phone.

The four subjects not proficient with Minesweeper commented that the computer players moved too fast for them to learn the strategies, and labeled the game experience as frustrating. One game round lasting four minutes is too short a time to either learn the SMS control scheme or the strategies behind a game like Kistenjäger. Some subjects wished they could have practiced the game without time limit and competing computer players. We met a conflict of interest here: on one hand, the conditions of a time limit and competing players are realistic circumstances as new players get to know an iTV application. On the other hand, under those circumstances the experience was frustrating for the subjects. Apparently, the game concept was not a good iTV-SMS game for beginners after all.

The usability interviews provided a number of valuable suggestions for refining the game. To encourage player moves, there should be at least one computer player making moves early into the game. Alternatively, question-marks might indicate unrevealed fields or players might be given direct on-screen instruction to start making moves. The last seconds of the game should be announced by a prominent countdown on the screen. Some subjects stated that the coins as designation of adjacent treasures by the number of coins were confusing and difficult to distinguish.

We conclude by stating that the information gathered by eye tracking during the play of iTV-SMS games tells us mostly about playing styles and strategies of the players examined. As explanation, we offer that fixation, which is usually interpreted as the user being occupied with the fixated element (as in [12]), here mostly occurs during game state analysis.

Eye tracking is not applied easily to iTV-SMS games. The game on the TV display is just a one-way interface. The subject gains information from it, but no direct interaction takes place since the input is made on the mobile phone. The part how the subject tries to interact with the application, e.g. to make an input or cause a change, is lost.

What we see instead is how the subject tries to obtain information from the screen. We see how the subject plays the game and what strategies are employed. We can learn if the subject understood the game and how long it takes. However, this is information we can obtain more easily by conducting a usability interview or watching the subject play.

6 Summary

In this work, we examined the user requirements for interactive TV games using SMS as return channel and determined key success factors for such games. We further surveyed what expectations potential users have. We made a number of findings about criteria that make a game appealing or not. We also found key motivations and concerns people might have with regard to iTV-SMS games.

We further developed an iTV-SMS game and conducted a usability study for it, employing eye tracking to find out how people actually play specific games. We found that eye tracking usability tests of iTV-SMS games are limited due to the way the games are played and the games are interacted with. As expected, we found the usability interview very useful for identifying specific problems with the game.

ITV-SMS games are a very specific breed of games. While they successfully overcome the technical barrier, they suffer many restrictions due to the medium TV and SMS. The survey result suggests that iTV-SMS games will have a hard time until they are accepted. This is partly due to the image of electronic entertainment in general, but also because the thought of using SMS to play games on a TV appears to be unusual. High prices for SMS in Germany won't make it easier for iTV-SMS games.

We found that future usability studies of iTV-SMS games should try to place the subjects in a more credible environment and position, i.e. in front of a TV screen, ideally in a comfortable, living-room like environment, with a mobile phone the subject is familiar with.

Acknowledgements

We would like to thank our test subjects and the staff of ContentLogic, Hamburg, for their invaluable help and support.

References

1. Blythe, M. and Hassenzahl, M.: Interview with Don Norman. In: *interactions*, vol. 11 no. 5, September + October 2004, pp. 43 – 46 (2004)
2. Grigg, R. J..: Pulp Gaming: Taking An Episodic Approach To Interactive Entertainment. In: *ACM International Conference Proceeding Series*, vol. 123, pp. 75 – 82 (2005)
3. Wallace, M. (ed.) and Robbins, B. (ed.): *International Game Developers Association 2006 Casual Games Whitepaper*. Retrieved July 20th, 2006 from http://www.idga.org/casual/IDGA_CasualGames_Whitepaper_2006.pdf (2006)
4. Pagulayan, R. J., Keeker, K., Wixon, D., Romero, R. L. and Fuller, T.: User-centered Design in Games. In Jacko, J. A. and Sears, A. (eds.): *The Human-Computer Interaction Handbook: Fundamentals, Evolving Techniques and Emerging Applications*, Lawrence Erlbaum Associates, Mahwah, NJ, pp. 883 – 906 (2003)
5. Frøkjaer, E., Hertzum, M. and Hornbæk, K.: Measuring Usability: Are Effectiveness, Efficiency, and Satisfaction Really Correlated? In: *Proceedings of the SIGCHI conference on Human factors in computing systems*. April 1-6, The Hague, Netherlands, pp. 345 – 352 (2000)
6. Monk, A., Hassenzahl, M., Blythe, M. and Reed, D.: Funology: designing enjoyment. In: *CHI'02 extended abstracts on Human factors in computing systems*, April 20 – 25, 2002, Minneapolis, USA, pp. 924 + 925 (2002)
7. Hassenzahl, M.: Emotions Can Be Quite Ephemeral. We Cannot Design Them. In: *Interactions*, September + October 2004, vol. 11, pp. 46 – 48 (2004)
8. Hassenzahl, M. and Tractinsky, N.: User experience – a research agenda. In: *Behaviour & Information Technology*, vol. 25, no. 2, March – April 2006, pp. 91 – 97 (2006)
9. Klimmt, C.: The Science of Fun. In: */GameStar/dev*, August 2006, pp. 10-15 (2006)
10. Hassenzahl, M., Beu, A. and Burmester, M.: Engineering Joy. In: *IEEE Software*, vol. 18 no. 1, pp. 70-76 (2001)
11. Kjeldskov, J., Skov, M. B. and Stage, J.: Instant Data Analysis: Conducting Usability Tests in a Day. In: *Proceedings of the third Nordic conference on Human-computer interaction*. 2004, Tampere, Finland, pp. 233 – 240 (2004)
12. Joos, M., Rötting, M. and Velichkovsky, B. M.: Die Bewegung des menschlichen Auges: Fakten, Methoden, innovative Anwendungen [The Movement of the Human Eye: Facts, Methods, innovative Applications]. In Herrmann, T., Deutsch, S. and Rickheit, G. (eds.): *Handbuch der Psycholinguistik [Handbook of Psycholinguistics]*. Berlin, De Greyter (2000)

Acceptable System Response Times for TV and DVR

Michael J. Darnell

Microsoft TV User Experience
1065 La Avenida, Mountain View, California, USA
mdarnell@microsoft.com

Abstract. An experiment was conducted to identify system response time criteria for commonly-used TV functions based on acceptability judgments of TV viewers. Sixteen participants used four different response time profiles on the same digital TV system and rated the acceptability of the response times of eighteen commonly-used TV functions. Results showed significant differences in the acceptability ratings of different response times for different TV functions. This data may be used to estimate how TV viewers would rate various system response times for specific TV functions.

1 Introduction

One important factor that influences the perceived quality of the user experience of digital TV systems is the system response time. The system response time is the time between pressing a button on the remote control and perceiving the result to occur. If response times are too long, an even otherwise great user interface can be judged as undesirable.

There are many factors that may affect the perception of time and judgments concerning acceptable response time for a given function.

One factor that may affect people's judgment of acceptable response time is their recent experience with similar systems. For example, if a person perceives that it takes substantially longer to change the channels on a new TV system, they will probably judge the change negatively. If system response time is longer than expected, people may be more likely to make certain kinds of errors. [1] For example, they may press the same button on the remote control repeatedly. When using a function that requires multiple repetitions of the same button, such as moving the selection highlight to an item in a list, people may be more likely to miss their target. Making such errors may negatively affect judgments of system response time acceptability.

Other features of the user interface may effect the acceptability of a given response time for given function. For example, people may judge a response delay to be more acceptable if the system responds quickly with immediate feedback to a button press even though it takes longer to fully complete the requested action.

Variability of the response times may also affect people's judgments of acceptable system response time. For example, if the response time for a given function is sometimes noticeably longer, this may reduce the overall acceptability.

P. Cesar et al. (Eds.): EuroITV 2007, LNCS 4471, pp. 47–56, 2007.

Various guidelines have been published listing common computer functions and assigning recommended system response times to them based on various sources. [2, 3] These guidelines are of limited value for TV domain because they are difficult to map from the computer domain to the TV domain.

Some authors have assembled general recommendations for system response times based on human perceptual capabilities ranging from the perception of instantaneous (0.1 s) to immediate (1 s) to losing attention (10 s). [4, 5] These recommendations may not be specific enough for TV systems because within a range, people's perceived acceptability of system response times may vary greatly. For example, a response time of 0.3 s may be judged largely acceptable for a given function, whereas 0.9 s is judged as unacceptable. Both of these values are within the range between 0.1 and 1.0.

The aim of the current study was to use empirical methods to determine acceptable TV system response times for a set of common TV functions.

Representative people used a digital TV system to do common functions using four response time profiles. To investigate the effects of people's response time expectations, half of the people who participated had digital TV at home and half had analog TV. People rated the acceptability of the response times for each function on a rating scale. TV system designers and engineers can use this data to determine which specific response time would be required for a given function to be judged by TV viewers to have a given level of acceptability.

2 Method

2.1 Participants

Sixteen people, 9 males and 7 females, participated. Their ages ranged from 21-70 in proportion to US Census figures. They reported watching at least 20 hours of TV per week. Half the participants had analog cable without a digital video recorder (DVR) at home and half had a digital TV system: satellite, digital cable and/or DVR.

2.2 IPTV System

The TV system used in this study was the Microsoft TV IPTV Edition. [6] It has live TV channels, an electronic program guide (EPG), DVR and Video On Demand. This system was used because it is of specific interest to Microsoft. However, the results are intended to be generalizable to similar TV systems.

2.3 Tasks

A relatively small number of functions account for most of people's interaction with TV and DVR systems. [7] See Table 1.

Table 1. Common TV Functions[1] and Response Time (RT) Profiles Used In this Study

Functions	RT Profiles (seconds)			
	A	B	C	D
1 a Change Channels in Full-screen TV	0.4	0.7	1.2	1.6
2 a Go to Program Info	0.5	0.8	1.2	1.6
3 b *Type in Channel Number in Full-screen TV	0.2	0.5	0.6	0.8
4 b Go to Previous Channel	0.4	0.7	1.1	1.6
5 c Go to Guide	0.5	0.9	1.6	2.2
6 c Arrow Down in Guide	0.3	0.6	0.9	1.2
7 c Page Down in Guide	0.3	0.9	1.5	2.1
8 c Arrow Right in Guide	0.3	0.9	1.7	2.3
9 d Pause	0.2	0.5	0.9	1.2
10 e Go to List of Recordings	0.3	0.9	1.5	2.2
11 e Arrow Down in List of Recordings	0.2	0.5	0.7	0.9
12 e Page down in List of Recordings	0.3	0.4	0.7	0.9
13 e Play a recording	0.5	2.3	4.2	5.0
14 e *Begin to Fast Forward in a Recording	0.4	0.9	1.4	2.0
15 f Go to Browse	0.4	0.8	1.2	1.7
16 f Change Channels in Browse	0.3	0.7	1.0	1.3
17 g Go to Menu	0.3	0.9	1.4	1.8
18 g Go to Video On Demand from Menu	0.8	1.4	2.2	3.1
Overall Means	**0.37**	**0.85**	**1.39**	**1.86**

2.4 Tasks

For each of the 18 functions, a simple task was created to describe how to perform the function. The task was composed of a written instruction with a picture showing the relevant button on the remote control or screen on the TV. For example, the instruction for Task 1 was:

"Use the Channel button to change the channel a few times."

2.5 Response Time Profiles

Four response-time profiles were used. Each profile defined the system response times for the 18 functions in Table 1. Profile A, having the shortest response times, was simply the actual response times for the 18 functions in the IPTV system. Profile B was approximately[2] 2 times (2x) the Profile A response times. Profile C was 3x and

---

[1] Functions 15-18 are not common, but are of specific interest to Microsoft.
[2] Table 1 shows mean response times based on a sample of 3 measurements.

Profile D was 4x. Profiles B, C and D were implemented by adding a time delay to each function in the IPTV system. For example, the system response time to change channels in full-screen TV (Function 1) was 0.4, 0.7, 1.2 and 1.6 seconds, respectively, for profiles A, B, C & D. In comparison, the overall mean response times for the comparable functions in the TiVo Series 2, DirecTV DVR and Comcast iGuide are 0.95, 0.96, and 0.73 s, respectively. The correlation coefficients between the response times for the comparable functions in the IPTV system and the TiVo Series 2, DirecTV DVR and Comcast iGuide are 0.33, 0.44 and 0.81, respectively.

2.6 Procedure

Participants were run individually in a usability lab for about 2 hours. They sat on a sofa 10' (3 m) from a 32" (81.3 cm) diagonal TV. They used a remote control to control the IPTV system. Half the participants read the task instructions on a laptop computer screen. The other half read the same instructions printed on sheets of paper.

Participants first completed a free-form comment session and then completed 4 acceptability rating sessions. In the free-form comment session, participants completed each of the 18 tasks 2 times. The tasks were grouped together into logical activities indicated by the letters a-g in Table 1. For example, participants performed the tasks in the order: 1, 2, 1, 2, 3, 4, 3, 4, 5, 6, 7, 8, 5, 6 ... and so on. They were asked to "think aloud as you explore this new TV system." They were told nothing about the true purpose of the study and response time was not mentioned. The 16 participants were randomly divided into 4 groups of 4. Each group used a different response time profile during the free-form comment session.

Following the free-form comment session, each participant completed 4 acceptability rating sessions, each session corresponding to a different response time profile. Each of the 4 groups of participants completed the 4 acceptability rating sessions in a different order following a 4x4 balanced Latin Square.

During each acceptability rating session, participants completed each task 3 times in the order described above. After the third time, they rated the acceptability of the function's system response time on a 9 point scale (Table 2.) They were told to "rate how acceptable the function's response time would be if you were using it at home."

Table 2. System Response Time Acceptability Rating Scale

1	Extremely unacceptable
2	Largely unacceptable
3	Moderately unacceptable
4	Slightly unacceptable
5	Neither unacceptable nor acceptable
6	Slightly acceptable
7	Moderately acceptable
8	Largely acceptable
9	Extremely acceptable

3 Results

3.1 Free-Form Comments

During the free-form comments session, comments about the system response time, either positive or negative, were noted. Also noted were errors related to response time (e.g., pressing a button extra times.) The results are shown in Table 3.

Table 3. Total number of participants with response-time-related comments and errors for each response time (RT) profile (Four participants used each profile.)

RT Profiles	Number of People Commenting about System Response Time		Number of People Making Response Time Related Errors
	Negatively	Positively	
A	0	2	0
B	1	1	1
C	4	0	2
D	4	0	3

The people who experienced the response time profiles C and D, the two slowest profiles, all had negative comments about response time and no positive comments. Profiles A and B, the two fastest profiles received 3 positive and 1 negative comment concerning response time. An X^2 test for non-equal distribution (among profiles) of people, who had negative comments, was not significant $X^2(3) = 6.25$, $p>0.05$. An X^2 test for non-equal distribution (among profiles) of people, who made response-time-related errors, was not significant $X2(3) = 7.5$, $p>0.05$.

3.2 Acceptability Ratings

Each participant rated, on a 9-point scale, the acceptability of the response time of each of the 18 functions for four different response time profiles. The ratings were analyzed using Analysis of Variance (ANOVA). Two of the functions, 3 and 14, (See Table 1) were eliminated because some people misunderstood what aspect of the system response time of the function they needed to rate.

The mixed ANOVA model included 2 between-subjects factors: Type-of-TV-at-Home (analog vs. digital) and Type-of-Task-Instruction-Media: (computer vs. paper). There were 2 within-subjects factors: Response Time Profile (4 profiles) and Function (16 functions.)

The effect of Response Time Profile was significant[3] $F(2.1, 24.7) = 38.2$, $p<001$. The mean ratings for profiles A, B, C and D were 8.1, 7.0, 5.4 and 3.8 respectively. Overall, the shorter the response time was, the higher its acceptability was rated.

---

[3] Using the Huynh-Feldt correction.

The effect of Function was significant F(9.5, 113.9) = 8.4, p<001. Different functions were given different overall response time acceptability ratings.

The interaction of Response Time Profile and Function was significant F(21.6, 259.6) = 2.78, p<001. The pattern of ratings across functions depended on the response time profile. No other effects were significant.

The mean response time acceptability ratings for each function for each response time profile are shown in the Appendix as individual graphs. All 16 functions had significant linear trends. No higher-order trends were significant. The best-fit straight line is plotted on each graph.

Another ANOVA was done to examine the effects of practice on acceptability ratings to see if the overall ratings changed over the 4 rating sessions. This ANOVA was the same as the one described above except that the 4 rating sessions were included as a within-subjects factor instead of the 4 response time profiles. There was no significant difference between rating sessions and the rating sessions factor did not interact with other factors. Thus, there was no systematic change in people's ratings over the rating sessions.

4 Discussion

The free-form comments session was intended to provide an absolute measure of acceptability of the different system response time profiles. It was a blind procedure in that participants didn't know that response time was of any interest in the study. Yet, all 8 participants in the two slowest response time conditions (profiles C & D) commented negatively on the response time, whereas only 1 of 8 participants in the two fastest conditions (profiles A & B) commented negatively on response time. Although not statistically significant, this result suggests that if a TV system achieved response times at least as fast as profile B, that people would not perceive it to be slow.

During the free-form comments session, participants were also observed to make various errors, particularly in the slower response time conditions (profiles C & D). For example, people commonly mistyped channel numbers. Five of 8 people in the two slowest conditions (C & D) made response time related errors, whereas only one of 8 people in the two fastest conditions made such errors. These errors were generally correlated with people's negative comments.

The acceptability rating sessions were intended to provide specific response time acceptability criteria for each of the 18 functions. These are presented as individual graphs in the Appendix. The graphs can be used to determine the response time that corresponds to a given acceptability rating for each function.

For example, if an engineer adopted a rating of 8 (Largely acceptable) as the target response time acceptability criterion for a TV system, the corresponding target response time to change channels (function 1) would be about 0.5 seconds.

How well would these results generalize to other TV systems? These findings would seem likely to generalize to other similar TV systems because different systems share many functions. For example, most systems have an "info" button that when pressed displays a screen of information about the selected TV program. However, there are differences in the way functions are implemented on different TV systems that could affect people's perception of response time. For example, some systems give immediate auditory or visual feedback when a button is pressed that occurs before the actual function is performed. Some systems have animated screen transitions. Some systems repeat when a button is held down. Any of these differences could affect people's judgment of acceptable response time for a specific function. To generalize the current findings to another TV system, one should make sure that the salient aspects of the functions of the two systems are similar. If the two TV system's functions are too dissimilar, one could still use the current methodology to test the other TV system.

People's expectations were predicted to play a significant role in their judgments of acceptable system response times. Thus, participant's TV system at home (digital vs. analog) was included as a factor in the study. Since analog TV users don't have certain functions (e.g., EPG), they may not have strong expectations concerning those function's response times. However, there was no significant difference between the overall acceptability ratings for people with digital (6.0) vs. analog TV (6.1) or between their patterns of ratings for the different functions. Also there was no evidence that people's overall ratings changed over the 4 acceptability rating sessions. These results suggest that the effects of expectation on acceptability judgments of a function's response time are much smaller than the effects of the actual response time.

In summary, this study provides both data and methodology that may be used to determine acceptable system response times for TV functions.

Acknowledgements

The author would like to thank Afshan Ali for supporting this research and Linda Chan for creating an IPTV client with configurable system response times.

References

1. Iatrino, A. and Modeo, S.: Text Editing in Visual Terrestrial Television: a Comparison Of Three Interfaces. Proc. 4th European Conference on Interactive Television (Athens, Greece, 25-26 May, 2006) 198-204.
2. Maximum Acceptable System Response Times. Department of Defense Design Criteria MIL-STD-1472F, (1999) 196.
3. Miller, R. B.: Response Time in Man-Computer Conversational Transactions. Proc. AFIPS Fall Joint Computer Conference Vol. 33, (1968) 267-277.
4. Card, S. K., Robertson, G. G., and Mackinlay, J. D.: The Information Visualizer: An Information Workspace. Proc. ACM CHI'91 Conf. (New Orleans, LA, 28 April-2 May, 1991) 181-188.
5. Nielsen, J.: Response Times: The Three Important Limits. Retrieved Feb. 26, 2007 from http://www.useit.com/papers/responsetime.html
6. Microsoft TV IPTV Edition. Retrieved Feb. 26, 2007 from http://www.microsoft.com/tv/IPTVEdition.mspx
7. Darnell, M.: How do people really interact with TV? Naturalistic Observations of Digital TV and Digital Video Recorder Users. Proc. 4th European Conference on Interactive Television (Athens, Greece, 25-26 May, 2006) 91-99.

Appendix: System Response Time Acceptability Ratings for Common TV Functions

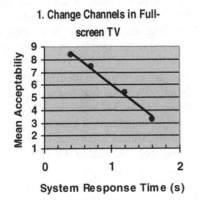

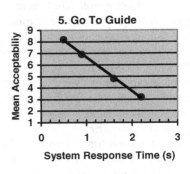

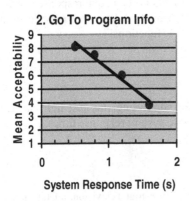

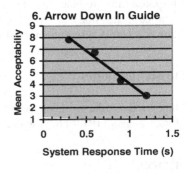

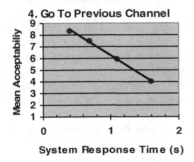

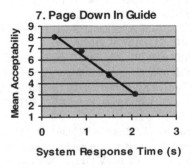

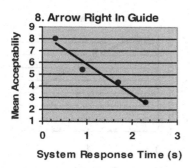

8. Arrow Right In Guide

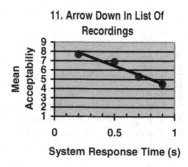

11. Arrow Down In List Of Recordings

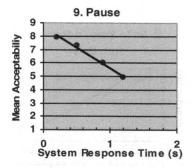

9. Pause

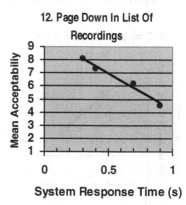

12. Page Down In List Of Recordings

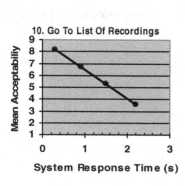

10. Go To List Of Recordings

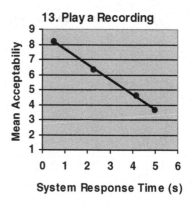

13. Play a Recording

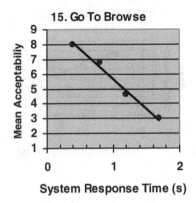

15. Go To Browse

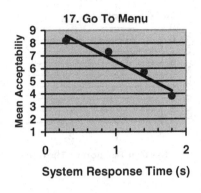

17. Go To Menu

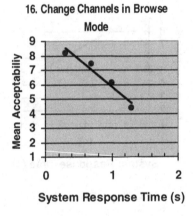

16. Change Channels in Browse Mode

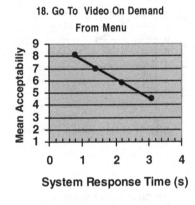

18. Go To Video On Demand From Menu

Exploring the Effects of Interactivity in Television Drama

Stacey Hand and Duane Varan

Interactive Television Research Institute (ITRI), Murdoch University, Western Australia
s.hand@murdoch.edu.au

Abstract. Interactive television dramas have long promised to deliver entertaining experiences. In practice, however, successful interactive television dramas are rare. This paper suggests that the fault lies in attempts to abandon narrative structure in favour of interactive freedom and hypothesized that a model of interactive drama which encases interactivity within a strong narrative structure would be successful. This hypothesis can be seen as part of a larger research goal of which this paper represents the first step. This paper attempted to establish that the addition of interactivity to a narrative could enhance audience enjoyment. In order to test this hypothesis a research experiment was conducted which directly compared an interactive television programme to its linear counterpart. The research tested 180 participants and attempted to ascertain the differences in the viewer experience. The research found overall significantly higher averages in entertainment, appetite, immersion, and empathy among those who viewed the interactive television drama.

Keywords: Interactive Narrative, Interactive television, Drama, Audience Research.

1 Introduction

The television landscape has changed more dramatically over the last few years than in its entire 50 year history. Television can now be distributed and consumed in a myriad of ways, ranging from Internet Protocol Television (IPTV) through to mobile TV. "Traditional media services are being challenged by new digital technologies resulting in the emergence of new players, content, services and delivery platforms." (DCITA report 2006: P.3).

The television industry is beginning to recognize this changing landscape by acknowledging that new forms of distribution and consumption need to be met with new forms of content creation. Television content needs to capatilise on its new interactive, personalizing and content sharing capabilities.

It is in this new television environment that we can revisit the genre of interactive drama. Interactive drama, as a concept, has long promised many exciting possibilities for enhancing audience enjoyment by bringing together the interactive pleasures of gaming and the enjoyment of storytelling. "Immersive interfaces provide a great sense of presence and freedom while narration or narrative structure allows an author to weave an engaging presentation. The hope is, that by bringing together the best of these compelling experiences, a new type of experience can be made and that this new experience may even be more compelling..." (Gaylean 1995: P.19)

P. Cesar et al. (Eds.): EuroITV 2007, LNCS 4471, pp. 57–65, 2007.

While there has been a litany of one-off interactive drama projects, the genre has yet to fulfill its promise. There is very little audience research which has been able to ascertain why such projects have failed.

Some argue that the reason for the failure of previous interactive projects lies in interactivity's innate incompatibility with story structure and suggest that interactive narratives are simply an attempt by narrative theorists to colonise new interactive media. "As a theory, this narrativistic colonialism might seem aesthetically problematic (Aarseth 1997, chapter six), as well as technologically unachievable (Bringsjord 2001)..." (Aarseth 2004: P.49) This paper does not suggest that new media technology will not be met by new forms, but that to dismiss story as being incompatible with interactivity is premature and short sighted.

Instead of abandoning the notion of narrative structure as incompatible with newer interactive technologies; this paper hypothesizes that a successful model of interactive drama is one which encases interaction within a strong narrative structure.

Such a model was found to be the most effective in research conducted at the Interactive Television Research Institute (ITRI) of Murdoch University. In working with Nike in 2001 to create an interactive narrative-based advertisement, it was found that the most effective model was one which allowed for interaction which did not compromise the narrative structure of the advertisement.

This model, which ITRI dubbed the 'yo-yo' structure of interaction, is a branching form of interactive narrative which allows the audience to interact but which always uses bridging storylines so as to bring the audience back to the central storyline. In this way the 'yo-yo' structure accommodates structured interaction which allows the audience a sense of agency without negating the narrative structure of the overall story. Similar structures of interactive narrative have also been outlined by Meadows (2003) as the "nodal plot structure" (P.64) and by Garrand (1997) as the "branching from scenes" structure. The main difference between Meadows' (2003) and Garrand's (1997) structures and the 'yo-yo' structure is the identification, in the 'yo-yo' structure, of the bridging scene. The diagram below outlines the 'yo-yo' structure at the first point of interaction.

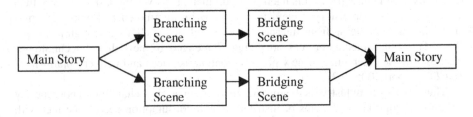

In order to begin testing the more long-term hypothesis, that the most successful model of interactive narratives would in fact be the 'yo-yo' structure, it was necessary to first establish that an interactive narrative could successfully enhance audience entertainment. Previous audience research in the field has been unable to establish whether interactivity could enhance audience entertainment.

Research by Lee, S; Heeter, C and LaRose, R (2005) comparing an interactive film to a linear film in individual and group viewing sessions did not find significant differences in terms of interactivity's effect on viewer enjoyment, story involvement and arousal. The authors suggest that the use of a 5-point Likert scale and a small student sample (eighty) may have minimized their ability to find the differences between the interactive and linear versions of the film.

Vorderer, P; Knobloch, S and Schramm, H (2001) conducted audience research on the effects of an interactive suspense film on audience entertainment, empathy and suspense. This research tested three versions of the suspense film; no-involvement, low-involvement and high- involvement. The findings suggest that interactive narratives may only increase entertainment among those viewers with higher cognitive capacities. This research is problematic, however, in terms of its definition of a participant's cognitive capacity. Participants were judged as having higher cognitive capacities based partly on their response times during the interactive film. The research suggests that cognitive capacity is a correlate of intelligence, or cognitive capacity, and cites Neubauer's (1990) research on psychometric testing (P. 349). The use of response times as an indicator of intelligence is problematic as Neubauer suggests that while response times among those with higher cognitive capacities are faster in simple tasks, this is the opposite in terms of more difficult tasks. (1990: P.151) It is difficult to determine whether asking an audience to consider the direction of a narrative can be considered a simple or difficult task, and thus it is problematic to judge an audiences' response times as indicative of their cognitive capabilities. Vorderer, P; Knobloch, S and Schramm, H (2001) do not report any significant differences between those participants in the no-interaction; low-interaction and high-interaction groups without this measure of cognitive capacity and thus questions still remain on the effects of interactivity on the general audience.

In order then to establish that interactivity could enhance audience entertainment, as the first phase of a research goal to study interactive narrative structure, it was necessary to design an audience research experiment. The research experiment directly compared two versions of a television programme, one linear and the other interactive, in order to evaluate whether the interactive model could successfully improve the audience experience.

2 Research Methods

2.1 Design

A controlled audience research experiment was used to investigate the effects of a structured interactive drama on audience entertainment, empathy, immersion, appetite and narrative difficulty. The experiment had a 2 X 1 design. There was one between-subjects condition: Interactivity with two levels- the interactive programme vs. the control [linear] programme.

2.2 Developing the Interactive Drama Programme

The need to build the research instrument for the research experiment required the production of an interactive drama programme from scratch or the use of existing content. Existing content did not, however, exist within the confines of the specific research needs. Interactive television drama which followed the 'yo-yo' structure, which this paper hypothesized would be the most successful, was not readily available for use. Thus the need arose to explore producing original content. When combined, however, with the demands associated with the research aspect of the study, it became clear that the production of an original interactive drama would transcend the scope of the study.

Thus it became evident that a hybrid solution was necessary in order to create an interactive television programme that could conceivably be viewed on television.

Accessing medium fidelity animation provided an alternative, given the high quality of computer console games it appeared feasible that the interactive content could be produced drawing on animation extracted from games. Thus the hybrid solution that was eventually used for the research instrument used the animation from a playstation game edited into a television drama. The console game used in the research instrument was *True Crime: Streets of LA*.

Interaction within the programme centered on the decisions of the main character, Nick. Thus the audience would be given choices that were presented to Nick throughout the narrative, for example the choice of whether to shoot Rosie's kidnapper or whether to negotiate with him. Following each decision the audience would be shown a branching scene, for instance Rosie's kidnapper being shot, before the drama would bridge back to the central storyline.

Another factor in deciding the form the interactivity would take was the source material itself. Since the research instrument was not created from conception, but instead used the animation from an existing game, the possibilities of interaction points within the narrative were not endless. The game lent several possibilities where sufficient footage allowed for points of interaction- of these points there were five that were selected as they were determined to be meaningful interactions which showed sufficient change, but which also allowed us to take the audience back to the main storyline. The total running time of the drama was 30 minutes.

2.3 Procedure

Participants were drawn from the 'TV Panel' database at the Interactive Television Research Institute (ITRI) of Murdoch University, Australia. This is a panel made up of a wide spectrum of the public who regularly participate in studies at the Institute.

180 members of the TV Panel were first allocated to three age groups: 18 to 34 years old, 35 to 54 years old and 55 yeas old or older. These groups were further divided along gender lines (male/female) to create six equal demographic categories.

Participants viewed the television programmes within ITRI's Audience Research Labs where identical rooms simulate an ordinary living room. Prior to the beginning of the viewing session participants were told that they were about to view a drama, which they were to imagine was the pilot episode for a new television series that was being considered for production. Participants were also told that while the pilot episode was animated- if the series was commissioned then live actors would be used. Those participants within the treatment group were then given further instructions on how to interact with the programme using the red and green buttons on their remote control.

After viewing the programme participants were asked to fill in a pen and paper questionnaire.

2.4 Measures

Measurements were collected with a post-test questionnaire. Many of the questionnaire scales were adapted from the advertising and marketing sector, which has a more established tradition of testing for entertainment. Thus several of the questions within the survey were adapted from the marketing scale developed by Lastovika (1983: P.294/5).

Measurements for audience immersion were derived from literature by Green and Brock (2002: P.324) on the symptoms of audience immersion.

In order to cater towards television programming, and the interactivity within the treatment version, further questions were developed by the researchers specifically for this study. All questions, then, asked the participants to rate their opinion to a statement on a seven point Likert scale- with 1 being strongly disagree and 7 being strongly agree.

3   Research Hypothesis

The research hypotheses have been outlined in terms of each of variables to be tested. The variables are derived from a literature review; the following table outlines each of these hypotheses formally.

Hypothesis 1	The interactive drama will deliver a higher entertainment value to its audience when compared with the linear drama.
Hypothesis 2	The interactive drama will deliver a more immersive experience for its audience when compared with the linear drama.
Hypothesis 3	The interactive drama will deliver a greater appetite for the programme content than the linear drama.
Hypothesis 4	Participants viewing the interactive drama will have greater empathy for the main character, than those participants viewing the linear drama.
Hypothesis 5	Participants viewing the interactive drama will not find the narrative more difficult to comprehend than those viewing the linear drama.

4   Research Results

4.1   General Findings

The chart below outlines the mean scores of the variables of entertainment, appetite, immersion and narrative difficulty for each of the treatment and control cells.

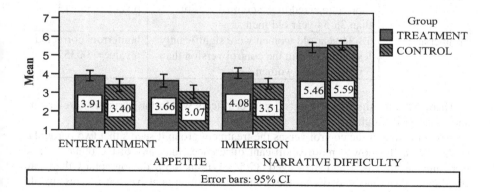

When looking at the differences between the treatment and control groups as a whole, the results are promising for interactive dramas. As a whole the interactive version proved to have significantly higher entertainment (.024 p value), immersion (.005 p value) and appetite (.017 p value) scores. The highly significant empathy score (.008 p value) also suggests that this form of interactivity, where the audience chooses the course of action for the main character, may increase empathy even further. Concerns of narrative difficulty seem to be unfounded, as the results show no significant differences between the groups in terms of narrative difficulty (.483 p value).

4.2 Gender and Age Effects

The research hypotheses did not take into account the possibility of varied gender and age results. These are, however, perhaps the most interesting aspect of this research. The research suggests that there is a significant age and/or gender effect occurring in the variables of entertainment, appetite and immersion. These results are outlined below.

The table below outlines the significant gender and age effects:

VARIABLE	EFFECT	P VALUE
Entertainment	18-34 year old men were significantly more entertained by the treatment version than by the control version.	bonferroni corrected p value= .00250
Entertainment	35-54 year old men were significantly more entertained by the treatment version than by the control version.	bonferroni corrected p value= .00294
Entertainment	35-54 year old women were significantly more entertained by the control version than 35-54 year old men.	bonferroni corrected p value= .00250
Appetite	Women, aged 35-54, had significantly higher appetite for the control version over the treatment version.	bonferroni corrected p value= .00263
Immersion	35-54 year old men were significantly more immersed in the treatment version than in the control version	bonferroni corrected p value= .00333
Immersion	35-54 year old women were significantly more immersed in the control version than 35-54 year old men.	bonferroni corrected p value= .00313
Immersion	18-34 year old women were significantly less immersed in the control version than 35-54 year old women.	bonferroni corrected p value= .00357

There were no significant age and gender effects within the variables of empathy and narrative difficulty.

When looking at the control versus the treatment group it seems that two particular age/gender cells showed more significant differences than any of the others. These were men aged 18-34 and men aged 35-54. Within these demographics there are significant differences between the control and treatment versions. This would suggest that these two demographics are more open to interactivity and thus this has led to a greater enjoyment of the treatment version over the control version.

This greater enjoyment of the treatment version could be due to the fact that men within these age groups are more likely to be gamers and thus are already quite adept at interacting. "However, digital gaming has often been viewed, in both the media and academia, as a traditionally male preserve (Cassell and Jenkins, 2000)." (Crawford, G 2005: P.260)

Another possible factor is remote control use. Men are far more likely to dominate the remote control in the home and to use it more frequently. (Eastman,S & Newton, G 1995; Krugman, D, Cameron, G, White-McKearney, C 1995) "In fact, research consistently reveals that males dominate the remote control and are more likely to be in control of the TV remote control device." (Frisby, C 1999: P.60)This suggests that men would thus be more comfortable when called to use the remote control to interact.

4.3   Interactive Variables

The diagram below outlines how the participants felt about the interactivity in terms of its effect on their sense of entertainment, appetite, immersion and narrative difficulty.

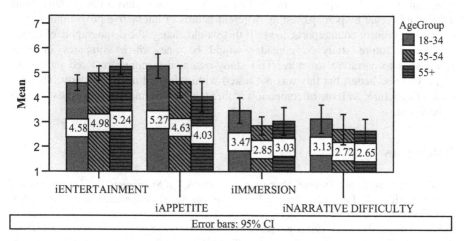

4.4   Age and Gender Effects: Interactive Variables

The research shows an interesting contrast in terms of gender and age effects. While there seems to be a significant gender effect between the control and treatment groups, this effect does not exist in terms of the variables connected to interactivity. In fact all the demographics scored interactive entertainment highly with mean scores hovering around the 5 point mark. This suggests that while all gender and age groups enjoyed interactivity- this enjoyment only carried over into general enjoyment of the programme for men aged 18-34 and men aged 35-54.

The reasons for this could be multiple. But a strong reason may be the programme genre itself. The programme was an action crime genre with a strong lead male character, in this way it was already more likely to be enjoyed by males. The leanings of certain genders to certain genres are a widely acknowledged and well reported phenomenon. (McCarty, J & Shrum, L 1993; Oliver, M 2000; Fishchoff, S; Antonio, A; Lewis; D 1998) Thus men were perhaps already more open to liking the programme, and were thus more receptive to the interactivity. Women and the older age group of men were less receptive to the programme initially, perhaps, and this may have led to the interactivity being less effective in terms of programme enjoyment as a whole.

The only age group which showed a significantly different score (p value .003) in terms of the interactive variables was men aged 55+ within the variable of interactive appetite. The data in this study suggests that while the 55+ age group enjoyed the ability to interact they did not have an appetite for increased interactivity.

5 Future Studies

The contrast between there being significant gender and age effects between the control and treatment groups but not within those interactive variables suggests the need for further research in this area. This contrast could suggest that in order for interactivity to improve an audiences' overall enjoyment of a programme; that programme must first appeal to the audience demographic. Thus a future study could address this issue by perhaps testing different genres of interactive programmes, with their linear control counterparts, to see if this would change the demographic effects.

Another future study to consider would be one which compares different approaches to narrative structure. This study assumed a more structured interactive narrative to be better, but this was not tested within the realms of the study. Thus the issue of structure, an issue of contention within the field of interactive narrative, needs to be tested.

References

Aarseth, E (2004) Genre Trouble: Narrativism and the Art of Simulation. In Wardrip-Fruin, N and Harrigan, P (Eds.) First Person: New Media as Story, Performance and Game. USA: MIT Press

Crawford, G (2005) Digital Gaming, Sport and Gender. Leisure Studies, Vol. 24, iss. 3, p.259

Department of Communications, Information Technology and the Arts, Australian Government (2006) Meeting the Digital Challenge: Reforming Australia's media in the digital age [electronic version] Retrieved April 2006, from DCITA website, www.dcita.gov.au

Eastman, S and Newton, G (1995) Delineating Grazing: Observations of Remote Control Use. Journal of Communication, vol. 45 (Winter), 78-96

Frisby, C (1999) Building Theoretical Insights to Explain Differences in Remote Control Use Between Males and Females: A meta-analysis. Journal of Current Issues and Research in Advertising, vol.21, pp.59-76

Garrand, T (1997) "Scripting narrative for interactive multimedia" in Journal of Film and Video, vol. 49, ½;

Gaylean, T (1995) Narrative Guidance of Interactivity. Unpublished PhD thesis, Massachusetts Institute of Technology, Retrieved: 4/09/2005 from http://ic.media.mit.edu/

Green, M and Brock, T (2002) "In the Mind's Eye" in Narrative Impact: Social and Cognitive Foundations ed. Melanie C. Green, Jeffrey J. Strange, Timothy C. Brock, New Jersey, USA: Lawrence Erlbraum Associates

Kim, P & Sawhney, H (2002) A Machine-like new Medium: Theoretical examination of Interactive TV. Media Culture and Society, Vol 24, No. 2

Lastovicka (1999) Relevance, Confusion, and Entertainment. In Bearden, W & Netemeyer, R (Eds.), Handbook of Marketing Scales, 2nd edition, USA: Sage Publications

Lee, S; Heeter, C and LaRose, R (2005) Viewer Responses to Interactive Narrative: A comparison of interactive versus linear viewership in alone and group settings; Presented at the Communication Technology Division of the International Communication Association Conference: New York City.

Meadows, S (2003) Pause & Effect: the art of interactive narrative, New Riders: Indiana, USA

McCarty, J and Shrum, L (1993) The role of personal values and demographics in predicting television viewing. Journal of Advertising, Vol.22, Iss.4, p.77

Neubauer, AC (1990) Speed of Information Processing in the Hick Paradigm and Response Latencies in a Psychometric Intelligence Test. Personality and Individual Differences, Vol. 11, No.2

Oliver, M; Weaver, J; Sargent, S (2000) An Examination of Factors Related to Sex Differences in Enjoyment of Sad Films. Journal of Broadcasting & Electronic Media, Spring

True Crime: Streets of LA, developed by LUXOFLUX, copyright: Activision

Vorderer, P; Knobloch, S and Schramm, H (2001). Does Entertainment Suffer From Interactivity? The Impact of Watching an Interactive TV Movie on Viewers' Experience of Entertainment. Media Psychology, vol.3, no.4, pp.343—36

Focusing on Elderly: An iTV Usability Evaluation Study with Eye-Tracking

Marianna Obrist, Regina Bernhaupt, Elke Beck, and Manfred Tscheligi

HCI & Usability Unit, ICT&S Center, University of Salzburg, Sigmund-Haffner-Gasse 18
5020 Salzburg, Austria
firstname.secondname@sbg.ac.at

Abstract. Elderly people often experience difficulties using interactive TV. This paper presents the findings of a usability evaluation study in combination with eye-tracking conducted for an information oriented interactive TV application. We explored two user groups: elderly users (50 years and above) and users between 20 and 30 years of age. Our focus was on how elderly people perceive and interpret a navigation oriented iTV application. Apart from the standard usability data we used eye-tracking data to gain more insight on why iTV usage seemed to be more difficult for the group of elderly.

Keywords: interactive TV, usability evaluation, eye-tracking, elderly.

1 Introduction and Background

New technologies often exceed the capacity of humans especially of elderly people, as the technological development is very rapid. It can be imagined that the deficit due to the aging process can lead to a larger gap between certain technologies and users in the case of elderly people compared to younger people. This is especially relevant for interactive TV (iTV), as elderly people represent a large TV viewing group, which is often less familiar with the practices of today's information presentation [2].

In this paper we report on a usability evaluation study within the iiTV@home (information oriented interactive TV at home) project. The project mainly focused on the development of new forms of news and information oriented regional iTV services. This usability study was conducted in February 2006 and aimed to evaluate the application prototype with two different user groups. We compared young people (aged between 20 and 30 years) with elderly people (older than 50 years of age). We focused on how elderly people compared with younger people perceived and interpreted a navigation oriented iTV application. Moreover, we used eye-tracking to further explore difficulties in task completion for the group of elderly people.

Eye-tracking is a technique where individual's eye movements are measured to find out where a person is looking while conducting a task. "Tracking people's eye movements can help HCI researchers understand visual and display-based information processing and the factors that may impact upon the usability of system interfaces" [10]. Measures most commonly used are the number of fixations and the mean fixation duration, gazing time and saccade rates [10]. The number of fixations

P. Cesar et al. (Eds.): EuroITV 2007, LNCS 4471, pp. 66–75, 2007.
© Springer-Verlag Berlin Heidelberg 2007

in each area of interest (AOI) is said to be negatively correlated with search efficiency and task efficiency [6]. Jacob et al. [6] reviewed 21 studies that have involved the use of eye-tracking in usability evaluations. They demonstrate the broad range of measures that can be used as well as the difficulties related to the conduction of such studies. "The generally accepted assumption behind eye-tracking is that of a direct correspondence between where people look and where they focus their attention. Thus, by examining people's eye movements, we can gain insight into their attentional processes and learn more about what they find important, interesting, or confusing" [1]. For a comprehensive overview on the theory and practice of eye-tracking see also Duchowski [3]. However, there are still a lot of open questions regarding the usefulness of eye-tracking in general, and which measures to use in particular [11]. We believe in the useful contribution of eye-tracking data to standard usability data, especially to underpin problem areas identified during the usability study. In the presented study, we used the eye-tracking data to understand user's difficulties during task performance in more detail.

Our hypothesis was that elderly people have more problems than young people when navigating through the application interface of the iTV application prototype, in terms of task duration times and search behaviors. We assumed that elderly people are slower in understanding the navigation concept than younger people. Both user groups had only limited experience in using PC and Internet. To prove our hypothesis we performed a usability evaluation study with this two target groups.

We based our usability evaluation study on standard usability data and eye-tracking. We used the ClearView eye-tracking software for analyzing the data. We represent the areas of the screen receiving either more fixations or receiving the longest dwell times in a color-coded "hot spot" image of the interface. The closer to red the hot spot image is the more fixations occurred in an area of the interface and intensity decreasing with movement down the spectrum. Also "gaze plot" images are analyzed, which deliver feedback on participants' searching behavior while performing a task. We also decided to use the thinking aloud method during the usability evaluation study to help in understanding the difficulties of the participants while performing the task, even though it is sometimes recommended not to use the two methods in combination, as they make people self-conscious and not behave naturally [4]. We decided to use thinking aloud, because people are used to talk while watching TV and performing iTV [7].

2   Usability Evaluation Study

The goal of this usability study was to evaluate design and navigation of an interactive news application with two different user groups and to show that eye-tracking can deliver additional data to the defined problem areas and can support the definition of design recommendations.

2.1   Tested Application

An information based iTV application was tested. It was an MHP based application also using broadband Internet over the cable network as a back channel for dynamic content delivery (e.g. news updates each 5 to 10 minutes). The user interface was developed around a simple navigational concept using up/down, left/right and color keys as well as the OK button. The content for the news application was provided by the local newspaper. Figure 1 shows some screenshots of the evaluated application.

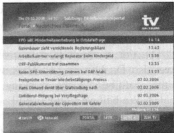

Fig. 1. Two screenshots of the tested application. On the left the main menu showing the start page of the iTV Portal and on the right a submenu in the news rubric.

2.2 Participants

Sixteen people were recruited to participate in the usability evaluation study. Two different user groups, each with eight participants, were selected to test the iTV application. The first group of people was between 20 to 30 years, with some PC and Internet experience, and the second group was elderly people older than 50 years with no or minimal PC and Internet experience. For each group we selected four female and four male. The participant's age ranged between 22 and 66 years, with a mean of 25.3 years within the first group and 58.6 years in the second group. The average usage of the PC ranged between two and four hours per day, whereas two persons did not own a PC (59 and 66 years old participants) and seven use the PC only about two hours a day. From each group we additionally selected two female and two male (in sum eight participants) to test the application also with eye-tracking. We used the Tobii X50 eye-tracker (see Figure 2, on the left).

Fig. 2. Set up with eye-tracking (left) and without eye-tracking (right)

All participants, apart from 1 (male, 66 years old) had also experience with teletext. Nine participants (7 younger and 2 elderly participants) are using teletext on a daily basis for getting the newest program information. Six participants (mainly the elderly participants) are using teletext only from time to time to get informed about the upcoming programs, when they have no program magazine at home or to quickly check specific information (e.g. weather, lotto numbers, etc.).

2.3 Test Set Up

The domestic setting of TV consumption is complex and difficult to emulate in all its facets [9]. We created a living room experience in our lab by putting in a couch, some plants, and in the tests without eye-tracking we also positioned a table with drinks, snacks and magazines in the lab. Each person was tested alone (see Figure 2).

For the usability evaluation study the participant was seated on the couch with two meters distance to the TV screen. The eye-tracking device was placed in front of them on the table, with no more than 60 cm distance to the user's eyes. Additional to the eye-tracking, the participant's behavior and usage of the remote control during the test was recorded by three cameras. Figure 3 shows the recorded camera perspectives and the recorded TV screen.

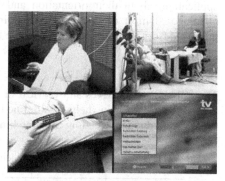

Fig. 3. Test set up for the usability study with three cameras and the TV screen

2.4 Procedure

The participants were briefly introduced about the usability evaluation study and were asked to think aloud. They answered some preliminary questions regarding their TV usage, how many hours they watch TV per day, what they use it for, and which other digital media they are using. Following these steps the eye-tracking system was calibrated using five points on the screen and two example stimuli to familiarize the participant with the device and to try to find best position on the couch, so that the tracking works well. Eight of the participants were wearing eye-glasses and two participants had lenses. The calibration was acceptable for all users.

The usability study included 6 tasks. Task 1 was to open the iTV application and to find traffic information. This task should demonstrate a typical situation at home, where people would like to use the iTV application while watching TV. In task 2 we focused on the navigation concept of the application. The task should show if people are able to find an article in a more complex sub-structure and if they recognize the possibility to use the navigational cues and color keys to solve the task. Task 3 was also concerned with the navigational aspects of the application. Task 4 focused more on the design details of the application interface. The main goal of this task was to evaluate the additional information visible on the screen, like finding article number 30 in a certain news area. We wanted to know if people see the information about the article (like article number or amount of pages). For these tasks we expected eye-tracking data to explain emerged difficulties during the test. Task 5 was more concerned with switching between the iTV application and the TV. In the last task the participants had to find the daily horoscope and then to leave the application. The purpose of task 6 was to get user feedback about the labelling of menu and if they are able to envisage where to find the proper information.

After each task people where first asked to rate the difficulty of the task completion on a scale from 1 to 5 (where 1 is very easy and 5 is very difficult). Second they were asked to give feedback on how to improve the application. At the end of the test, each participant had to fill out a standard usability score (SUS) questionnaire and a questionnaire to address user experience (based on the AttrakDiff [5]). Finally they were asked some questions about their general impression of using the iTV application, about their orientation and navigation within the platform, what they remembered most of the services and information and how the system should be improved from their personal perspective to better fit their expectations.

2.5 Results

The following table gives an overview of the number of tasks successfully solved, the tasks solved with help (help was defined for each task), and tasks not solved or not solved at all due to exceeding the time limit for each of the two user groups.

Table 1. Overview of solved tasks and their ratings (split for each of the two user groups)

Participants aged between 20 and 30 years			
Task	Solved	Solved with help	Not solved	Rating (Mean/SD)
T1	7	1	0	1.25 (0.46)
T2	7	1	0	1.75 (0.71)
T3	8	0	0	1.63 (0.74)
T4	8	0	0	1.75 (0.71)
T5	8	0	0	1.13 (0.35)
T6	8	0	0	1.38 (1.06)

Participants older than 50 years old			
Task	Solved	Solved with help	Not solved	Rating (Mean/SD)
T1	4	4	0	2.25 (0.71)
T2	2	4	2	2.50 (1.31)
T3	6	2	0	2.25 (0.89)
T4	6	2	0	2.00 (0.76)
T5	7	0	1	1.63 (0.52)
T6	8	0	0	1.38 (0.52)

Table 1 shows that five participants (one young and four elderly participants) solved task 1 only with help from the test leader. Especially the elderly participants searched on the remote control an "iTV" key or pressed the menu key and entered the set top box menu to start the iTV application. To open the application, participants had to press the blue color key on their remote control which was visualized as blue button (rectangle – see Figure 4) in a transparent horizontal bar on the bottom of the TV screen. After 1.30 minutes of searching and exploring wrong ways, the test leader gave them the hint "to focus not too much on the remote control only, but to look more carefully on the TV screen."

Fig. 4. Screenshot of the TV screen with the information bar on the bottom to access the iTV application (by using the blue color key on the remote control)

Fig. 5. Gaze plot showing user's eye movements while performing task 1 – open the iTV application. First fixation on the blue button, but the participant continues searching.

Participants explained they did not use the blue key on the remote control to open the application, because they did not associate the interface element on the TV screen with the blue color key on the remote control. One participant also explained his behavior with the comment: "I saw that there is something blue on the screen, but I couldn't read it... so it didn't make sense to me at that time" (66 year old man).

The eye-tracking data support this statement by showing that people looked at the blue button on the screen without recognizing its meaning; because they continued their search on the left upper side of the TV screen (see gaze plot image in Figure 5). This supports existing research on eye movements on homepages whereby "eyes most often fixated first in the upper left of the page, then hover in that area before going left to right. Only after persuing the top portion of the page for some time did their eyes explore further down the page" [12].

Moreover, we compared the time to first fixation for the two user groups. The younger group ranged from 849 to 10992 ms compared to the elderly group ranging from 4662 to 21761 ms. Time to first fixation typically shows where people put their first focus and what kind of interface elements attracted them. The longer fixation time for elderly people shows, that they could not find a common interface element to focus on. We defined additional two major AOIs (areas of interest) – "information bar" and "TV screen" – for the first part of task 1 (namely "open the iTV application") and also looked at the amount of fixations as well as on the average fixation duration in each user group. Data indicates that the amount of fixations is higher for the group of elderly. We compared the average number of fixations per second showing that elderly and younger people do not differ in the average number of fixations. Elderly people are able to explore the interfaces as fast as younger people, but less accurate. Interesting is the fact, that elderly users tended to return from the area of the information bar to the TV screen in task 1 around 50 % of all eye-tracking movements. The group of younger participants did not return at all to the TV screen area, after looking at the information bar. It clearly indicates that the group of elderly people had difficulties to understand and interpret the information bar.

The task showed that especially elderly participants were not able to immediately associate the entry button (named "ZUM ITV", which means "to the ITV") in the blue box on the right bottom of the TV screen with the blue key on their remote control. Table 2 illustrates the time participants needed to complete the different tasks in the usability study.

Table 2. Allowed and needed time per task for each of the two user groups

Participants aged between 20 – 30 years				
Task	Maximum time allowed per task	Average time per task	Minimum time needed per task	Maximum time needed per task
T1	360 sec	47.75 sec	21 sec	138 sec
T2	480 sec	75.38 sec	43 sec	111 sec
T3	480 sec	65.63 sec	40 sec	93 sec
T4	480 sec	41.50 sec	20 sec	93. sec
T5	360 sec	41.75 sec	35 sec	56 sec
T6	360 sec	38.88 sec	22 sec	98 sec

Participants older than 50 years old				
Task	Maximum time allowed per task	Average time per task	Minimum time needed per task	Maximum time needed per task
T1	360 sec	169.63 sec	37 sec	251 sec
T2	480 sec	293.12 sec	98 sec	502 sec
T3	480 sec	152.12 sec	90 sec	478 sec
T4	480 sec	147.37 sec	81 sec	226 sec
T5	360 sec	120.87 sec	43 sec	385 sec
T6	360 sec	53.50 sec	37 sec	81 sec

In task 2 the main difficulties for the group of elderly was the usage of the navigational keys and their association with the color keys in the applications. Participants did not recognize that there was more than one page available on the TV screen. They had no PC or Internet experience and were not used to scroll on the TV screen. Moreover, the elderly participants were not experienced teletext users (only two participants mentioned that they use teletext on a daily bases).

In task 2, almost all participants (14 out of 16) used the up and down keys (article per article) to select the article and to go to the end of the three-sided article, which was part of the task. Only five participants used the color keys (page up and down) to reach the article and then the end of the article. Interestingly, three of the participants who used the color keys were from the elderly group and only two from the group of the younger participants. Figure 6 illustrates that an elderly participant did not look at the navigation elements (like color keys) on the bottom of the screen compared to the eye-tracking data (see hot spots in Figure 7) of a younger participant.

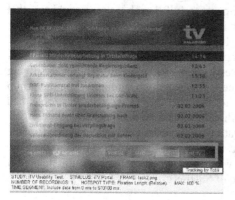

Fig. 6. Eye-tracking data (hot spots) from an elderly test person, who solved task 2 only with help (color keys were not recognized – see orange selection)

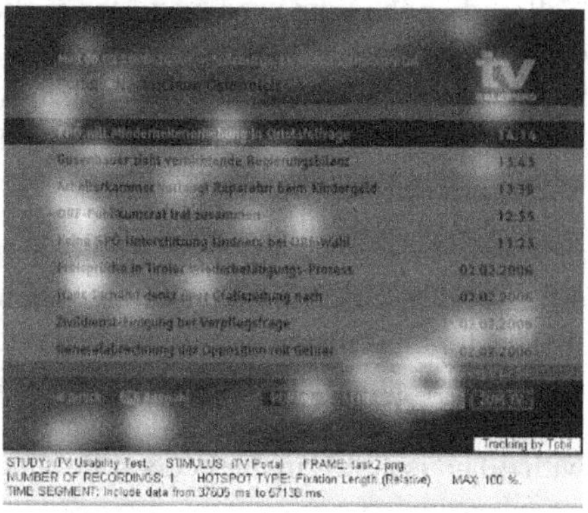

Fig. 7. Eye-tracking data (hot spots) from a young test person, who solved the task 2 without help (color keys were used, quick search forward behavior)

Figure 8 and 9 compare the gaze plot images of an elderly and younger participant while performing task 4 – finding article number 30 in a certain news area.

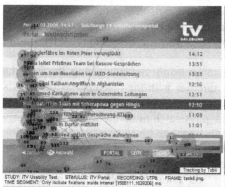

Fig. 8. Eye-tracking data (gaze plot) from an elderly test person, who solved the task 4 with help only (additional information recognized but not used for solving the task – see orange selection)

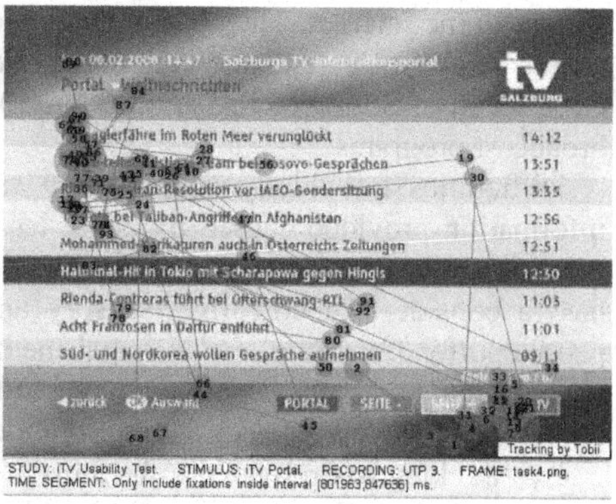

Fig. 9. Eye-tracking data (gaze plot) from a young test person, who solved the task 4 without help (straightforward navigation by using the additional information on the right bottom)

Task 3 and 4 tested the navigational aspects of the interface design in more detail. Based on the success rates of these two tasks we can state, that young people had no further problems to solve the tasks, whereas elderly people (female as well as male) had still problems to finalize task 3 and 4. Major problems were related to the font size and the color combinations, which made it even more difficult for the elderly to read the information (like white font and green background).

Based on the time used by all the participants to fulfill each task we could see, that elderly participants were always slower in their viewing, searching and finding behavior than the younger participants. Results of mean time for task solution, number of tasks solved, participants rating and several measurements from the eye-tracking data indicate, that the group of elderly people had more difficulties in solving the task, based on the design of the interface and unusual navigation. While the group of younger participants quickly learned to use the interface, elderly people had difficulties in task completion during the whole usability evaluation study.

The findings from this usability evaluation study were further considered in the development and design of the iTV applications within the iiTV@home project. The final information based iTV application was evaluated in a three-month field trial with 40 households in the Federal Province of Salzburg.

3 Conclusion and Outlook

Interactive TV is of particular interest to elderly people as it would allow them to access several services at home [8]. Elderly people represent the biggest group of TV consumers, also in Austria, where people older than 60 years are watching TV on average more than four hours a day, which is about one hour below the European average (see http://mediaresearch.orf.at/). Interactive TV provides the elderly and other active viewers with the opportunity to extend their use of the TV to activities similar to the Internet. They can browse information, personalize their viewing habits, access databases, carry out e-commerce related activities (shopping, banking, betting, etc.), ideally also interact with other viewers, and play an increasingly active role in broadcast programs.

Difficulties for elderly people often arise in using and navigating through the information provided caused by being less familiar with the conventions of today's information presentation and navigation concepts [2]. The design of iTV applications has to consider the cognitive, sensory and physical limitations that many elderly people suffer from (e.g. visual impairments). Supported by our usability evaluation study, it can be assumed, that the navigation concept and choices of color have to be strongly considered when designing for elderly people.

Eye-tracking has provided to be a useful methodology to evaluate and inform user interface design. For instance, we could identify which features (cues) of the user interface of the interactive application received more visual attention during task performance, which in turn, points to the potential problem areas of the interface, especially for elderly people. For example elderly participants had longer times to first fixation during solving the tasks than younger participants, indicating that higher contrast and font sizes could support elderly people.

The usage of metaphors from other information and communication technologies should be kept to a minimum as this group may have no prior knowledge of the domain. Visual cues should be designed more clearly to avoid errors during eye movements. We will work on this area to enhance usability and accessibility of iTV services for elderly people not only focusing on design, but also on new interaction techniques to support elderly with better screen design and special forms of feedback.

Acknowledgements

We like thank all our project partners from iiTV@home, especially the team involved in the usability evaluation study.

References

1. Bojko, A.: Eye Tracking in User Experience Testing: How to Make the Most of It. Proceddings of the UPA (Usability Professionals' Association) 2005 Conference. Retrieved November 22, 2006, from http://www.usercentric.com/UC/upa/
2. Carmichael, A.: Style Guide for the Design of Interactive Television Services for Elderly Viewers. Retrieved December 15, 2006, from http://www.computing.dundee.ac.uk/projects/UTOPIA/publications/Carmichael%20-%20DesignStyleGuideFinal.pdf/
3. Duchowski, A. T.: Eye Tracking Methodology: Theory and Practice. London: Springer Verlag (2003).
4. Godding, T.: Eye tracking vs Think aloud? Retrieved December 15, 2006, from http://staff.interesource.com/priority4/october2006/eyetracking.htm/
5. Hassenzahl, M., Burmester, M., Koller, F.: AttrakDiff: Ein Fragebogen zur Messung wahrgenommener hedonischer und pragmatischer Qualität. In Ziegler, J., Szwillus, G. (Eds.). Mensch & Computer 2003. Interaktion in Bewegung. Stuttgart, Leipzig: B.G. Teubner (2003) 187-196.
6. Jacob, R. J. K., and Karn, K. S.: Eye tracking in human-computer interaction and usability research: Ready to deliver the promises. In Hyona, J., Radach, R., and Deubel, H. (Eds.). The Mind's Eye: Cognitive and Applied Aspects of Eye Movement Research. Amsterdam: Elsevier Science (2003), 573-605.
7. Lull, J.: Inside Family Viewing. Routhledge, 1990.
8. Obrist, M., Bernhaupt, R., Tscheligi, M.: Interactive Television for the Home: An ethnographic study on users requirements and experiences. Proceedings of EuroiTV 2006, Athens, Greece, May 25-26, (2006) 349-358.
9. Pemberton, L., Griffiths, R.: Usability Evaluation Techniques for Interactive Television, In C. Stephanidis (Ed.). Proceedings of HCI International 2003 (4), Universal Access in HCI (2003) 882–886.
10. Poole, A. and Ball, L. J.: Eye Tracking in Human-Computer Interaction and Usability Research: Current Status and Future Prospects. In Ghaoui, C. (Ed.). Encyclopedia of Human Computer Interaction. Idea Group (2000).
11. Renshaw, J. A., Finlay, J., and Webb, N.: Getting a Measure of Satisfaction from Eyetracking in Practice. Workshop at CHI 2006, Montreal, Canada (2006), 1723-1726.
12. Ruel, L., Outing, S.: Viewing patterns for homepages. Retrieved December 7, 2006, from http://www.poynterextra.org/eyetrack2004/viewing.htm/

Accessibility of Interactive Television for Users with Low Vision: Learning from the Web

Mark V Springett[1] and Richard N Griffiths[2]

[1] Interaction Design Centre, Middlesex University, Ravensfield House, The Burroughs,
London, NW4 4BE, UK
m.springett@mdx.ac.uk
[2] University of Brighton, School of Computing, Mathematical & Information Sciences,
Watts Building, Moulsecoomb, Brighton, BN2 4GJ, UK
r.n.griffiths@brighton.ac.uk

Abstract. Contemporary developments in digital and interactive television in the UK are reviewed to assess their accessibility implications for viewer/users with low vision. Of particular significance is the likelihood of divergence between sectors of the population receiving digital television in an enhanced form through new broadband distribution (thin client) technology and those remaining with older broadcast set-top-box (thick client) technology, comprising proportionately more visually disabled viewers. With this second segment particularly in mind, and utilising findings from our previous research with visually disabled people, we examine the applicability of the W3C web accessibility guidelines to interactive television. We conclude that, while technical limitations may prevent their wholesale adoption, guidelines relating to the display of interactive features, and brightness and contrast may be directly interpreted for this medium, whilst other guidelines involving magnification and audio equivalence and feedback are highly relevant and should inform technical developments in set-top box functionality.

Keywords: Accessibility, Low vision, Guidelines, IDTV, Set-top boxes.

1 Introduction

Accessibility is desirable in systems providing public information and services—and its absence can have legal consequences. For many, a primary source of information is television. The interactive capabilities that digital broadcasting has brought should enhance its capabilities. This may be particularly important for those otherwise excluded from the 'e' world (email, web, etc.) by lack of computing equipment and connectivity, but only if it is accessible. Unfortunately in the rush to deliver interactive digital television (IDTV) the needs of the visually disabled have not been taken fully into account (The Tiresias font for television being a notable exception [16]). In section 2 of this paper we review developments with regard to visual disability issues. Of particular importance is the move away from broadcast television onto broadband and the web. The services offered and underlying technologies are increasingly converging with the web. In section 3 we briefly rehearse the reasons for

P. Cesar et al. (Eds.): EuroITV 2007, LNCS 4471, pp. 76–85, 2007.

promoting accessible digital television, referring to the divide being opened up between those with access to the newer broadband television services and the older broadcast set top box (STB) viewer/users. An information resource where accessibility has made considerable progress is the web. In section 4 we consider the applicability of guidelines developed by W3C to IDTV. We conclude with indications as to development and application of television guidelines.

2 Developments in Digital TV

This section focuses on developments in the UK, where the presence of commercial implementations of all DTV technologies reflects the state of the art world wide. The past 10 years since the introduction of digital TV in the UK have seen an enormous increase in the rate of technical development. First available via satellite, then cable and terrestrial, and in some parts of the country phone line via asymmetric digital subscriber line (ADSL), now to be extended much wider through the newly launched British Telecom service and BSkyB's separate broadband add-on. Each of these technical developments confers its own advantages and disadvantages, which from the point of view of service subscribers often translates into winners and losers. The original STB systems currently installed should really be though of as a transitional technology. In systems architecture terms they are thick-clients; systems in which much processing (particularly rendering and animating interactivity) is done locally. Given the continuing advance of Moore's Law, the difference in memory capacity and processing power between the earliest installed STB's and the latest is enormous. However, services must be delivered to both the oldest and the newest boxes; a legacy problem that becomes ever more acute for the broadcaster.

The availability of high bandwidth multicast and unicast transmission together with efficient back-channel as provided by ADSL broadband and improved cable provides the opportunity to escape the legacy problem by deploying thin clients. The thin STB has only both to render the incoming stream into video and audio, and detect control inputs before relaying them back to the head-end. Interactive elements can be generated at the head-end before being encoded in the video stream. Essentially an installed base of thin STB's is future-proofed, and improvement in service can be implemented by enhancing the processing power of the head end; a much more manageable task than upgrading thick STB's in the field. This method of distribution, known as internet protocol television (IPTV) is almost certainly the future of broadcast television and its associated interactive services.

So, who are the losers? The likelihood is that the demographic segments who have not acquired personal computers and internet access will be left behind to continue with the older thick STB technology (until it becomes commercially unviable for the broadcasters to support). The quality of interactive services between the two strands of technology will diverge widely. All things being equal, it is likely to be the elderly and the economically disadvantaged (who may include a higher proportion with disabilities) who are left with the older technology. There is a double disadvantage here in that the newer technology has the capability to significantly enhance both the viewing and interacting experience for people with disabilities.

It must be pointed out that developed technology exists to retrospectively configure thick STB's as thin clients. This is already in operation in cable systems, and in principle could be applied to digital satellite (DSat) STB's, where necessary with additional hardware if the STB does not have a broadband port (though we are not aware that BSkyB has any plans to take this option).

A significant advantage of unicast delivery is the provision of true video-on-demand, with instant switching of the video stream. This may well lead to the development of interactive applications that move away from the web-on-TV textual style of presentation, to a TV style where video and audio carries the content. Whilst this may reinvigorate television interactivity by providing an experience more akin to 'natural' TV (and of the sort most people expected and were disappointed by its lack), it may present even more challenges to disabled viewers.

The TV screen itself has also been developed, with cathode-ray tube technology (CRT) giving way to flat screen liquid-crystal and plasma. These have been rapidly upgraded to large high-definition displays. The accessibility consequences of these changes need to be investigated. It may be expected that they can only be positive, but this is not necessarily so. In general CRT screens are brighter and may have better contrast. Additionally the artefacts of digital compression are more visible on high definition screens; this may have accessibility consequences.

Alongside development of the 'living room TV'; television has been migrating onto the personal computer, and the mobile phone. On the PC video distribution by download and subsequently streaming has been available for some time and has been widely exploited by the pornography industry. The lowered costs of video storage and distribution facilities have recently lead to the 'Web 2' amateur and copyright infringing video 'communities' exemplified by You Tube. However, commercial broadcasters are now moving into this field with programme assets streamed or delivered by download. Ironically, interactive enhancements currently do not work in this environment, though in principle they can be made to work much better here. This goes for accessibility enhancements too.

On mobile phones, the development of Digital Video Broadcasting - Handheld and other broadcast technology promises a new environment for TV consumption. From the accessibility point of view, this may be a mixed blessing. Depending on the disability of the viewer, it may be impossible to use, or allow better access. For example, viewers with peripheral vision defect can hold the handset very near to their face and scan the image by moving the handset rather than kneeling in front of the TV set and scanning their head across the screen. The possession of an individual mobile TV may actually facilitate group viewing where the visual and auditory settings may be best adjusted to support a disabled viewer without irritating other viewers in the same room viewing on a conventional TV.

One final development should be mentioned; the re-emergence of web access via the TV through the development of WTVML technology as used in the recently launched SkyNet portal. Here specially developed web sites (coded in WTVML) can be accessed via the BSkyB STB back-channel and the inbuilt WTVML micro-browser. For people without a PC and internet connection this offers an alternative access to the 'e' economy; all be it an extremely limited one. Due to the innate limitations of the technical environment and a commercial decision to disallow audio content, accessibility is not explicitly supported.

Our conclusion from this rapid overview of contemporary development in DTV is that there will be a parting of the ways between more affluent and technically sophisticated viewers who obtain IPTV services, and the remainder of the population who stay with broadcast DTV and its inherent limitations. Whilst IPTV, and in particular its reception through a personal computer with its innate flexibility, provides tremendous potential for accessibility enhancements, many (perhaps the majority) of disabled people will not have access to it. Thus the relevance of developing accessibility within the domain of broadcast DTV and iTV remains.

3 Reasons for Promoting Accessible Interactive Digital TV

The potential utility of interactive TV is exemplified by a recent initiative from the UK. In 2001 the UK government stated its wish for local government services to be offered online by 2005, under the Implementing Electronic Government (IEG) initiative, explicitly citing IDTV as a primary medium for this development. From the IEG statements both in 2001 and 2002 it is clear that UK central government saw IDTV having a particular potential for delivering key services more effectively and making new services possible. The UK government's thinking was based on their perception of TV as the popular medium. The aim of the initiative is to enfranchise those who tend often to be excluded. Amongst the key target groups are the elderly, and also people with learning difficulties. A significant proportion of this population segment suffers from varying forms of visual impairment.

In random survey of 12 UK local authorities' responses to the IEG initiative conducted in 2005, more than half reported that they had not made any tangible progress in developing IDTV-based services [9]. Most had placed more emphasis on the development of public kiosks rather than move towards providing local authority services via IDTV. However, some examples are more encouraging, e.g., Islington council's pilot initiative IDTV information service. The site provided information about: Jobs, safety, health, local services, events, life-long learning, and appeared to be regarded as a success. However their follow-up report stated that external collaboration would be needed to fully implement it [6].

The potential of TV as an accessible and useful technology is high, but this is a long way from being fully realised. However, contemporary developments may afford similar developments in accessibility as the web. Accessibility guidelines for the web are now relatively established, and have had an effect in making key sites such as public information portals accessible to a wider population. Similarly commercial web sites have an agenda for increasing outreach to a wider market by following accessibility guidelines (and a legal requirement). Some of the most significant and also relatively soluble accessibility problems relate to users with low vision. The next section considers the World Wide Web Consortium (W3C) accessibility guidelines [17] as a benchmark for assessing a sample of currently available IDTV services for viewers with low-vision.

4   Portability of W3C Guidelines to IDTV

We carried out an expert evaluation of the applicability of the W3C accessibility guidelines to a sample of current Sky and BBC IDTV services. We compared the recommendations in five key categories to data collected from contemporary requirements gathering studies previously conducted [4,11,12,13,14]. Whilst specific guidelines refer to the use of HTML features and other environment-specific items such as Applets, a substantial amount of the content refers to aspects of the presentation and interactivity. Our review assesses the applicability of these guidelines to IDTV design, and in turn assesses the design of contemporary IDTV services with reference to them. Of the fourteen W3C web guideline sections we identified five that previous studies would suggest are particularly relevant. These were examined and relevant points extracted.

The design of a number of existing DTV displays appears to contravene the principles of W3C. The recommendations from these guidelines combine the need for specialist features for impaired users, and more generic recommendations for the design of displays and interactive features.

4.1   Cursor Issues

An inspection of Sky Active (a collection of public and commercial information and interactive resources available via Sky STB's in the UK) revealed two problems relating to cursors. One was the considerable variation of cursor designs both in terms of physical appearance and in rules of operation. Related to this was the problem of identifying and operating the cursor, i.e. finding it when entering a page and completing a selection operation. Studies of use [14] also revealed compounding problems with recovery after errors. Errors may be caused by mistakenly identifying options [8] or simple physical slips [10]. The likelihood of slips occurring is strong given the nature of the remote controlled interaction, and the possibility of divided attention in a TV-viewing environment. Therefore ease of recovery is an important general principle for any user. Evidence from studies reported in [12,14] suggests that recoverability is a particular problem for low-vision users. If a wrong selection is made or navigation within pages is misdirected, it is typical for users to re-scan the page in order to specify corrective actions. Where subjects' central or peripheral vision was impaired this proved to be a particularly difficult process.

The variation in cursor design and operation principles effectively forces the user to recognise and explore the use of cursors on a repeated basis as a series of pages are visited. In effect, the user generates a hypothesis of how the cursor on each page can be manoeuvred and selection actions performed. Exploratory action will either confirm that hypothesis or assist the user in specifying further exploratory action. For fully-sighted users the confirmation of the initial hypothesis and reasoning about alternatives is based on a scan of both the area of the screen where cursor action is anticipated, and on the page contents as a whole. This issue is referred to as 'consistency mapping' in [11].

(a)   (b)   (c)

Fig. 1. (a),(b) and (c) show three screens from one Sky Active application in which three variations on menu item selection are used

The application opens with a menu listed as a vertical column of buttons, selection of the active item being shown by reverse text (Fig. 1a.). From the opening screen, pressing the green button on the handset opens a menu consisting of a vertical list of items enclosed in a rectangular panel (Fig. 1b.). Using the up and down arrows on the handset causes the active item to change colour and be marked with a bullet on its left. Selecting an item from the previous menu replaces the initial menu with one in which an item is activated by pressing the associated number button on the key pad (Fig 1.c). The up and down arrows have no effect here.

4.2 Brightness, Contrast and 'Advanced Features'

The W3C guidelines on colour displays recommend strong foreground/background contrast, and warn against blinking or moving elements on-screen. Where there is a combination of TV viewing content and interactive content such as pop-up screens it is difficult to avoid peripheral movement that may affect the focusing of attention for users with low vision. There is also a potential conflict in that designers' desire to make screens visually appealing as well as providing a continuous 'presence' of TV content whilst interactive content is accessed is likely to diminish accessibility for low vision users. The text overlays used by BBC digital text services provide an example of this (see figure 2). Text overlays in deep red with white text display a visible 'shadow' of the underlying TV content, diminishing readability for low-vision users. Presently this does not appear to be adjustable. The ability to adjust such pages, or set preferences for sharp backgrounds without background movement seems critical for users with low vision. This issue is also identified in [11].

4.3 Identifying and Selecting Options

The W3C web guidelines point to the utility of enlarging options, magnifying the currently selected cursor item. This appears to be useful for users with low vision. One general utility would be to address the issue of feedback and visibility of system status [3, 7] for IDTV services. The enlarged option would act as a tracker allowing users to detect whether the current option was the intended one and continuously monitoring coverage of navigation around the page. The enhancement of readability to overcome difficulties in scanning text is another desirable aspect. Feedback from

Fig. 2. In this screen, a permanent scrolling marquee of black text on an opaque white background is in constant movement. On the right a semi transparent overlay has been opened through red-button selection. The presenter can be seen moving behind its text.

study participants in [14] suggests that viewers with low peripheral vision tend to scan parts of words, often having to make assumptions about the identity from a few letters. The addition of magnification would alleviate this problem.

The issue of magnification and its utility is in part conditional on the issues with page layout and cursor design described above. It is anticipated that for simple page metaphors such as the Sky electronic programme guide (EPG) the expanded cursor is easier to track. Compare this with a page where shape and form are irregular and changeable, or not represented by text objects. Many objects are not comprehensible without contextual information provided by the array or page in which they are situated. Therefore it is difficult to imagine even the expanded version being without problems where iconic representations are used without text.

4.4 Audio Equivalence and Audio Feedback

The use of speech input/output is emphasized in W3C guidelines and screen reader devices are available for web readers. The use of auditory equivalence is relatively common in web use, although it requires sites to provide meaningful content in alt-tags, something that is not always provided. No equivalent yet exists in DTV, although the BBC recently published a white paper describing the nature and utility of audio description in future DTV services [15]. Users suffering from low central vision seem to have much to gain from audio description where navigating screen containing dense text such as the Sky EPG shown in figure 3.

A representative task model for operating the EPG is described below:

1. Locate remote control directional button → 2. Locate cursor → 3. read current channel option → 4. move cursor to next option → repeat 2,3,4 until channel found, 5. move cursor to next content/schedule option → 6. read current content/schedule option → repeat 5 and 6 until option found 7. select option.

Fig. 3. The SKY EPG with its dual cursor highlights focusing on the selected channel and a specific scheduled item

Previous study evidence [14] shows that viewers with low vision have problems locating (and re-locating) the cursor and reading textual options on the screen. The utility of auditory feedback potentially turns this from a desperately slow (or even impossible) process into one in which task steps can be carried out with sufficient information resources to support the execution and evaluation of each action. The reading of options of the screen can serve both as confirmation of the user's arrival at the desired option and a navigation aid, guiding them through the menu operation process. The use of non-verbal auditory output also has a potential role in providing feedback. This type of output helps the user to recognize and monitor cursor movement. The non-verbal identification of basic repeated actions allows the user to listen to the screen-reader describe the actual options with minimal distraction.

4.5 Input Devices

One of the most significant features of web accessibility is the considerable variety of input devices ranging from customized mice through track-balls, joysticks and more specialized equipment such as sensor pads and mouth operated devices. The W3C guidelines emphasize designing for device independence. Conventional remote control design tends to exclude many sight impaired users, raising issues such as text size, labelling and tactile feedback [3]. For TV use the complexity of the input device makes it a second 'interface'. Remote devices have similar issues of option labelling, functionality and feature clustering to the screens with which they interact. Typical problems include difficulties in identifying the current mode in relation to multifunctional buttons, reading the textual labels on dedicated buttons. Furthermore, sight-impaired users report problems searching for mislaid remote control devices, suggesting that either fixed devices or direct communication with the set-top box may be useful alternatives. The use of keyboards has proved useful for some users, particularly in support of skills that make the visual channel relatively redundant for STB control tasks. This type of skill requires little in the way of visual cueing, with spatial and sensory information providing the necessary sensory input. Supporting such skilled behaviour allows those with central vision problems to interact fluently rather than painstakingly inspect the remote device for visual information. This relatively static input device also has the advantage of being less likely to be mislaid.

The space of possible input devices has yet to be explored fully, although developments in related fields such as game technology suggest a range of tailorable input support is possible. The use of gesture has also been shown to have potential utility for users with low vision [14]. In general minimising the movement of attention between the screen and handset is beneficial, especially where viewers may require different glasses for each.

5 Conclusions and Future Work

Many of the W3C guidelines are equally appropriate for IDTV. For the new IPTV, particularly when viewed in a non-traditional TV environment (PC, mobile) they will be directly applicable to subsidiary interactive material which will be presented as web pages. For the older 'red-button technology' STB environment considerable development is required, as it lacks the flexibility to support customization and tailorability to user preferences. This is the technology that a substantial proportion of the older population will be most likely to have available. Problems such as low vision and compounding health issues associated with age accentuate the need for accessible DTV services. Whilst it may not be possible to import every advance in accessibility from the web into DTV, attention to aspects such as device independence, display design and navigation support can provide significant improvements.

TV interactivity remains significantly rooted in the traditions of its desktop-based predecessor. Longer-term research and development goals include new metaphors for design that improve on the 'desktop' inherited from the PC [1]. Given that accessibility in the wider scope combines instrumental and hedonic factors, research into more human-like mediators between viewer and device may be explored. Some exploratory work into avatar-based interaction to specific services for vision-impaired users is reported in [5]. Further leading-edge exploratory research such as the 'virtual companion' considers an alternative style of interface in which human-like forms interact mediate between user and device [2]. This approach seems to have the potential to enhance both instrumental and hedonic aspects of TV use. This suggests that the low-level refinement of current interactivity may be a temporary forerunner to a new era of accessible television. However vulnerable sections of the population are likely only to have access to the current STB technology for the foreseeable future, making further work on guidelines for this environment important.

References

1. Chorianopoulos, K., Lekakos, G. and Spinellis, D. (2003), *The virtual channel model for personalized television*. In Proc. the 1st European interactive television conference
2. Cringeon, S., Benyon, D., and Leplatre, G. (2005) *Exploration of personality rich mobile comanions* In. Proc, Human-Animated Character Interaction Workshop
   http://www.dcs.shef.ac.uk/cogsys/workshop/StewartCringean_H-ACI2005.pdf

3. Freeman, J., Lessiter, J., Williams, A. and Harrison, D. (2003) Easy TV 2002 Research Report. ITC and Consumer's Association, available online: http://www.which.net/campaigns/other/communications/0301easytv.pdf
4. Gill, J. & Perera, S., *Accessible universal design of interactive digital television*, Proceedings of 1st EuroITV Conference
5. Hamilton, F., Petrie, H. and Carmichael, A. (2003). *The VISTA Project: universal access to electronic programme guides for digital TV*. In C. Stephanidis (Ed.), Proceedings of HCI International Mahwah, New Jersey: Lawrence Erlbaum Associates.
6. Islington Borough Council UK (2004) Implementing electronic government: return, http://www.islington.gov.uk/DownloadableDocuments/CouncilandDemocracy/Pdf/ie g4_2004.pdf
7. Klein, J, Simon K & Sinclair,K. (2004) Attitudes to Digital Television. Preliminary findings on consumer adoption of Digital Television. www.genericsgroup.com
8. Nielsen, J. and Molich, R. (1990)   Improving a Human-Computer Dialogue, Communications of the ACM, March 1990
9. Office of national statistics(UK), (2006). www.statistics.gov.uk
10. Reason, J. (1990) *Human Error,* Cambridge University Press
11. Rice, M., and Fels, D., (2004). *Low vision the visual interface for interactive television*. In J. Masthoff, R. Griffiths and L. Pemberton (Eds). Proceedings of the 2nd European Conference on Interactive television
12. Rice, M., 2003. *A study of television and visual impairment: Prospects for the accessibility of interactive television.* In J.Masthoff, J. Griffiths, R. and Pemberton, L (Eds). Proceedings of the 1st European interactive television conference
13. Cereijo Roibas, A., Nur Anthashs Syed Ahmad, S., Sala, R. & Rahman, M. (2005). *Beyond the remote control: Going the extra mile to enhance iTV access via mobile devices & humanizing navigation experience for those with special needs.* In Jensen, J. (Ed.) User-Centred ITV Systems, Programmes and Applications: Proceedings of EuroITV 2005, Aalborg University, 30 March – 1 April, 2005.
14. Springett M. and Griffiths R. (in press) *The use of stalking-horse evaluation prototypes for probing DTV accessibility requirements*, to appear in, Interactive Digital Television: technologies and applications, IGI press
15. Tanton, N.E. Ware, T. and Armstrong, M. (2006), Audio Description: what it is and how it works, http://www.bbc.co.uk/rd/pubs/whp/whp051.shtml
16. 16Tiresias.org, http://www.tiresias.org/
17. W3C Web content accessibility guidelines 1.0 (1999) http://www.w3.org/TR/1999/WAI-WEBCONTENT-19990505

Will Broadcasters Survive in the Online and Digital Domain?

Andra Leurdijk

TNO-ICT, P.O. Box 5050,
2600 GB Delft, The Netherlands
Andra.Leurdijk@tno.nl

Abstract. Digital television and the internet are fundamentally changing media markets. Consumers have access to an increasing amount of news, information and entertainment. In addition to traditional media companies such as publishers and broadcasters new players enter the market as content producers, packagers, marketers and distributors. These changes threaten the position of traditional broadcasters. This paper explores the ways in which broadcasters have responded to these challenges and identifies opportunities and bottlenecks for broadcasters' development of digital media services. Based on desk research and case studies it points at audiovisual archives and distinct criteria for quality and editorial standards as the main assets of traditional (public service) broadcasters. Copyright issues, regulatory constraints on public service broadcasters and differences between broadcast and internet culture are among the main bottlenecks.

Keywords: broadcaster, digital television, internet, business model, user generated content, audiovisual archives.

1 Introduction

Digital television and the internet – especially web 2.0 – are fundamentally changing media markets. These changes threaten the position of traditional broadcasters and publishers for a number of reasons. Firstly, in a multichannel environment individual television channels will have relatively small audience shares. Most traditional general interest broadcasters (public and commercial) have seen their audience shares decline in digital and multichannel households. Secondly, people spend an increasing amount of time on the internet. Although this has until now not been at the detriment of television viewing, especially among young people there is a noticeable shift from television viewing time to internet use. Young people are also very skilled in multitasking and often consume different types of media simultaneously. Thirdly, with growing numbers of broadband households and users of advanced mobile phones and other mobile devices, users can watch television and video on the internet and through mobile networks. Traditional broadcasters do try to jump on the bandwagon and also offer content for these platforms, but in these markets they compete with many other companies that offer audiovisual content. Among them are network providers and web portals that try to attract consumers by offering attractive or

P. Cesar et al. (Eds.): EuroITV 2007, LNCS 4471, pp. 86–95, 2007.
© Springer-Verlag Berlin Heidelberg 2007

exclusive content, but also content producers themselves who have now a direct and relatively cheap way of access to their audiences and are no longer completely dependent on broadcasters with exclusive access to scarce spectrum or television channels to reach their audience.

Finally niche content producers find on the internet ample opportunities to publish their own content and, according to Anderson's long tail theory (Anderson, 2006) can still find a sufficiently large audience, because they can reach small and scattered audiences worldwide and over time. Even users themselves can publish and exchange photographs and films, some of which are also used in professional media outlets. User generated content is the term for a trend that has rapidly become hugely popular.

What do these developments mean for the position of traditional broadcasters? Will they become obsolete, as content producers now offer their content directly to viewers, without the intermediary role of broadcasters? And because they are no longer needed as packagers and schedule makers for users who are increasingly able to find content of their own interest, also outside the traditional television channels and even turn into producers themselves? Or will they be able to survive and successfully exploit their audiovisual archives on digital platforms as well as develop popular new services and new ways of engaging their audiences?

Some believe that traditional broadcasters have responded too slowly and inadequately to the new opportunities of a digital and networked world. As traditional media organisations their staunch, hierarchical and rigid production routines, work style and professional ethics do not fit very well with the much more anarchistic and hybrid internet culture. At the same time traditional broadcasters also have some strengths. An important advantage is their ability to cross promote digital services and websites through their open television channels and vice versa. In addition some broadcasters possess considerable amounts of audiovisual archive footage that they can exploit on digital channels; others have a reputation for quality or a strong brand name. The current market changes affecting broadcasters lead to the following question:

What strategies do (public service) broadcasters adopt in the digital domain and what opportunities and bottlenecks do they face?

This paper will analyze some of the strategies that broadcasters adopt in the digital domain and attempts to assess the strengths as well as the bottlenecks for the further development of these services. Broadcasters offer digital channels, video-on-demand services, interactive programmes, websites with extra information on programmes and celebrities and platforms for communication and debate. Out of a number of different ways in which broadcasters have become active players in the digital domain, this article focuses on two prominent trends: a) broadcasters' attempts to exploit content across different platforms and devices and b) broadcasters endeavours to incorporate user generated content in their offers.

1.1 Method

This article is based on data gathered for a number of TNO research projects; firstly two projects on policies and regulation concerning public broadcasters' new media services (Leurdijk, 2005b and 2005c) and secondly a number of in-depth case studies into (public service) broadcasters' digital services that were used for two different European research projects in which TNO is responsible for exploring new business models for so called ShapeShifted TV (in NM2) and user generated content (in Citizen Media) (Leurdijk and others, 2005a, 2006)[1].

For each service the business and content strategies were analysed, based on interviews and desk research, identifying both opportunities and bottlenecks for traditional broadcasters in the digital domain. The cases represent only part of broadcasters' current and varied digital offers by only three different broadcasters. The cases do however represent broadcaster's dilemma's in exploiting archive content and in incorporating user generated content in their offer and the opportunities and bottlenecks that we have identified are likely to be of relevance for other digital services, especially when offered by public service broadcasters.

2 Case Studies

2.1 BBC Creative Archive

In April 2005 the BBC launched the pilot version of the BBC Creative Archive (http://creativearchive.bbc.co.uk/). The Creative Archive offered free access to selected and legally cleared BBC television and radio programmes. Its users were able to search, preview, download (in non-broadcast quality) and modify (extracts of) programmes. They could use this material for class room presentations, personal projects or other non commercial uses and share their creations with others on a non commercial basis. The Creative Archive content has been released on topical BBC websites and includes Radio 1 VJ, clips on different regions in the UK, Open School material and news clips. Viewers have access to 500-600 video clips in total. In the pilot phase the audiovisual material has been limited to factual content; in the future there might be content across all BBC genres.

At the core of the Creative Archive project is the Creative Archive Licence, inspired by the Creative Commons movement. The Creative Archive Licence recognises and preserves copyright, but releases the opportunity to engage in non-commercial sharing and integration of personal derived work. Commercial use is prohibited and users must share their own content on the same terms.

The Creative Archive Licence was launched by the BBC together with public and private partners such as Channel4, the British Film Institute and the Open University. Since its launch Teachers' television, the Community Channel, The Museums, Libraries and Archives Council and ITN Source (formerly ITN News Archive) have joined the Creative Archive Licence Group. Most partners are still in the process of making (more) material available. At the end of the pilot in October 2006 the service went through a public value test, commissioned by the BBC Board of Governors (now: the BBC Trust), whose outcome was not yet known at the moment of completing this article (end 2006)[2].

---

[1] See for more information on these projects: www.ist-nm2.org and www.ist-citizenmedia.org
[2] During the review BBC Creative Archive was closed down, only general information pages are still available.

Many of the possible ways in which end-users will use the material in BBC's Creative Archive are still unclear. The present offer is a starting point from which other uses and models can be developed. It is foreseen that in the future more of the BBC's archive material will be made available to the public.

2.2 Vara Comedy, Dutch Public Broadcaster

The Dutch public broadcaster Vara is in the process of reorganising its production process in order to become a cross media organisation. Comedy is one of Vara's key genres and a genre that is central to its brand. Vara's Comedy offer is exploited on different platforms. On its open channel Vara broadcasts live and recorded comedy registrations. On its digital thematic comedy channel Vara recycles archive content. It will also produce a few hours of low cost, original content for this channel. The Comedy web portal (http://variatee.vara.nl/) offers access to over 40 hours archive material in the form of 3-5 minutes comedy clips. The clips can be rated by viewers and viewers can suggest to include material that is not yet represented on the site. The site also offers biographies of the comedians that are showcased on the site. In addition there are an online comedy magazine (Greinz.nl), content for mobile devices and real life events such as comedy battles between schools organised by the broadcaster.

The digital channels and the live events are used as a platform for young talent; Vara will scout young talents and will invite them to produce low cost short films for the digital channel. If successful these can then move on to the other platforms (web portal, open channel). There will also be space for user generated content within Vara's comedy offer, but this is not yet considered to be of strategic importance. The content will be moderated, to guarantee certain quality and decency standards.

2.3 Four Docs, Channel 4

FourDocs (http://www.channel4.com/fourdocs/) is a broadband internet channel designed by Channel4 for people to showcase their documentaries. Users can upload and download four minutes' long documentaries. In addition to this the website provides a large knowledge base of practical, audiovisual guides on how to make documentaries.

People who have uploaded a documentary to FourDocs receive comments from the FourDocs' professional editorial team as well as from other users. All reviews are published on the website. By October 2006 approximately 200 films had been published on the website.

The website also contains a rushes library of free, already cleared material that people can use in their own four minutes' documentaries and background information on the history of British documentary and interviews with documentary makers.

Channel4 and the editors of the site want to bring their ideas on high quality documentary, decency and public values to the users, therefore the site is moderated. Also the video quality on FourDocs is higher than the video quality on sites like Google Video, MySpace or YouTube. The editorial team checks the legal aspects of the films (copyrights infringements, libel, infringement on legal procedures, etc.).

All contributors to FourDocs are required to make their work available under a Creative Commons licence. This means that everyone can download and use the material on the site, "provided they make their own work available on similar conditions, and provided that they use it for their own purposes in a non-commercial, attributive, no-derivative way. That means that you must give credit and others can not make any money from your film. Neither can they take any clips from your film out of context." (From FourDocs FAQ)

3 Digital Services and the Broadcasters' Strategies

The case studies of BBC Creative Archive, FourDocs and Vara Comedy are all part of the broadcasters' strategies to follow their audiences to digital platforms. Each of the services discussed is considered to be successful by its owners. The use, numbers and frequency of visits and/or contributions of users live up to the broadcasters' original expectations. The BBC might be able to obtain some extra income by making the service available on the international market. The Vara has banner advertisements on its website as well as bumper-ads at the start of its comedy clips and streaming audio files. FourDocs is currently advertisement free. People are asked to upload their documentaries for free; therefore Channel4 feels it can not directly earn money from people's contributions through sponsorship or advertisements. Especially in the beginning this was thought essential, in order to build up trust and persuade people to upload their films. FourDocs' target is also considered to be more critical than other people on how businesses operate and would probably not have been willing to contribute their films to FourDocs if it was seen to earn money off their backs. Now that FourDocs has established a good reputation, some advertising or sponsorship might be conceivable, for instance by inviting industries to sponsor bursaries or competitions for Channel4 or allow some small banners on its web pages.

However, the main goals of the three digital services are not to attract huge audiences or to generate money, but are of a different nature. The BBC Creative Archive fits with the BBC's philosophy to make its content available to as many people as possible, on all platforms. Public access to the BBC's archives, is considered as one of the ways in which the BBC' s licence fee is justified. For the Vara its comedy offer helps to build Vara's strategy to become a cross media organisation that exploits its brand name in a number of key genres. For Channel4 FourDocs is a way of securing its brand name and reputation in the field of documentary and to fulfil its public service remit to provide innovative programmes in both form and content. Another way in which Channel4 benefits from the service is that it uses the website as a pool for new talents. Some of the people that have uploaded their films were invited by Channel4 to work on other projects.

4 Opportunities and Bottlenecks

In this paragraph a number of opportunities for broadcasters will be discussed as well as some bottlenecks that might hinder further development.

4.1 Contradictory Interest in Exploitation of Copyrights on Digital Platforms

One of the main assets of (public) broadcasters is their large audiovisual archive that they can exploit online and through digital channels. When programmes are made in-house, copyrights are in most cases possessed by the broadcaster. However, this is not always the case for all the underlying copyrights for the use of music, décors, and performing artists. These copyrights usually remain with the artists. The contracts with these underlying right holders have until recently only included the rights to a first screening and one or two repeats on open channels, but not for online exploitation or for digital channels and video-on-demand services. Copyright issues thus present broadcasters that want to exploit their archives with a major bottleneck. Sorting out all the varying provisions in copy right contracts, as well as clearing those copyrights, requires a considerable investment of time and money. Even when the exploitation of content on other platforms is included in contracts, they often take different forms and there are still many conflicting interests between stakeholders. This is particularly the case for content commissioned by broadcasters to independent television producers and for recordings of the performing arts (theatre, music, dance, etc.). Some content genres, such as sports and film, but also – like in the Vara case - comedy, humour and satire, are examples of highly exploitable content. Artists are reluctant to give away or sell copyrights beyond the two to three times broadcast exposure on television's open net channels that they have initially agreed on. They either think that they can exploit the content themselves, or they are afraid that online exposure or broadcasts on digital channels will cannibalize on the number of visitors of their live theatre shows. They fear that recycling their shows on digital channels reduces their market value. This is particularly true for recordings of full shows. Acquiring content rights to clips is generally a lot easier.

When the copyrights have remained with production companies issues are even more complicated for broadcasters, as production companies could also decide to re-exploit popular programmes in collaboration with for instance network operators, other platform or portal owners or even launch their own distribution channels, because distribution scarcity has diminished and television producers are no longer solely dependent on channel owners to broadcast their programmes.

The BBC Creative Archive has a different copyrights problem. Most of the non fiction material is produced in house, so the BBC already owns the copyrights of the footage. However the copyrights are only cleared for the UK. This means that users are restricted in publishing material from the BBC Creative Archive on their websites, unless they employ geo-IP filtering technologies that restrict the use of their productions to UK residents. It is expected that in the future Creative Archive material could be made available through a distribution partner outside the UK that would pay for the copy rights of distribution abroad. This foreign partner could generate revenues from for instance online advertising or sponsorship and thus be able to pay for the rights. Users of the BBC Creative Archive would then be able to publish the derivative works on their websites without restricting access to UK residents, because he underlying rights would already have been cleared by the international distribution partner.

Channel4's FourDocs does not have this copyright problem because it includes only a limited amount of archive material and works with producers who, by uploading the material to the FourDocs website, agree to make their works available online, worldwide under the Creative Commons Licence.

Archive material provides broadcasters with an important asset. But the case studies show that there are competing stakeholders, such as platform and web portal owners, television production companies and in some cases the right holders themselves, who are interested in exploiting the same content and are becoming less dependent on broadcasters for distribution of their works.

4.2   Public Service Broadcasters and Competition Issues

Two of the three case studies concern services by public service broadcasters that receive income from the licence fee or government funding and have thus been able to build a large archive with valuable content that can be re-exploited on digital platforms. It also allows them to produce additional original content for these digital platforms. Without these assets the Vara and the BBC would not have been able to build the services discussed in the case studies. Therefore public service broadcasters are still in a strong position vis-à-vis other market players (television producers, ISPs, network operators). They can guarantee a considerable investment in original content production that other market players can not afford, apart from some of the very big ones. At the same time it makes them vulnerable to accusations of unfair competition and crowding out markets, especially when they start to exploit these assets in the digital media domain, where other stakeholders (publishers or commercial broadcasters for instance) have sometimes similar ambitions, but not equal funding possibilities.

Companies that sell archive footage to broadcasters and other businesses (b-to-b), such as ITN and BBC Motion Gallery originally objected to the BBC Creative Archive on the grounds of unfair competition. Even though the quality of the material offered through BBC's Creative Archive is below professional standards and commercial use is prohibited, these companies feared piracy and competition for their business. Free access to audiovisual archives and the availability of high quality audiovisual material was thought to hamper their possibilities to commercially exploit this type of material.

However, the BBC believes that the pilot phase has proven that there is little or no piracy and that instead the service has made archive material better known among the audience. According to the BBC it has even stimulated the demand for commercial audiovisual archive material. They expect that in due course a mass market for audiovisual material will develop, in which people are prepared to pay small amounts of money for upgrading their productions to high quality video content.

The BBC has offered the creative archive licence to other public bodies, but also to commercial ones. Thereby commercial companies (ITN and BBC Motion Gallery) have been able to participate and have come to acknowledge that making available audiovisual archive content has widened market possibilities and might develop from a predominantly b-to-b market into a mass consumer market.

Generally speaking there is still a debate on the extent of government funding that is allowed for public service broadcasters' online and digital activities. Commercial stakeholders have filed several complaints with the European Commission on this issue. At present the agreement is that public broadcasters are allowed to develop digital services on digital platforms, but governments should make these an explicit part of the public service broadcasting remit. Often the start of new services has to undergo separate procedures for approval by regulators. An analysis of the impact on the market can be part of this procedure and in some countries there is a limit to the funding allowed for certain new services.

4.3 Control over the Context of the Content

One of the main characteristics of the web is its networked character, whereby services are interlinked by intricate webs of hyperlinks. Being visible on search engines and being linked to on blogs, vlogs, portals and websites are crucial to survive in the online world. Another way to plug ones content to end users is by syndicating it to third parties. In this way a broadcaster's most interesting or popular clips can be showcased on another company's web portal. For public service broadcasters this may in some cases conflict with legal restrictions on public-private partnerships. But there are also strategic and ethical issues, such as how to maintain one's integrity and editorial independency if one's content is shown in an environment over which one has no control. This might be more problematic for public service broadcasters than for commercial broadcasters. The Vara for instance turned down Google's offers to have Google host all Vara's internet content for free on its servers, in order not to risk its status as a provider of independent and objective information. In other cases there have been debates on whether PSBs would want to distribute their services through MSN web portals, where they would be surrounded by highly commercial services that might in some cases conflict with PSB's own editorial policies and where end users might not always be able to distinguish between PSB and non-PSB's services.

This the issue does not only arise with public broadcasters and because of legal reasons only. Often it is also a clash of cultures between traditional broadcasters that want to retain full control over their content and the context in which it appears on the one hand, and internet culture that thrives on mixing, sharing and linking on the other hand.

4.4 Broadcasters' Quality Standards and User Generated Content

Traditional broadcasters and the concept of user generated content have a complex, sometimes contradictory relationship. Most broadcasters recognise that viewers are developing from 'just' viewers into co-creators of content. FourDocs fully depends on users submitting their own films. Also the BBC and Vara wish to include user generated content on their websites or digital channels. The BBC Creative Archive has showcased the films made with the BBC's archive material by organizing competitions of which the best submissions were made available on BBC's websites. The Vara intends to broadcast user generated comedy material on its digital comedy channel. The relationship between broadcasters and user generated content is a complicated one though, because unrestricted publication of content by users might conflict with their reputation for quality and editorial independency. For instance: material on Google Video is unmoderated; it is hard to find what you are looking for, and the material on offer is often of low quality. In order to safeguard their own standards broadcasters will have to adopt a strategy for editing and moderating the user generated content that they publish on their websites or elsewhere. This requires considerable investments though and the more successful these services become, the more costs they generate. FourDocs currently works with a team of approximately three fte's that judge about 14 submitted films per month. The BBC has organised contests, which means that they also have a strict selection mechanism and do not allow users to publish anything that they want on the BBC's websites.

5 Conclusions and Discussion

The analysis of BBC Creative Archive, Vara Comedy and FourDocs leads to three conclusions. Firstly the three case studies clarify the distinct and innovative nature of the broadcasters' services, not only in opening up high quality material for more extensive (re-)use, but also in guaranteeing open access to this material while at the same time preventing piracy of copyrighted material, and in the case of BBC Creative Archive and FourDocs, experimenting with a new form of copyright protection, based on the creative commons principles.

Secondly, the case studies point at contested position of current public service broadcasters' online and digital activities. There are many other competing stakeholders, such as the underlying right holders of broadcasters' audiovisual archive material, as well as network operators, publishers, or portal owners that are also interested in exploiting television programmes on digital platforms and that challenge public funding for digital services. At the same time a cross media production and distribution strategy are crucial for public service broadcasters in order to remain a viable and relevant brand in the digital domain. Moreover, in this domain cooperation and networking with third parties, both commercial and non commercial, are inevitable to provide a relevant service for end-users, remain visible and findable or aid in covering the investments required for the services.

Thirdly the analysis shows how the logic of the internet world and the more authoritative logic of public broadcasting are not always easy to reconcile. User generated content confronts public service broadcasters with urgent questions on how and to what extent they should function as the upholders and caretakers of quality, morality and good taste and where exactly the need for professional production, selection, interpretation and guidance lays in a world where, as some say, everyone can become a journalist or an artist. On a more optimistic note, public service broadcasters' endeavours could also lead to highly valued new services for a general audience, increasing their ICT skills and stimulating creativity as well as to new and fruitful exchanges between professional and amateur programme makers (content producers).

Acknowledgments. The case studies were carried out in the context of the European 6th Framework Programme New Media for an New Millennium, and as part of collaborative work with TNO colleagues Nico Pals, Sander Limonard, Fleur Mevissen and Jop Esmeijer. The author also wishes to thank Anthony Lilley (Magic Lantern, FourDocs), Patrick Uden (FourDocs), Wessel Valk (Vara) and Paul Gerhardt (BBC Creative Archive) for their interviews. The analysis and conclusions fully remain the author's responsibility.

References

1. Anderson, Chris (2006). The Long Tail. Why the future of business is selling less of more. Hyperion.
2. BBC (2006). BBC Annual Report and Accounts 2005-2006. Governors Review of Services. New Media.
3. Leurdijk, A. en O.D. Rietkerk (2005a). Market perspectives for interactive and reconfigurable media. Report for EU 6th Framework Programme New Media for a New Millennium (NM2), public deliverable, available on www.ist-nm2.org.
4. Leurdijk, A. (2005b). Overheidsbeleid publieke omroepen en nieuwe diensten in vijf Europese landen (Government policies concerning public broadcasters and new ICT services). TNO report 33578. Delft: TNO 2005.
5. Leurdijk, A. (2005c). Quick Scan Beleid publieke omroep in Europa, Nieuw Zeeland en de Verenigde Staten. TNO report. (Quick Scan of PSB policies in Europe, New Zealand and the US). Delft TNO 2005.
6. Leurdijk, A., N. Pals, S. Limonard, F. Mevissen & J. Esmeijer (2006). Market Perspectives for ShapeShifted Television. Report for EU 6th Framework Programme New Media for a New Millennium (NM2), public deliverable, available on www.ist-nm2.org.
7. Poel, M and R. Tee (2006). Business Model Analysis as a tool for policy analysis. Digital television platforms in France and the Netherlands. Freeband, B@home, TNO deliverable.

Conceiving ShapeShifting TV:
A Computational Language for Truly-Interactive TV

Marian F. Ursu[1], Jonathan J. Cook[1], Vilmos Zsombori[1], Robert Zimmer[1],
Ian Kegel[2], Doug Williams[2], Maureen Thomas[3], John Wyver[4], and Harald Mayer[5]

[1] Department of Computing, Goldsmiths, University of London, SE14 6NW, London, UK
[2] Future Content Group, BT, Adastral Park, Ipswich, IP5 3RE, UK
[3] Cambridge University Moving Image Studios, Cambridge University, UK
[4] Illuminations, London, UK
[5] Institute of Information Systems, Joanneum Research, Graz, Austria
m.ursu@gold.ac.uk

Abstract. iTV does not yet have truly interactive programmes, that is programmes whose content adapts to the preferences of their viewers. In commercially deployed iTV productions, the programmes themselves are essentially linear and therefore non-interactive. In the research arena, the main bulk of work in computational support for interactive narratives focuses on wrapping interactions up in meaningful and interesting narratives, rather than on expanding traditional linear narratives with interactivity. This paper presents a validated approach to the development of truly interactive programmes called ShapeShifting TV. In focus is a representation language for narrative structures.

Keywords: itv, interactive, programme, storytelling, narrative, space, structure, representation, intelligence, reasoning, automatic, editing, authoring, testing.

1 Introduction

iTV has become an established entertainment mode, adopted by most major broadcasters, and a rich research area. Despite the increasing attention it has received in the past few years, iTV has still not delivered *truly interactive programmes* (such as news or drama), that is interactive audio-visual narratives, made with recorded material, that adapt on the fly to suit the preferences of individual viewers.

As most of the research in computational models for interactive storytelling has focused on games and virtual reality environments, where audio-visual content is *computer-generated*, solutions for producing and delivering truly interactive programmes made with recorded material failed to arise. The commercial world, understandably, tends to choose simple but robust formats. It employs limited interaction modes that can be implemented straightforwardly and whose effects can be evaluated without dedicated tools. Consequently, the existing iTV programmes are not *themselves* interactive; interactivity happens alongside them. Conversely, without appropriate software support, it is very difficult for programme creators and producers even to explore ideas for viable truly interactive programmes, as the non-linear structures they require cannot go beyond the concept stage.

P. Cesar et al. (Eds.): EuroITV 2007, LNCS 4471, pp. 96–106, 2007.

This paper presents a validated approach to the development of truly interactive programmes, which we call *ShapeShifting TV*, accompanied by a generic, programme-independent, software system for their production and delivery. They were devised by software developers in collaboration with content creators and producers. The software system has been validated through the production of a number of ShapeShifting TV productions, some of which have been or will be deployed in the commercial world.

It is easy to see why such programmes offer a timely paradigm. They will provide a better solution to the information explosion that we currently witness; truly interactive programmes can offer levels of personalisation not achievable otherwise. They could offer richer and more engaging personal entertainment. Thirdly, and very importantly, in a world where the need for innovative content for broadcast and webcast is urgent, they offer a far more powerful medium for creative expression than their linear counterparts.

2 Current Commercial iTV Formats

One mainstream method for interactivity is to allow the individual viewers to move forwards and backwards within a programme stream or to swap between streams. This method could be called *brute force interactivity*, as it relies on broadcasting large number of programmes in parallel or on powerful recording equipment. Viewers can choose between streams delivered synchronously, can watch a number of them in parallel on a screen mosaic, and, in time shifted TV, can access favourite programmes in larger time windows than precisely at the time of broadcast. Viewers are also able to get content on demand, and to pause, rewind and fast-forward through the programme. The programmes themselves, however, are not interactive. They are made in a *linear fashion* and *independently* from one other, under the assumption that they would be watched from beginning to end. Other interaction modes, such as choice of parallel supplementary footage or of camera angle to view (in crime investigation drama), short mini-episodes and catch up extracts services (in soap opera drama), headline and summary clips (in current affairs) may appear more sophisticated, but, in principle, fall within the same category.

Other two mainstream methods for providing interactivity are the "show-me-more" format and voting. The former is realised via parallel services for broadband and mobile devices and includes interviews, biographies, newsletters, chat groups, quizzes, competitions and games. They act as satellites to, and have little direct impact upon, the mainstream programmes themselves. Voting is realised mainly via SMS or the "red button". It is a popular method of interaction, but it has not been used to determine the shape of the TV programmes themselves.

There are a limited number of productions that integrate more sophisticated interaction modes and so begin to become truly interactive. Examples include observation tests, logical puzzles and reaction trials that determine the development of the events (as in the BBC's *Spooks Interactive*), explicit choice of different audio-visual components or between multiple narrators (as in the BBC's *Walking with Beasts*), explicit selection to watch cutaways from the main stream, such as mini-documentaries and biographies (as in Schematic's *Woodrow Wilson*), or the ability to navigate chronologically or thematically within the programme (as in Schematic's *Love and Diane: An Interactive Timeline*). However, the narrative structures employed are extremely simple, such as two parallel paths with intermediate decision and transition points. Furthermore, each such programme is hard-coded in a bespoke implementation, rendering this solution expensive and unfeasible to support real creativity and innovation.

Programme independent tools for the creation of PC-based interactive media exist, such as Macromedia Director and Flash, but they operate at a too low level to enable narrative concepts to be expressed and reasoned with[1]; notably, the authoring happens along an explicitly represented timeline. Programme independent tools are needed that allow authors to experiment with, create and deliver truly interactive programmes [1]. This is a strong motivation for our work.

3   Research in Computational Support for Interactive Narratives

Research in computational support for interactive narratives – denoted as *interactive narrative-based systems* [2] – has focused mainly on applications where the audio-visual content or the media essence is *computer-generated*, such as games and VR environments, rather than recorded, as in TV programmes and movies. Its final aim is the development of virtual worlds in which stories unfold and the user, considered a character in the story, is able to interact with the other characters and the environments of the worlds [3], whilst achieving cognitive and affective responses as those seen in conventional narrative media such as film [4]. However, to date, they focus mainly on wrapping up interactions in meaningful and interesting narratives, rather than on expanding traditional linear narratives towards interactivity. They are situated in the interactive-rich but narrative-simple area of the interaction-narrative complexity space. iTV productions are in a complementary area, namely narrative-rich but interactive-simple. ShapeShifting TV aims for both: *rich narrativity* and *rich interactivity*.

Most research in interactive narrative-based systems is concerned with the *automatic generation* of interactive narratives. Two mainstream approaches seem to have become prevalent [3, 5] namely *autonomous agents*, possibly mediated by drama managers, and *narrative mediation*. They both employ planning, but the former concentrates mainly on characters (character-based interactive storytelling), whereas the latter concentrates on actions and events (plot-based interactive storytelling).

A representative example of the former approach is described in [6] and [7]. The user is allowed to interfere at any time with the story line progression by influencing the characters or the environment. Feature characters and objects of the environment are modelled as autonomous agents, formalised as hierarchical task network plans. A plan determines how best to achieve the agent's goals. The execution of a plan generates character behaviour at run time. Story variants emerge from the characters' interaction. The emphasis of this work is on the behaviour of the characters, rather than on explicit plot representation. There are other examples of modelling characters

---

[1] Incidentally, this also applies to the majority of the tools created for mainstream game development.

as agents. The work described in [8] experiments with both guessing and influencing the psychological state of the engager. The work described in [9] approaches agent-based characters from the point of view of their beliefs. In [10] agents are investigated as means of automatic narration. In all cases, the emergent stories were simple but credible within the chosen genres. However, there is no evidence that the approach could be transferred to a more narrative complex genre.

Drama managers can be employed to enforce narrative coherence [3]. An example is Façade [11] which aims to create a dramatically interesting world that the user navigates by engaging in natural language dialogues with virtual characters [12]. The plot is coarsely structured on major events, called beats. Dialogues happen within beats and result in micro-narratives. They also affect the "social scores" which are considered by the drama manager in moving the narrative to the next beat. Façade concentrated on micro-narratives to the detriment of the overall plot.

Narrative mediation, on the other hand, concentrates on narrative structures, by globally controlling characters' actions (plot) and their audio-visual materialisation (discourse). Mimesis [4], for example, is a planning-based controller for virtual worlds that generates and maintains coherent story-lines. Its main components are the story planner, the discourse planner, the execution manager and the mediator [13]. The story planner takes an "initial world state", a set of possible "character actions" and "goals" (states in which the story could end) and composes sequences of actions, called "story plans", leading from the initial state to a goal. The discourse planner takes a story plan and a set of possible "communicative actions" and creates a sequence of actions that is executed by the media rendering engine. The story world and the discourse plans are combined into a "narrative plan" by the execution manager. The narrative emerges from the parsing of the graph. User actions may deviate from the plan, in which case the mediator can cause the attempted action to fail or request re-planning. Simple narratives can be generated in this approach, but, to date, they are far from the narrative quality of a TV programme or a movie.

Interactive narrative-based systems can also be modelled as branching narratives, containing a fixed number of points at which the decisions or actions of the engager determine the way the narrative unfolds [2]. Generally, they are represented as directed graphs, in which nodes are scripted scenes and arcs correspond to possible decisions [3]. An example is presented in [14]. Rich interaction could happen within nodes, but scenes are more or less independent episodes; the events of a scene do not adapt to interactions that happen in other scenes.

In conclusion, most work in interactive narratives remains centred on the generation of meaningful actions staged as 3D animations [5]. It looks at means for the *automatic* generation of narratives, whilst ShapeShifting TV is focused on *giving humans* new means of expression. It uses *automatically generated* audio visual material, through graphics rendering and audio generation, whist ShapeShifting TV uses *recorded* material. It is centred on games and VR environments, whilst ShapeShifting TV is about drama, news and documentary. The generated narratives are still a long way from the aesthetic qualities of traditional film [7]; in ShapeShifting TV, this is a necessary characteristic. All these motivate our approach from narratives towards interactivity, and, consequently, ShapeShifting TV.

Viper [15] is one of the very few systems that allow the creation of programmes that could change during viewing in response to preference or profile information, presentation devices or real-time sensor feedback. Automatic editing is carried out on the basis of "editing guidelines", expressed via a number of primitives implemented in the programming language Isis, and media clips annotations, made via a dedicated interface. Viper illustrates, in part, the principles of ShapeShifting TV, but, among other limitations, provides neither a language nor an authoring environment for expressing narrative structures.

4   ShapeShifting TV – Generalities

We define a ShapeShifting TV programme (for brevity called S2TV) to be an *interactive* programme that is *automatically edited at viewing-time* to reflect the choices and preferences of individual viewers or of communities of viewers. S2TV programmes are made with *pre-recorded* audio-visual material, called *media items*, such as video-clips, audio recordings, and graphics, but material generated on the fly could equally well be used. Each viewed programme is a sequence of media items. S2TV programmes are *authored*. Currently, the authors are human, but the principle does not prevent them from being software agents. The potential entertainment value of an S2TV programme – including coherence, meaningfulness, information and aesthetic quality, and level of engagement and enjoyment – should at least equal that of traditional, linearly edited, programmes. We refer to potential, as poor S2TV programmes may be made similarly to some of the unfortunately poor traditional programmes. The definition makes no specification regarding the level or complexity of the interactivity, leaving it entirely to the latitude of the author. Finally, it is worthwhile to note that S2TV programmes are inherently *non-linear*.

Each individual interaction between an S2TV programme and an engager must resolve into a linear narrative that is cogent, interesting and entertaining. How can these many facets of an S2TV programme be conceived and effectively represented as a consistent whole? How could the scriptwriter be supported in conceiving and capturing *plot grammars* for non-linear programmes? Similarly, how does the director manage the *shot grammar*, and how is the corresponding *editing expertise* going to be captured? These questions are made more difficult by the fact that the language of interactive screen media itself is still developing (see, for example, [16, 17, 18, 19]). A potential answer to these questions is presented in the remainder of this paper.

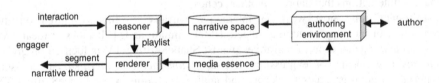

Fig. 1. A Declarative approach to modelling ShapeShifting TV programmes

Individual S2TV narratives ought to be considered from two perspectives. From the standpoint of an individual engager, there are *narrative threads*. From the standpoint of the authoring team, there is the *narrative space*. For a given programme, the narrative space is the union of all the possible individual narrative threads.

We take a *declarative approach* to modelling S2TV programmes (refer to Fig. 1) according to which the *narrative structures* of narrative spaces are represented *symbolically* and separately from both reasoning procedures and the media essence. For each programme, the narrative threads are realised automatically, via an iterative process. Each interaction received or sensed from the engager triggers the interpretation, by the *reasoner,* of the narrative structures, resulting in the generation of a play-list. Each such play-list is passed onto a *renderer* which assembles the actual media essence into corresponding *narrative segments,* that the engager will experience lasting until their next interaction. Each narrative thread is made of a sequence of narrative segments. The separation of narrative strictures from reasoning procedures eliminates all the drawbacks associated with hard-coding. The separation from media essence could provide for reusable *computational programme formats.*

We devised a logic-based language, called the *narrative structure language* (NSL), for the expression of narrative structures. There are two main requirements that NSL should satisfy. On one hand, it should be sufficiently *intuitive* and *effective* for authoring. Despite NSL being used mainly via the authoring environment, this is still a requirement for it, as NSL defines the *concepts* that structure the authors' thinking. The authoring environment through which it is used is just syntactic sugar. On the other hand, NSL representations should be *computable in 'reasonable' time* to ensure continuity for individual programme threads. This, too, is a requirement for NSL, despite the existence of solutions that can be used to speed up reasoning. A poorly designed NSL would result in a major overhead in terms of such satellite solutions.

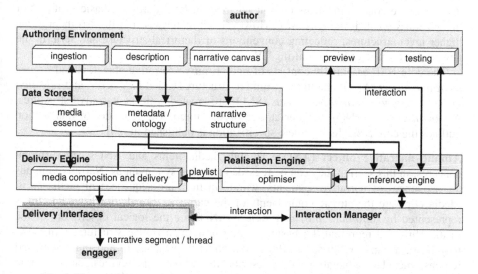

Fig. 2. The architecture of the system for authoring and delivering ShapeShifting TV

To date we have developed a *core NSL* and a fully working software system for authoring and delivering S2TV programmes. The architecture of the system is depicted in Fig. 2 (arrows denote data-flows). The media items – logical descriptors of the media clips – are created via the *ingestion tool.* Media item descriptors are further refined with metadata, semi-automatically, via the *description tool*. The *narrative canvas* is where the narrative structures are authored. The *preview tool* allows authors to view parts of the narrative. The *testing tool* implements NSL syntax checking and a number of other meaningful checks, such as determining whether a certain point in the narrative structure could ever be reached. The *realisation engine* creates the playlist for each narrative thread. The *delivery engine* assembles the actual media content. An *interaction manager* mediates between the delivery interface and the realisation engine. Each interaction triggers the realisation engine to compute the narrative segment that is to be delivered next. We introduced an *optimiser* in order to enhance the efficiency of the reasoning. Amongst many other functions, the optimiser can compute, before an interaction arises, the most probable narrative thread, when a quick response is necessary. The delivery interfaces are platform and programme specific.

The inference engine is implemented in SICStus Prolog. The rest of the system is implemented in C++. The authoring environment uses Qt for the graphical user interfaces. The realisation engine generates SMIL that, subsequently, can be converted to other formats, allowing the use of any scriptable multi-layer compositors to be used. XML-RPC is used for communication between most of the constituent components.

5 Narrative Structure Language

The narrative structure language (NSL) is the language in which S2TV interactive narratives are conceived. In its current incarnation NSL defines a basic syntax. For this reason we call it the *core NSL*. However, ultimately, NSL will also incorporate higher level structures, reflecting conventions of rhetorical structure and style in the new creative space of ShapeShifting TV.

The core NSL essentially consists of one primitive narrative object, called *atomic narrative object* (ANO), and three primitive structures called *link*, *layer*, and *selection group*. *Structured narrative objects* (SNO) are created with the narrative structures. A *narrative object* (NO) is either atomic or structured. The reminder of this section outlines the core NSL. Its complete specification is published in [20].

Atomic narrative object (ANO). Though media items and ANOs are different concepts, in this section they can be regarded as being synonymous. Narrative threads are sequences of narrative segments, which, in turn, are sequences of media clips. Media clips are the atomic components of the narrative threads. Each media clip is represented by an *atomic narrative object*. ANOs are the logical descriptors of the media clips and represent the basic building units of narrative structures. An ANO may have: a name, reference to the media clip it represents, in and out points and regions, metadata annotations that describe the whole clip, regions, or only time points thereof, and unstructured text. Reaching an ANO during the interpretation of a macro-narrative leads to its referred media clip being added to the play-list.

ANOs may refer to no media items, in which case they are called *placeholders*. They are useful in designing narrative spaces before recording high quality material, and in structuring scripts. For this, we extended the properties of the ANOs to include script fragment and a reference to a low cost media item (such as a still). Placeholders are expected be associated with media items at some point in the authoring process.

Link structure. A link structure is a *directed graph*, possibly *with cycles*. Each node specifies a NO. Each edge specifies a potential path that the narrative could take from the origin to the target node. Each edge has an enabling condition, which is a Boolean expression referring to the metadata of NOs, input from the engager and context information (such as the play-list compiled so far). If an enabling condition evaluates to true during the compilation of a narrative thread, the target node can immediately follow the origin in the play-list. If a node is to be followed by more than one node, then it should first lead to a *decision point*, which is then linked to the other nodes. One reason for introducing decision points as explicit objects is the need to disambiguate the situations where either more than one or no direct path is enabled. This is done by associating default rules the decision points.

A starting node for a link structure must be specified. This can be done either by naming the node or via en expression that evaluates to a node. Interpreting a link structure involves starting at the start node and following enabled edges through the graph, until an end point (a point from which there are no links) is reached.

It is possible to move from a decision point in one link structure (see below) to a point in another link structure. This supports the higher-level structure of a *narrative arc*. Such jumps are bridges that allow the narrative to move between the arcs as well as to progress within one arc. Such jumps always return to where they left off when the destination link structure finishes.

Layer structure. A layer structure has a number of layers, each consisting of an NO. Reaching a layer structure in the interpretation of a macro-narrative leads to the media referred to by each layer being added *in parallel* to the play-list, meaning that they are played concurrently, starting at the same time. Layer structures can be used, for example, to associate audio (soundtrack) with video.

Layer structures provide *synchronization* mechanisms between its objects. For example, reaching a point in one NO on a layer, during interpretation, could result in a forced exit from a NO on another layer, allowing the object that directly follows it to being considered. Computing synchronisation is facilitated by NSL's support for specifying priorities between layers. *Collision rules* disambiguate contradictory synchronisation messages. We chose to adopt this procedural solution for reasons of efficiency. However, we will replace it with a more elegant declarative solution provided in terms of *alignment* conditions.

Selection group. A selection group has content, selection criteria and constraints. The *content* is a set of NOs. It may be specified explicitly, by naming the objects, implicitly, via a *filter* expression, or be *dynamically provided*. The filter is evaluated on the whole repository of media items each time and just before a narrative thread is started. This allows the reuse of a narrative structure with different sets of media items. This mechanism is useful, for example, for news. Dynamic content reaches the group during programme delivery. This allows, for instance, the use of user generated content in ShapeShifting TV programming.

A group, when reached in the narrative structure, is interpreted either into one narrative object (in the case of a *single selection group*) or a sequence of objects (a *multi selection group*) from its content. This interpretation is based on the *selection criteria* which are specified as expressions that evaluate to narrative objects. They, too, employ metadata, input values from engager and context information. Support for disambiguation is provided, but, for this structure, we found it useful to separate *refinement* rules, for situations when more than one solution exists, from *alternative* rules, which resolve empty selections. Hierarchies of conditions can be expressed by nesting selections, refinements and alternatives.

The constraints are only applicable to multi-selection groups. They specify the sequence in which a subset of the selected objects should be arranged. NSL offers a number of predefined criteria, including the specification of the minimum or maximum time length for the overall sequence, of content that should always appear in the sequence, and items that, if selected, should be neighbouring in the play-list.

Each selection groups has an optional *termination condition* which may be used to loop its interpretation.

Special annotations. Interactions, actions and editing rules are among the special annotations available in NSL. An *interaction annotation* is expressed through attributes including type, such as selection from a set or free text, cue to the engager, duration, referring to how long the engager's should be waited for, and a default value, which denotes what should be used in the absence of the user's input.

Action annotations are employed for side effects. An action is effected when the inference engine reaches its corresponding NO in the interpretation process. NSL provides a number of predefined actions, such as to trigger the start of a dormant selection group or terminate a NO that is playing, but it also allows the use of custom specified procedures. In the latter case actions are called *code points*. Actions may also be associated with time points and regions within ANOs.

Editing rules can modify the standard behaviour of the primitive structures. As the mechanisms associated with them are quite complex, they are not further described here.

Interpretation. In generating a narrative thread, the Inference Engine interprets the narrative structures of the narrative space and produces playlists for narrative segments between consecutive interactions. The Inference Engine decides what is to be selected in a structure as it reaches that structure in the narrative space and is able to look ahead in order to apply constraints and editing rules. When an interaction requires a change in an already computed fragment that is yet to be rendered, the engine reverts to an earlier state and continues from there.

NSL is a very powerful means of expression, whilst being interpretable in sufficient good time. Its recursive nature allows it to represent very complex narrative and interactive structures, and in various forms. So far, it has proved to be a good instrument for thinking and for expressing ideas, and successful in experimentations.

6 Evaluation and Conclusions

We have introduced an approach to creating truly interactive iTV productions which we call ShapeShifting TV and an accompanying representation language, the narrative structure language (NSL). Despite NSL being only a core, its power and potential have been demonstrated through the production of a number of robust ShapeShifting TV programmes, in drama, documentary, current affairs, and art. *Accidental Lovers* [21], a black romantic comedy, broadcast by the Finish National Television (YLE) in December 2006 and January 2007, is one of them. It is rewarding to see "programming styles", as individual forms of expression, emerging with NSL. They are the seeds for NSL's syntax extensions and for further developments for capturing rhetorical and stylistic structures. The accompanying software system supports the whole production and delivery workflow. However, many extensions have already been designed, some of which are already in the development stage.

Acknowledgments. This work was carried out within the European Union's 6th Framework Programme Integrated Project "NM2: New Millennium, New Media" (IST-2003-004124).

References

1. Murray, J.: Towards the Holodeck. Free session at International Broadcast Conference (IBC), Amsterdam, The Netherlands, 7-12 September 2006
2. Young, M.R.: Notes on the Use of Plan Structures in the Creation of Interactive Plot. In the Working Notes of the AAAI Fall Symposium on Narrative Intelligence, USA (1999)
3. Riedl, M., Young, R.M.: From Linear Story Generation to Branching Story Graphs. IEEE Journal of Computer Graphics and Applications, May/June (2006) 23- 31
4. Young, M.R.: An Overview of the Mimesis Architecture: Integrating Intelligent Narrative Control into an Exiting Gaming Environment. In the Working Notes of the AAAI Spring Symposium on Artificial Intelligence and Interactive Entertainment, Stanford, USA (2001)
5. Cavazza, M., Charles, F.: Dialogue Generation in Character-Based Interactive Storytelling. In Proceedings of AAAI First Annual Artificial Intelligence and Interactive Digital Entertainment Conference, Marina del Rey, California, USA. AAI Press (2005)
6. Cavazza, M., Charles, F., Mead, S.J.: Character-Based Interactive Storytelling. IEEE Intelligent Systems, Special Issue on AI in Interactive Entertainment (2002) 17-24
7. Lugrin, J-L., Cavazza, M.: AI-Based World Behaviour for Emergent Narratives. In Proceedings of the ACM SIGCHI International Conference on Advances in Computer Entertainment Technology, Hollywood, California, USA. ACE (2006)
8. Shapiro, S. C., Anstey, J., Pape, D. E., Nayak, T. D., Kandefer, M., Telhan, O.: The Trial The Trail, Act 3: A Virtual Reality Drama Using Intelligent Agents. In Proceedings of the First Annual Artificial Intelligence and Interactive Digital Entertainment Conference (AIIDE-05), Menlo Park, CA (2005) 157-158
9. Shapiro, S. C., Anstey, J., Pape, D. E., Nayak, T. D., et.al.: MGLAIR Agents in Virtual and other Graphical Environments. *In* Proceedings of the Twentieth National Conference on Artificial Intelligence (AAAI-05), Menlo Park, CA (2005) 1704-1705
10. Tallyn, E., Koleva, B., Logan, B., Fielding, D., Benford, S., Gelmini, G., Madden, N.: Embodied reporting agents as an approach to creating narratives from live virtual worlds. In Proceedings of Virtual Storytelling 2005, Lecture Notes in Computer Science, Springer, Strasbourg November (2005)
11. Mateas, M., Stern, A.: Structuring Content in the Façade Interactive Drama Architecture. In Proceedings of AAAI First Annual Artificial Intelligence and Interactive Digital Entertainment Conference, Marina del Rey, California, USA. AAAI Press (2005)
12. Mateas, M., Stern, A.: A Behavior Language for Story-Based Believable Agents. In: Forbus, K., Seif, M.E. (Eds.): Working notes of AAAI Artificial Intelligence and Interactive Entertainment, Spring Symposium Series, Menlo Park, California, USA. AAAI Press (2002)

13. Young, R.M., Riedl, M.O., Branly, M., Martin, R.J., Saretto, C.J.: An Architecture for Integrating Plan-Based Behaviour with Interactive Game Environments. Journal of Game Development, 1 (2004)
14. Gordon, A., van Lent, M., van Velsen, M., Carpenter, M., and Jhala, A.: Branching Storylines in Virtual Reality Environments for Leadership Development. In Proceedings of the Sixteenth Innovative Applications of Artificial Intelligence Conference (IAAI-04), July 25-29, San Jose, CA. Menlo Park, California, USA. AAAI Press (2004)
15. Agmanolis, S., Boye Jr., M.: Viper: A Framework for Responsive Television. IEEE Multimedia, 10 (1) IEEE (2003) 88-98
16. Murray, J.: Hamlet on the Holodeck: The Future of Narrative in Cyberspace. MIT Press (1997)
17. Ryan, M-L. (ed.): Narrative Across Media: The Language of Storytelling. University of Nebraska Press, Lincoln (2004)
18. Rieser, M., Zapp, A.: New Screen Media: Cinema/Art/Media. BFI, London (2002)
19. Manovich, L.: The Language of the New Media. MIT Press, Cambridge, London (2001)
20. Ursu, M.F, Cook, J.: D5.9: Languages for the Representation of Visual Narratives. Restricted project deliverable in the EU FP6 IST-004124 IP project "NM2: New Media for a New Millennium" (permission required) (2006)
21. Tuomola, M.L. (director): Accidental Lovers ("Sydän kierroksella"), Crucible Studio, Helsinki University of Art and Design Finland. Broadcast on Channel TV1 by YLE, The Finnish Public Service Broadcasting Company (2006/2007)

User Interfaces Based on 3D Avatars for Interactive Television

Alex Ugarte, Igor García, Amalia Ortiz, and David Oyarzun

VICOMTech: Visual Interaction and Communication Technologies
{augarte,iolaizola,aortiz,doyarzun}@vicomtech.es,
http://www.vicomtech.es

Abstract. Digital TV has brought interactivity to television. Even though actual capabilities of interactive applications are quite limited due to immaturity of the sector and technical restrictions in the standards, the potential of interactive Television (iTV) as a multimedia and entertainment platform is enormous. The existing gap between PC world and iTV concerning graphics capabilities, may restrain the development of iTV platform in favour of the former one. Support for 3D graphics applications in iTV would boost this new platform with plenty of possibilities to be exploited.

1 Introduction

There is a long way until we can see 3D-TV broadcasts [14], where the user can choose the view point of the scene or where the user himself is immersed in the virtual world [18]. Magnor [13] states that *the new possibilities interactive 3D-TV offers to the user are too attractive to be ignored for long* (pp. 6-7). As a logical evolution, 3D-TV content will be first offered for conventional PCs, then to game consoles to be finally adapted to set-top boxes connected directly to the television.

With the arrival of Digital Television, first interactive applications are being broadcast in DVB-S, DVB-T and DVB-C. Due to immaturity in the area, these applications offer basic information, based mainly on text and some graphical widgets [3,2] that enable interaction. Nevertheless, it is expected to see more advanced applications when the market settles down and the hardware and software technology becomes maturer. The DVB consortium[1] has defined an open middleware system that specifies the transmission, reception and execution of interactive applications: DVB-MHP[2]. This open standard is being adapted to new emerging platforms, such as DVB-H[3] and IPTV.

Although 3D-TV will not reach us for a while, other 3D contents may provide enhanced experiences while watching iTV. Available set-top boxes in the market

---

[1] Digital Video Broadcasting (DVB); http://www.dvb.org
[2] Digital Video Broadcasting (DVB); multimedia home platform (MHP) specification. http://www.mhp.org
[3] DVB for handheld devices. http://www.dvb-h.org

P. Cesar et al. (Eds.): EuroITV 2007, LNCS 4471, pp. 107–115, 2007.

do not incorporate a graphic card mainly because they pretend to be cheap in order to reach as much market share as possible, and secondly because the DVB-MHP specification does not specify a 3D API. Cesar [1] proposes a revision of the MHP specification, dividing the possible configurations of receivers into several categories:

- Broadcast
  - Basic: digitalisation of audiovisual content.
  - Enhanced: support for DVB-J applications.
- Interactive
  - Basic: Support for a limited XML user agent.
  - Enhanced: complex XML support and thus convergence with WWW content.
  - High-End: support for all kinds of multimedia objects, such as video and 2D/3D graphics.

In the later profile a Java layer wrapping OpenGL ES functionality, such as TVGL [24], is proposed. This feature would blur the edges between set-top boxes and game consoles, allowing new services such as games and 3D commercials, but requires a modification of the current MHP standard.

In this work we aim to insert an avatar in a MHP v1.0.2[4] compliant application, which is the version supported by most commercial set-top boxes. Avatars are virtual characters that can be used to improve appearance of iTV applications [9]. Moreover, their capabilities to reproduce human-like behaviour can be used to improve human-computer interaction [20]. This new user interface paradigm seems quite promising for a platform that lacks a window manager and a pointer device, and where the traditional WIMP (Windows, Icon, Menu and Pointers) paradigm may be difficult to use even for experienced computer users [12].

In section 2 we evaluate different libraries available to implement 3D graphics in an application. Later we describe the steps we followed to integrate a scene graph API into a MHP application, in order to develop a user interface based on avatars. Finally we analyse de performance we achieved and expose our conclusions.

2   3D Support in MHP

The DVB-MHP standard defines a way to display 2D graphics on the screen, but lacks a 3D API. We will analyse a set of 3D libraries to finally decide which is the most suitable to work over the 2D API available in MHP.

2.1   MHP Graphics APIs

Java provides the Java Abstract Window Toolkit (AWT) to develop graphics applications for PCs. But due to differences between PCs an TV screens [6,21],

AWT is not optimal to be used in iTV applications. Therefore the DVB consortium has adopted the HAVI UI API[4] as the user interface solution for interactive TV applications [16]. Although AWT classes can be also used to develop graphic interfaces, they have some limitations in MHP world, from which the lack of a window manager and a free-moving cursor are the most important ones.

2.2 3D Rendering Libraries

There are several graphic libraries thought to develop 3D applications for different platforms. Some of them are complex scene graphs that provide abstraction layers in top of more basic and low-level libraries. Here we will discuss the most important ones:

OpenGL: allows creation of virtual applications offering a high performance level, as they run in native code. It is one of the most extended 3D APIs, with lots of abstraction layers (OpenInventor, Iris Performer, OpenGLOptimizer, etc) and support in various programming languages (C, C++, Java, Tcl, Ada, FORTRAN). It has versions for a lot of different architectures, but is not suitable to distribute applications through Internet or broadcast, as it must be recompiled for each architecture/operating system. The projects JOGL[5] and LWJGL[6] aim at providing access to all OpenGL API functionality from Java. Khronos group has proposed OpenGL ES[7] as a new standard for embedded systems. OpenGL ES is a subset of OpenGL instructions, creating a flexible and powerful low-level interface between software and graphics acceleration.

DirectX: Similar to OpenGL, DirectX only works on Microsoft systems. It does not provide software emulation for aspects not supported by the graphic card. It is mainly used for PC computer games.

Java3D: is a powerful API to be used in Java applications. It allows development of multi-platform, i.e. independent of the host system, applications capable of showing 3D objects. This characteristic makes Java3D a perfect option to build portable applications that will be executed through Internet or in machines with different configurations and operating systems. It is based on scenes, which makes it very easy to use. As a drawback, it is not a pure Java library and it calls system libraries (OpenGL or DirectX) to communicate with the graphic card. Systems with no available Java3D plug-in can not execute Java3D based programs.

Xith 3D: is another open source scene graph for Java. It relies on low-level APIs, such as JOGL or LWJGL, as the underlying renderer, but can be controlled and even exchanged.

Anfy3D: is a commercial reduced version of Java3D. It allows creation of three-dimensional universes and includes visual effects, such as shadows, texture

---

[4] http://www.havi.org
[5] Java for OpenGL: http://https://jogl.dev.java.net/
[6] Light Weight Java Gaming Library: http://lwjgl.org/
[7] http://www.khronos.org/opengles

mapping transparencies, fog, etc. Its small size (about 100kB) makes it ideal for applications where bandwidth is limited. It is completely written in Java, so it is not necessary to install any plug-in. In case a graphic card is available, Anfy3D may take advantage of its capabilities. Therefore any system with a Java Virtual Machine may run an application with this library; if hardware acceleration is possible, it will be used, otherwise all calculations will be done by software.

2.3   Conclusion on 3D APIs

Currently, MHP does not define an API to render 3D graphics, so external libraries must be used. Native libraries must be specifically compiled for each platform, so its impossible to broadcast them with the application; they must be pre-installed in the receiver. Relying on native software not defined by the standard does not guarantee interoperability, due to the diversity of manufacturers and middleware implementers. In some works[1,8] it has been suggested an extension or modification of the MHP specification. In this case we want the application to work on the current version of the standard. Therefore the external libraries must be written in Java and broadcasted with the application. Among the libraries described in 2.2, the only one that fulfills the requirements of being written in Java and not relying on native code is Anfy3D.

3   Implementation

The next step after choosing the graphic library (anfy3D), was to implement a simple test to be run on a set-top Box. For this purpose we implemented the tutorial provided by Anfy Team, in which a cube starts spinning around. This is a simple scene with very few polygons, very suitable to test the validity of the system. Except for some deprecated methods that are not available in MHP 1.0.2 API, this first application was quite successful. The cube was rendered by different commercial set-top boxes.

Due to the complexity of constructing a whole 3D scene with a significant number of polygons, we loaded a model stored in an *obj* file. We also added some interaction through the coloured buttons of the remoter. In this case, interaction was achieved successfully, but while some models where loaded and displayed correctly, in some cases we encountered problems rendering textures.

Images are stored in a *java.awt.Image* instance. and are loaded in a platform-specific manner, according to the JavaME documentation. In practice this means that images are stored outside the Java heap, in a specific zone of memory managed by, for example, C code.

Images must be processed to make them suitable to be used as textures. As *Image* objects don't offer the methods necessary to work on their data, Anfy3D copies images into byte arrays, which are stored in the heap. As we can see in Table 1, most of the available memory in a set-top box, is used for video, audio and data decoding and buffering; application storage; and for platform management (stacks, queues) [5]. This means that at the end only a small quantity of this

Table 1. Memory characteristics of the set-top boxes used to test the application

Model	Graphics/System memory	Heap Memory[8]
Humax DTT-4000	64 MB	5652 KB
Philips DTR 4600	32 MB	4095 KB
ADB T75 dev	72 MB	7168 KB
SAMSUNG DTB-S500F	64 MB	5859 kB

Fig. 1. 3D avatars. a)Model with simple textures. b)Memory needed to store big textures exhausts heap memory. b)Same Model without textures runs on commercial STBs.

memory can be used by the Java heap for application usage. Therefore, loading a 3D model with big textures will exhaust all available memory (Figure 1).

4   User Interface Based on 3D Avatars

Typically the main use of 3D applications has been in the game industry. Its success is so big that devices designed specifically to run games have been created: the consoles. This market is so competitive that pretending that a MHP alike platform will be competing with powerful game consoles is quite doubtful. Nevertheless, 3D graphics can be applied in other fields. But 3D graphics may have other uses in interactive television.

One of the most emphasized advantages of interactive TV is its easiness of use. As opposed to the PC world, where some technical skills are needed, the TV

---

[8] Calculated with method *java.lang.Runtime.freeMemory()*

is used almost by everybody, thus reaching most of the population. But when developing interactive TV applications some of the constraints attributed to PC world are maintained. Therefore, although everybody can use the television, not everybody knows how to interact with it.

To achieve natural communication, channels between people and the set-top box should be the same ones which people use in human communication. People usually communicate with other people through the senses of sight and hearing in order to interpret the input data of the communication. A natural interface should be capable of speaking and gesticulating to imitate this behaviour. Our approach is based on the use of avatars in simulating this kind of communication. Avatars are virtual characters which make communication between user and machine more natural and interactive. A growing number of research projects have begun to investigate the use of animated life-like characters in natural user interfaces because they present a priori a lot of advantages, which have also been validated by many authors:

- Social Interaction: In 1994, Nass [17] carried out five experiments which provide evidence that individual interactions between human and machine are fundamentally social. More recently, Prendinger et al [22] reached the same conclusion following another evaluation using a novel method based on tracking users' eye movements. His research also shows that users interact with life-like interface agents in an essentially natural way. He also realized that users follow the verbal and non-verbal navigational directives of the agent and mostly look at the agent's face. Human-like behavior occurs during interaction with the computer and human-like behavior is expected of the computer. Computer users turned out to be sensitive to flattery and humor; moreover, they were very much influenced by the properties of the synthesized voice in text to speech synthesis when assigning personality characteristics to a computer [19].
- User attention: Animated characters are capable of capturing users' attention, engaging users in active tasks, and entertaining them [7]. This is very important for learning environments where a virtual character can have a positive effect on the learning process, more so if it can show affective responses [10].
- Naturalness: Whether the virtual character is believable or not, the illusion of life is generated and [23] the user has the illusion of interacting with a real person.
- More information in the transmitted message: in the transmitted message: In communication, facial expressions provide a lot of information. This was demonstrated by Mehrabian [15], who shows in his research, that the 93% of our messages are transmitted through through non-verbal language. 55% is mainly based on facial and corporal motions, whilst 38% is based on the use of the voice.
- Trustworthiness and believability: Generally the agents act when the user authorizes them. If the user has to delegate some tasks to the agent, he/she should trust it. It is believed that the level of trustworthiness is increased by

the personification of the agent. Due to this, the design of the avatar is very important. Koda [11] found that a realistic face is rated as more intelligent, engaging, and likable than the less realistic faces.

The role of the avatar depends on the application; it can act as a guide or assistant, as an information presenter and can even represent the user in a virtual environment. In order to achieve natural behavior, both, non-verbal and verbal behavior is essential. We integrated the following rules into the system:

- Non-verbal behavior is automatically given to the avatar. This behavior is mainly based on an undulating head motion until speech is continued. The virtual character is never motionless, giving the illusion that it is alive and waiting for user feedback.
- Eye motion is randomly directed towards both sides and is very smooth. The pupils are dilated and contracted giving the illusion that it is watching different points of light.
- The avatar blinks randomly.
- The eyebrows are raised with changes of tone and pitch.
- In order to understand that there is a specific stress for semantic reasons. The facial animation is strengthened by raising the eyebrows and making the head nod.

5 Performance

The application has been tested in the following equipments:

- XletView on PC
- Osmosys emulator on PC
- ADB T.75 development set-top box (Osmosys middleware)
- Humax DTT-4000 set-top box (Alticast middleware)
- SAMSUNG DTB-S500F (Alticast middleware)

The final size of the avatar application is of 126 KB. The weight of the 3D engine itself is only of 57.5 KB. The model of the avatar must be sent with the application, and its size varies depending on the complexity of the model and the textures used. In 1 two different models can be seen; the simple one needs 112 KB to store its data, meanwhile the woman needs 211 KB. Here we can see that the size of the models supposes half of the total weight of the application, thus, making the weight of the 3D engine of less than 20% in this simple case.

The results of running the application on a PC[9] emulator showed that the 40% of CPU cycles where used to execute the application in the case of Xletview with no video rendering, and more than 90% in case of Osmosys emulator, with a video being displayed on the screen. When executing the application on real set-top boxes, with a CPU running at less than 200MHz, it could be seen that, even though the application run with no errors, the rendered frames per second where pretty far from those rates required for an animation with minimum quality

---

[9] Intel Pentium IV, CPU: 2'40GHz, RAM=512MB

requirements. When a minimum of 15 frames per second are needed to perceive movement, the time required to render a single frame was of several seconds.

6   Conclusion

In this work we have seen the way to render 3D graphics in MHP applications running on available commercial set-top boxes following DVB-MHP 1.0.2 standard. Current set-top boxes limitations in memory and processor capacity impose some restrictions that could be easily overcome by including a graphic processor in the device. Only High-End set-top boxes will be expected to support one such graphic card while it is supposed that Low-End devices will improve their features both in memory and processor capacity. Therefore we think that the extension of DVB-J with an API for 3D graphics should be flexible enough to run on Low-End set-top boxes with an all-Java implementation, and still being able to take the maximum advantage of capabilities offered by 3D graphics cards with a Java layer wrapping OpenGL_ES. Standardizing a low level API, such as TVGL, or JOGL would give enough freedom to use any high level scene graph, allowing even a solution that implements 3D functionality by software, in order to run applications with low requirements.

Support for 3D graphics applications would enable new ways of interactions between the user and the set-top box, as they may improve greatly the interactiveness experience of the end user. Using multimodal avatars as the human-computer interface would reduce the level of skills and knowledge required to interact with these applications, thus making easier the use of new technologies by more people.

References

1. Pablo Cesar. *A Graphics Software Architecture for High-End Interactive TV Terminals*. PhD thesis, Jelsinki University of Technology, December 2005. ISBN 951-22-7887-1 (printed version) ISSN 1456-7911 ISBN 951-22-7888-X (electronic version) ISSN 1455-9722.
2. Pablo Cesar and Petri Vuorimaa. A graphical user interface framework for digital television. *Proceedings of the 10th WSCG International Conference in Central Europe on Computer Graphics, Visualization, and Computer Vision, Plzen, Czech Republic*, pages 1–4, February 2002.
3. Tomislav Curin, Hrvoje Bai, and Mario agar. Framework for graphical user interface personalization in interactive television. *27th Int. Conf. Information Technology Interfaces ITI 2005, June 20-23, 2005, Cavtat, Croatia*, June 2005.
4. DVB. Digital video broadcasting (dvb); multimedia home platform (mhp) specification 1.0.3. etsi ts 101 812 v1.3.1, June 2003.
5. J.-P. Evain. The multimedia home platform - an overview. *EBU Technical Review*, pages 4–10, 1998.
6. Julian Florez, Igor Garcia, Iker Aizpurua, Celine Paloc, Alex Ugarte, Igor Jainaga, Jesus Colet, and Xabier Zubiaur. Seitv - interactive multimedia leisure/educational services for digital tv in mhp. *Entertainment Computing - ICEC 2004, Third International Conference, Eindhoven, The Netherlands, September 1-3, 2004, Proceedings.*, 2004.

7. Cholyeun Hongpaisanwiwat and Michael Lewis. Attentional effect of animated character. In *INTERACT*, 2003.
8. Tobias Daniel Kammann. Interactive augmented reality in digital broadcasting environments. Diplomarbeit, Institut fr Computervisualistik Arbeitsgruppe Computergraphik (Universitat Koblenz-Landau), November 2005.
9. M. Khadraoui, B. Hirsbruner, F. Meinkohn, Dj. Khadraou, and M. Courant. Interactive tv show based on avatars. *Proceedings of the 2005 Systems Communicationsk (ICW'05)*, 2005.
10. Yanghee Kim. *Pedagogical agents as learning companions: the effects of agent affect and gender on student learning, interest, self-efficacy, and agent persona.* PhD thesis, Tallahassee, FL, USA, 2004. Major Professor-Amy L. Baylor.
11. Tomoko Koda and Pattie Maes. Agents with faces: The effects of personification of agents. In *5th IEEE International Workshop on Robot and Human Communication*, Tsukuba, Japan, November 1996.
12. George Lekakos, Konstantinos Chorianopoulos, and Diomidis Spinellis. Information systems in the living room: A case study of personalized interactive tv design. *The 9th European Conference on Information Systems*, 2001.
13. M. Magnor. 3d-tv - the future of visual entertainment. *Proceedings of the workshop on Multimedia and Image Communication. Salerno, Italy*, pages 1–8, 2004.
14. Cornelius Malerczyk, Konrad Klein, and Torsten Wiebesiek. 3d reconstruction of sports events for digital tv. *Procedings of the eleventh International Conference in Central Europe on Computer Graphics, Visualization and Computer Vision, Plzen, Czech Republic.*, 2003.
15. A. Mehrabian. Communication without words. *Psychology Today*, 2(4):53–56, September 1968.
16. Steven Morris and Anthony Smith-Chaigneau. *Interactive TV standards. Aguide to MHP, OCAP, and JavaTV.* Focal Press, 2005.
17. Clifford Nass, Jonathan Steuer, and Ellen R. Tauber. Computers are social actors. In *CHI '94: Proceedings of the SIGCHI conference on Human factors in computing systems*, pages 72–78, New York, NY, USA, 1994. ACM Press.
18. Ulrich Neumann, Thomas Pintaric, and Albert Rizzo. Immersive panoramic video. *Proceedings of the eighth ACM international conference on Multimedia*, 2000.
19. A. Nijholt. Disappearing computers, social actors and embodied agents. In T.L. Kunii, S. Soon Hock, and A. Sourin, editors, *2003 International Conference on CYBERWORLDS*, pages 128–133, Singapore, 2003. IEEE Computer Society Press Los Alamitos. ISBN=0-7695-1922-9.
20. David Oyarzun, Amalia Ortiz, Carlos Andrs Toro, and Jorge Posada. Animation techniques for achieving avatar interaction in a virtual environment. *Proceedings of IADAT-MICV 2005. International Conference on Multimedia, Image Processing and Computer Vision. March 30-April 1, 2005, Madrid, Spain*, 2005.
21. Chengyuan Peng. *Digital Television Applications.* PhD thesis, Helsinki University of Technology, 2002.
22. Helmut Prendinger, Chunling Ma, Jin Yingzi, Arturo Nakasone, and Mitsuru Ishizuka. Understanding the effect of life-like interface agents through users' eye movements. In *ICMI '05: Proceedings of the 7th international conference on Multimodal interfaces*, pages 108–115, New York, NY, USA, 2005. ACM Press.
23. W. Scott Neal Reilly. *Believable Social and Emotional Agents.* PhD thesis, 1996.
24. Yongjun Zhang. A java 3d framework for digital television set-top box. Master's thesis, Helsinki University of Technology, October 2003.

Perceptions of Value:
The Uses of Social Television

Gunnar Harboe, Noel Massey, Crysta Metcalf,
David Wheatley, and Guy Romano

Motorola, 1295 E. Algonquin Rd., IL05 2nd Floor,
60196 Schaumburg, IL, USA
{gunnar.harboe,noel.massey,crysta.metcalf,
david.j.wheatley,guy}@motorola.com

Abstract. We present the results of two studies on social television concepts. In one study, a Social TV prototype was tested in the field, allowing groups of users watching television at home to talk to each other over an audio link. Specific patterns of use are described, showing that users did perceive the system to be valuable. In another study, focus groups were presented with several Social TV concepts, and their responses were collected. These participants saw only moderate to marginal value in the concept. We discuss the discrepancy with reference to the limitations of each method.

Keywords: Interactive Television, ITV, social television, field test, focus group.

1 Introduction

Although the popular stereotype presents television watching as a solitary, asocial activity, the social uses of television have long been recognized. Both at the time of watching and after the fact, television serves a number of social purposes, such as providing topics for conversations, easing interaction, and promoting feelings of togetherness [12]. Conversely, the sociable aspects can be important motivations for TV viewing, such as when someone watches a television program in order to participate in conversations about it later.

Much of the time people watch television they do not do so by themselves, but with family, with friends, or in public places such as sports bars [14]. However, it is not always possible to be together when watching a show. More and more people live alone [18], and while communication technologies make it possible to stay in touch over distance, they also mean that more of our relationships are with people in remote locations.

Providing a response to these developments, "Social TV" is a label for Interactive TV (iTV) systems that support the sociable aspects of TV viewing [9] [16]. Although in principle this includes improvements to collocated interaction, most of the work on social television involves integrating remote communication capabilities with a broadcast TV feed. Typical Social TV communication includes presence (what channel and program someone is watching), text, voice, video, or some combination of these.

P. Cesar et al. (Eds.): EuroITV 2007, LNCS 4471, pp. 116–125, 2007.
© Springer-Verlag Berlin Heidelberg 2007

Interest in enabling communication through the television has increased dramatically in the last couple of years. However, although there are compelling reasons to explore social applications for the TV, we should not for that reason take for granted that such offerings will be widely adopted. The previous attempt to integrate communication and broadcast television, AOLTV, proved to be a flop [11], one of iTV's many false dawns. Additionally, the notion of communicating through the TV set overlaps with video telephony, a technology that has been a perennial failure outside of a few specialized niches. These precedents are not promising.

It has been argued that Picturephone, AT&T's 1960s–70s videophone system, failed in part because it did not take into account how people actually interact [15]. And one reason for AOLTV's downfall may have been that it was not properly adapted for a situation with multiple simultaneous users, and the social dynamics that entails.

Therefore, as we try to use the television to bring people together, it is important to understand how people behave in this new situation, how they find the technology useful and valuable, and in which ways it creates problems for them. That is the goal of the research presented in this paper. We focus our discussion on people's reaction to the concept, and the evidence as to whether it adds value to the experience of watching TV. The answers to these questions may determine the success or failure of social television.

2   Related Work

Basic ways for viewers to communicate with each other through their TV sets have existed for some time, without the need for specialized technology. For example, some television stations let their viewers chat with each other by sending SMS text messages from their mobile phones, which are displayed on-screen as part of the broadcast. AOLTV, a set-top box launched in 2000, offered users the ability to send and receive instant messages (IM) and email on their TV, with programming playing simultaneously in a picture-in-picture window [5]. While AOLTV went off the market in 2002, these features are now part of many iTV services.

Several conceptual, prototype or research systems for social television have been described, and to various degrees implemented. AmigoTV includes a particularly rich set of interaction options such as animated emoticons [9]. 2BeOn is a workbench system for integrated interpersonal communication on a TV [1]. Coates sketches out some hypothetical social software for set-top boxes, including ways to make digital video recording social [8]. An argument for integrating IM with iTV is laid out by Chuah [7]. In Telebuddies, "laid-back" social interactions aim to bring people closer together by having them work together in a TV-related game [13].

In TV Cabo Interactiva, communication takes the place of a public, text-based, chat room offered for selected shows (football matches and debates) [17]. Cesar et al. go further to propose ways for viewers to enrich broadcast content and share the result with other users [6].

The systems mentioned so far are all presented through the TV. Fink et al., on the other hand, provide a TV channel chat room through a separate laptop computer, gathering presence information from the TV audio through the PC microphone [10].

Recently, websites such as BuddyTV[1] also allow users to chat while watching TV, though presence has to be managed manually.

While many systems, both conceptual and real, have been reported, we find only one study that focuses on the actual use of social television applications. Oehlberg et al. looked at groups of people watching TV in a lab setting, some in the traditional way and some with an audio connection to another group watching the same program in a different room [16]. Their interaction was studied using conversational analysis, and insights from this led to a number of proposals for how to design for distributed, sociable television viewing.

Oehlberg et al. observe that "more studies in 'natural' environments (e.g. a participant's own home)" would be the next step of the research, and this is the path we had independently started down in order to understand how social television could find a place in the living room.

3 Methods

Motorola's work on Social TV emerged from several studies that we conducted on family communication and use of media. These found that "people who want to build/maintain relationships but live far apart can use mediated communication technologies to develop 'close' relationships through a virtual experience of being 'physically' close," and that sharing the experience of commercial content is an important way to maintain a personal connection [2]. In one study in particular we noticed people calling each other during a TV show they were both watching, so that they could watch it "together." These observations suggested that people might want a Social TV application to foster social interaction around broadcast content.

In order to investigate how people act and interact through a system like we envisioned, what kind of value they got from it, and if it introduced new problems or issues, we combined a number of different methods. Our primary research has so far included paper prototyping tests, lab tests, field trials and focus group sessions. By comparing the results of each, we hoped to be able to triangulate the information and hopefully converge on more reliable answers to our research questions. The findings from the field trials and focus groups form the basis for this paper.

3.1 Field Trials

For the field trials, we used a prototype that simply set up an open audio connection between two or more televisions. We used an open microphone and the television speakers to enable conversation. Users could control the conversation volume and television volume separately with a remote control. This straightforward setup allowed us to test the most important Social TV functionality. The features of the prototype were similar to that of Oehlberg et al. [16], but we set ours up in the participants' own homes; for a live TV show of their own choosing; and connected them to their own friends or family. We ran four trials with this prototype. Each trial lasted for one hour, and the participants watched live programming that had been agreed on in advance. Participants were recruited from our social networks using the

---

[1] http://www.buddytv.com

friend-of-a-friend method. 11 were male and 8 female, and all were non-engineers. The programs consisted of an American football game (2 households, with 5 people watching), a basketball game (3 households, 5–10 people at various times), a home decorating show (2 households, 2 people) and an animated comedy followed by a sitcom (2 households, 2 people), respectively. In the first trial a mother connected to her son, daughter-in-law and grandchildren, in the other trials the participants were connected to friends and their friends' families. The participants were video taped during the trial (the researchers were not present), and interviewed immediately afterwards. We also recorded the programs they watched.

Fig. 1. Participants in field trials watching TV and talking. The images are from different trials.

We used a form of grounded theory analysis to understand the data, applied as an affinity diagram technique [3] [4]. Because we had well-defined research questions but also wanted to probe more deeply into the reasons for the answers, the analysis was both deductive and inductive. We began by watching and listening to the video tapes, synchronized with the recorded program. We pulled out raw data from the sessions and interviews that addressed the research questions. These items were grouped based on the patterns that emerged, and the resulting organization of the data surveyed to answer the research questions. The findings were then compared with the results of the other methods.

3.2 Focus Groups

In addition to the direct observation of people using the system, we ran a concept study to test the appeal of communication and interaction through the TV, as well as four other, more advanced concepts which have no direct bearing on this paper. The study consisted of 7 focus groups (and a pilot group) followed by a data analysis workshop. In the focus groups, which lasted for two hours, participants were shown a number of storyboards depicting possible Social TV scenarios and were asked to discuss the ideas with respect to their own needs and lifestyles. They also filled in worksheets with ratings and other information.

Fig. 2. Storyboards shown to participants in the focus groups to illustrate Social TV scenarios

In all, 53 people participated in the focus groups. Each group represented a particular gender and age bracket, with participants from 17–61 yrs. The groups were selected so as to include people with and without children, and for other demographic characteristics considered to be relevant. The concept study was run by an independent consultancy, with researchers from Motorola Labs involved at each step of the design and execution.

Quantitative data from the focus group was analyzed statistically. Observations from the conversations were extracted, and we performed an affinity analysis on these items to identify key themes and see patterns emerge. A report described the findings and insights from the qualitative and quantitative data, which were held up against the findings of the other studies for comparison.

4   Findings

4.1   Focus Groups

In the focus groups, participants had mixed feelings about the overall idea of communicating through the TV. Some called it "intriguing," "interesting" and even "wonderful." At the same time there was considerable skepticism, with others describing it as "weird," "unnecessary" and "pointless." Despite the hyperbole, ratings showed a moderate response, falling mostly near the middle of the scale.

When we look more closely at the general lack of enthusiasm, a couple of possible explanations stand out. Several participants found no value in linking the personal communication to broadcast content. They considered that a television program would be an irrelevant distraction from their interaction with other people, for which existing communication technologies (telephone, email, IM, etc.) were sufficient.

The complementary argument—that having a communication channel open while watching would interfere with the TV viewing—was even more common. In a number of the groups, people argued that television was their "down time", the only chance they had to relax and unwind. The social demands of holding up their end of a conversation, of just relating to other people, was the last thing they wanted. They speculated that it would be time consuming, and argued that they simply couldn't fit it into their schedule. Some participants were also concerned that having others on the line would interrupt and disrupt their viewing, causing them to miss parts of the show they were watching.

Another way to frame these objections is to say that the participants in question claimed simply not to want to watch television with other people, except for special occasions. The unanimity of this response should not be exaggerated, however. There were other users who could see themselves using it on a regular, not just exceptional, basis. Sports broadcasts were the most oft-mentioned "regular" television events that our participants saw as good opportunities to use the system. This accords well with the observation that sports are often experienced in crowds, such as in an arena or a sports bar, and among groups of friends. Other examples included cooking shows and certain movies. Several participants suggested that men would use it mainly (or only) for sports, while women might be more inclined to talk during other programming.

There also seemed to be a group of participants who acknowledged the value of a social television system as a way to stay in touch with loved ones, particularly parents. These people were more positively inclined towards the concept, but some noted that the television broadcast was not an essential element of this contact. Each of the focus groups brought up the idea of adding a camera and using the TV screen as a videophone. However, they also raised privacy concerns over the idea of a video camera in their house.

There was no such ambivalence about audio. The participants rejected out of hand the idea of having to type in text in order to communicate. They were uniform in their opinion that communication should be mediated by voice, and that talking should be made as natural as possible.

4.2 Field Trials

In contrast with the focus group subjects, the participants in the field trials were on the whole very positive towards the concept and their experience with our prototype. Our users called the experience "a blast," "fun," "so cool," "a good time," and "the best thing to happen to TV since DVR." A minority had reservations, mostly about technical issues that cropped up during the trials. One participant felt that it was something of a novelty, although "not as frivolous as that word connotes." Another opined that although she enjoyed the experience, this was not a technology for her, because she would only rarely use it.

Interestingly, people were more enthusiastic after trying it than they were beforehand: "Before going into this I thought 'What would I ever use this for?' But it was a totally different experience actually doing it. Because I totally changed my mind. [...] I would totally use it!"

For all the participants, we found evidence that the social television experience added value over and above watching alone. In some cases it came close to the experience of actually being together: "I kind of forgot I was talking through the television at some point. I just was talking and could hear Mom." "It felt like she was in the room."

The social television system helped to relieve boredom and provide distraction during commercial breaks and slow segments of the show. Users rarely channel surfed during the commercial breaks. Instead they would indulge in small talk ("What did you do this weekend?"), continue discussions about the show, or even comment on the commercials themselves. Participants indicated that they enjoyed this aspect of the experience: "I never get a chance to tell someone 'I like that commercial,' 'I don't like that commercial.' " Having a conversation going on during the commercials did not keep our participants from performing other tasks in these breaks, such as sending kids to bed, playing with the dog, looking over homework, or getting a snack.

The communications link gave the participants someone who could provide them with information. In the sports sessions, this use of the system took the form of questions about players and their histories, requests for explanations of the state of play, and having others repeat bits they didn't catch. For the animated show, it meant pointing out pop culture references. "Maybe if we're talking while we're watching this I'll get more of the inside jokes." These interactions served a social as well as a utilitarian purpose. By helping each other out and validating each other's expertise, the participants affirmed and maintained their social ties.

The system allowed the participants to share their interests with other interested people. "Geeking out" over a common interest was one of the things that really got our participants excited. "I like listening to [my friend], and [we both] comment on 'Oh, that rug's cool!' or 'Oh, that rug's ugly!' " One of their exchanges: "Oh, they're going to use that as art!" "You're so funny! (Laughs)"

Finally, the sociability itself was valuable, because of the pleasure it gave our participants. We saw the system relieve loneliness ("You feel like you're not really alone in the home"), enhance the intensity of the experience, such as when two rooms would cheer together at an event in the game, and allow some participants to have contact with loved ones.

One of the most gratifying findings from the field trials was just how natural the flow of conversation turned out to be. The ease of verbal interaction appeared to be closely tied to how well the participants knew each other. In one trial where the participants were not close friends, turn-taking and pauses in the conversation were much less smooth than in the other sessions. This meant that their conversation interfered with watching the show. The type of show was probably also a factor in this, as this was the group watching the animated comedy, and risked missing both punch lines and plot twists, something the groups watching sports and home decorating did not have to worry about.

Other trials exhibited different problems. In the largest, three friends were connected together with audio while watching basketball, along with their wives and children. The sheer number of people talking was quite overwhelming, with conversation sometimes drowned out by noise. Of course, one could argue that bringing three families with seven kids between them together to watch TV would be overwhelming under any circumstances, but it does demonstrate that creating a "sports bar at home" could run into some difficulties.

An unanticipated effect of the prototype was a displacement of sociability. One of our participants confided that because he was interacting with his friends, he was paying less attention to his son than he would have done otherwise. By bringing outsiders into the family room, social television can intrude on important "quality time," and weaken the closest ties even as it builds relationships with more distant people. On the other hand, when the other person is not an outsider, the feeling of intimacy can extend across the connection, as expressed by a grandmother talking to her son's family: "If I close my eyes I can picture all of you in your family room, chit-chatting. [...] I can picture everything that's happening."

Although social television begins to approach the experience of watching something together, there are also important differences. The participants who watched basketball pointed out that the system did not provide the physicality of actual presence. Normally, they would jump up, "high-five" each other and hug when their team did well. Another difference is that because the interaction happens only through the TV set, the communication remains anchored in the shared content. One of our participants explained that having friends over to watch DVDs was different because they would also do other things, and just talk while leaving the TV on in the background.

Most of our participants agreed that Social TV was especially well suited for sports programs, and men in particular saw this as what they would use the system for.

5 Discussion

The field trials and focus groups came to the same conclusion on some questions. They both agreed that Social TV works well with sports. And they both suggested that Social TV is primarily a way for people who already know each other well to be together, not, for instance, a way to meet new friends. The value of an audio connection over text was affirmed in both.

However, while most of the focus group participants saw moderate to little value in the concept, the people in the field study liked it and demonstrated a long list of ways that it does add value. While the focus groups worried about the ways it would disrupt their TV watching, the field study participants were able to manage interruptions in most cases. How do we explain this?

Most of the field trials consisted of watching a particular show, agreed-upon in advance. However, in one of the trials the show only lasted half the length of the session, and the two participants had to find something else to watch for the last half. This proved to be a difficult and time-consuming process, and ended with the selection of a program one of the participants didn't really want to watch.

It is possible that even though the field trials are very natural in many ways, they are artificial in that most of the sessions involve shows that the participants have agreed upon in advance, that they are all interested in, and that they are all committed to watching. Perhaps this degree of harmony is a rare occurrence, and the field trials present the social television experience under ideal circumstances.

On the other hand, it is debatable how realistic the contrasting case is, with two users (or groups of users) sat down at a particular time and told that they have to find something to watch *now*, and with *each other*. More likely, Social TV will be used by people who already know each other and already watch the same program. Our users confirmed that there were things they watched regularly that they knew their family or friends also watched.

Many of the focus group participants said they preferred to watch TV alone. In this, they may be following a cultural expectation that television is not a social activity. Focus groups can be heavily influenced by such assumptions. Conceiving of TV in non-social terms could be the reason why they, along with the users in our field trials, were not able to predict that using Social TV would be so enjoyable. The difficulty of imagining something they have no experience with surely also factors in.

We found that people who knew each other well had a better experience with our prototype than less close friends. It is possible that the focus groups would have been more favorably disposed if the scenarios had emphasized close ties of family or friendship between the characters. In either case, the fact that field trial participants who were skeptical at first became more positive once they had actually tried the system suggests that the ambivalence of the focus groups might be turned around with hands-on experience.

6 Conclusions

Social television is an exciting topic within iTV. The real-world significance of Social TV depends on good understanding of the uses, purposes and problems of such systems, in order to design and position them correctly. Using complementary methods, we investigated these questions. On a number of issues the evidence converges on an answer. However, on several important points the methods seem to diverge. By considering the limitations of each technique, we suggest explanations for the apparent discrepancies and draw tentative conclusions.

People have a strong sense that sports is the type of programming most compatible with social television. Attempts to deploy Social TV features should consider optimizing for the characteristics of sports viewing.

Our field trials show that under favorable conditions, social television offers a compelling and valuable user experience. However, findings from the focus groups and other considerations raise some doubt as to how common these conditions would be. These concerns suggest that designers might wish to explore features aimed at easing and promoting watching together. For example, a system could use collaborative filtering or other recommender systems to suggest programs that two users might both want to watch.

The study as a whole underlines that the family is still the primary unit for television-watching. A Social TV system should take care not to break these family bonds. Instead, families that are split up and separated by distance, such as parents who work far from home or travel frequently, could be a group of early adopters.

The only way to know if the conditions are right for Social TV is through a longer field study, observing actual use over time. This is the next stage of our research, and will show whether social television is at best a niche application, or a pervasive part of the future television viewing experience.

Acknowledgements. We would like to thank Philip Hodgson and Lynne Tam at Blueprint Usability for their work on the concept study, and David Geerts for his work on lab tests of the prototype.

References

1. Abreu, J., Almeida, P., Branco, V.: 2BeOn: interactive television supporting interpersonal communication. In: Proc. EuroGraphics 2001, ACM Press (2001) 199–208
2. Bentley, F., Metcalf, C., Harboe, G.: Personal vs. Commercial Content: The Similarities Between Consumer Use of Photos and Music. In: Proc. CHI 2006, ACM Press (2006)
3. Bernard, H.R. (ed.): Handbook of Methods in Cultural Anthropology. AltaMira, Walnut Creek, California (1998)
4. Beyer, H., Holtzblatt, K.: Contextual Design: Defining Customer-Oriented Systems. Morgan Kaufman, San Francisco, California (1998)
5. Broom, T.: Philips AOLTV Review. In: CNET Reviews, 19 February 2001 (Retrieved 13 December 2006) http://reviews.cnet.com/Philips_AOLTV/4505-6487_7-4772942.html
6. Cesar, P., Bulterman, D.C.A., Jansen, A.J.: An Architecture for End-User TV Content Enrichment. In: Proc. EuroITV 2006, Athens U. of Economics and Business (2006) 39–47
7. Chuah, M.: Reality Instant Messenger. In: Proc. 2nd Workshop on Personalization in Future TV, Malaga Spain (2002) 65–74
8. Coates, T.: Social Software for Set-Top Boxes. http://www.plasticbag.org/archives/2005/03/social_software_for_settop_boxes/
9. Coppens, T., Trappeniers, L., Godon, M.,: AmigoTV: towards a social TV experience. In: Proc. EuroITV 2004, U. of Brighton (2004)
10. Fink, M., Covell, M., Baluja, S.: Social—and Interactive—Television: Applications Based on Real-Time Ambient-Audio Identification. In: Proc. EuroITV 2006, Athens U. of Economics and Business (2006) 138–146
11. Hu, J.: America Online confirms end of AOLTV. In: CNET News.com, 18 February 2003 (Retrieved 13 December 2006) http://news.com.com/2100-1023-984920.html
12. Lull, J.: The social uses of television. In: Inside Family Viewing, Routledge, New York (1990) 28–48
13. Luyten, K., Thys, K. Huypens, S, Coninx, K.: Telebuddies: Social Stitching with Interactive Television. In: Ext. Abstracts CHI 2006, ACM Press (2006)
14. Nielsen Top TV Ratings. (Retrieved 12. December 2006) http://www.nielsenmedia.com/
15. Noll, A.M.: Anatomy of a Failure: Picturephone Revisited. In: Telecommunications Policy, Vol. 16, No. 4 (May/June 1992) 307–316
16. Oehlberg, L., Ducheneaut, N., Thornton, J.D., Moore, R.J., Nickell, E.: Social TV: Designing for Distributed, Sociable Television Viewing. In: Proc. EuroITV 2006, Athens U. of Economics and Business (2006) 251–259
17. Quico, C.: Are communication services the killer app for Interactive TV? In: Proc. EuroITV 2003, U. of Brighton, UK (2003) 99–107
18. U.S. Census Bureau: America's Families and Living Arrangements: 2006. http://www.census.gov/population/www/socdemo/hh-fam/cps2005.html

Sociable TV: Exploring User-Led Interaction Design for Older Adults

Mark Rice and Norman Alm

School of Computing, University of Dundee, Dundee, DD1 4HN, UK
mrice@computing.dundee.ac.uk

Abstract. The adoption of digital television (DTV) could be particularly attractive for older people if appropriately designed. This paper explores the development of a novel interaction design approach specifically to support people who are reluctant or have difficulty using desktop technologies. Using a simplified remote control, four different navigational layouts were tested and evaluated with older users, primarily to assess their ease of use. The results presented indicate promising new directions in the development of visualization and navigation metaphors and concepts within the context of user-led activities on DTV for older adults.

Keywords: Interaction and participatory design, older users, information visualization.

1 Introduction

Over recent years, technological advancements and the convergence of more computer-based services within the home is an indication of the future possibilities of DTV. New opportunities exist in the development of applications that move away from the desktop paradigm into new realms of domestic technologies that support more socially oriented activities for a wider range of people. For older people, known variations of age-related changes to vision, cognition and manual dexterity [8] make a necessary and potentially advantageous area of research, the inclusive design of digital applications and services to support this heterogeneous segment of the population.

The research presented is part of an ongoing research project exploring how DTV could be appropriately designed to support older people, by adopting an overarching approach which puts the users' perspective at the forefront of every design decision made. This paper presents a study, which has examined new interactive and visualising techniques to support more dynamic operations involved in interaction with user-led, television-based sociable applications.

2 Early Requirements Gathering

Methods for eliciting needs in the design of user-centred systems have been found to be problematic when working with older users [7]. Although not true of *all* older

P. Cesar et al. (Eds.): EuroITV 2007, LNCS 4471, pp. 126–135, 2007.

adults, HCI researchers have found noticeable issues in relation to many older people, who lack the experience to understand, and thus criticise products and design concepts [6].

In view of these issues and known challenges, our early requirements gathering studies explored imaginative methods to gather appropriate information from older people, with little to no experience in using computer-based systems. Live theatre, comprising of older audiences, researchers, professional actors and a script writer, and user-centred paper brainstorming sessions with older user groups were used to provoke discussion on various sociable application areas via DTV. These sessions were successful in probing how older users would use such systems in 'real-world' settings, and raised a number of issues in relation to etiquette and social protocol, acceptability, usability and input control. Crucially, they helped confirm audience members' apprehension and uncertainty in using current DTV, and illustrated the need for new interactive approaches that are far more intuitive to this heterogeneous group. Of a range of possibilities, that included exploring reminder and prompting applications, one key area of interest was the development of an appropriate video-based application that would facilitate social communication with distant friends and family [12].

3 Hi-fidelity Prototypes

As a result of these studies, the research has focused on exploring alternative visualizing methods to organize information on DTV. This is particularly important given the tendency of navigation involving instantaneous 'snapping' from one screen to another (i.e. the status quo) to disorient many older users, leading them to get lost in the system. We have investigated more 'natural' and 'spatial' ways of thinking about the display and interaction of on-screen content within a domestic environment.

Within DTV, while studies have explored means of enriching sociable aspects of television viewing via voice [14] and integrated web-based communication [10], it is unclear the extent such application areas would interest more marginalized, and less technologically orientated audience groups. In the UK, a recent report by Office of Communications illustrated that *"nearly two in five (37%) of people aged 65 and over spend 'all or nearly all' of their leisure time at home, compared to 17% of all UK adults"* (p. 8. [11]). Based on findings like these, and given the extent television usage is known to give, among other assets, companionship for many older viewers [see 13], the design of more appropriate applications and services could offer huge benefits for many older adults. Unfortunately, despite such potential, a lack of user-centered research presently hinders more creative development in this area.

Given these issues, four prototypes were developed to explore different ways older users may interact with on-screen content, within the context of developing applications to support areas of 'sociability'. In particular, they were developed around a 'multimedia scrapbook concept', in which the support of asynchronous forms of communication, namely the sharing of photographs and music, text-based, and more prominently video messages would be available to the user as a separate activity in addition to watching a programme or interacting with an EPG. In more detail, it was envisaged this system would allow for the storage, organization and viewing of personal multimedia content, with the added facilities to share it with other people within the users' social circle. Primarily web-based, the system was designed to work both on PC and STB platforms, with real-time support from web-camera facilities. Given current advances in home multimedia and STB systems, it is expected that equivalent facilities could be available in the near future, deliverable over IP and cable networks.

Largely influenced by the visualization work of Bederson et al [e.g. 2], Card et al [3] and Fry [9] a selection of interfaces were developed and tested using various graphical techniques aimed at enhancing a sense of *continuity*, primarily to avoid disorientation due to snapping from one on-screen item to another, by exploring more physical means of representing graphical information within a 2D screen (see figures 2-5). These interfaces were all developed to be used with a simplified remote control, comprising of six navigational buttons, of which one (the "In" button) had a dual function as a 'in' and 'select' button (see figure 1). Given current usability issues with remote control handsets [4], buttons were much larger and appropriately grouped. Critically, all the interfaces were consciously designed to be equally applicable to the navigational functions of the remote control.

Fig. 1. Illustration of the remote control handset

As conventional interface models have been designed using principles drawn from the workplace, and built using principles such as efficiency and productivity [5], the interactive techniques applied in this study, focused on the ideas of continuity, exploring concepts of engagement and 'ease of use', 'affordances' and a form of 'navigational narrative'. In more detail, the prototypes took into account the generational differences of potential users, by exploring more 'natural', and 'real world' metaphors and visual cues to directly and visibly guide users through the tasks at hand, while trying to reduce the complexity of displaying multiple amounts of information at one time. As a control comparison to these novel approaches, a fourth, more traditional, interface was built based upon the familiar linear navigational structures found on current digital interactive systems.

 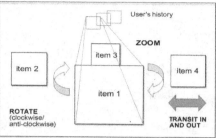

Fig. 2. (*Left*) Screenshot of the *Carousel* interface; (*right*) Items can be selected by pressing the left and right navigational buttons to smoothly rotate around the carousel. Typically, once the item in the forefront of the screen is selected, it zooms to the back of the screen to form a continuation of the history list. The remaining layer then slowly transits towards the right of the screen and the next layer subsequently emerges to allow selection.

 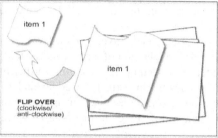

Fig. 3. (*Left*) Screenshot of the *Flipper* interface; (*right*) Items are organized, in this case monthly, by separating them onto individual sheets of paper. To select a message, users flip over the paper by consecutively moving the left and right navigational buttons. Users can also zoom in and out of the paper to select and watch a pre-recorded message.

 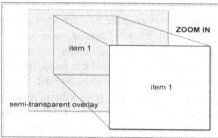

Fig. 4. (*Left*) Screenshot of the *Transparency* interface; (*right*) Once a menu item like 'video messages' is chosen, the application automatically zooms onto the menu item, becomes semi-transparent and the subsequent layer is revealed. Users then have the options to zoom back, or to zoom in to reveal the underlying item.

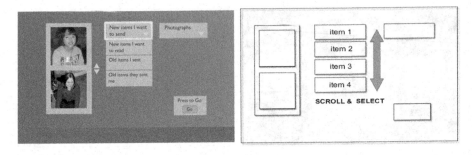

Fig. 5. (*Left*) Screenshot of the *Standard* DTV interface; (*right*) Users can scroll up and down each item by pressing the up and down buttons. To select an item, they press the 'in' button. Users move across menus by pressing the left and right navigation buttons.

3.1 The Procedure

In total 19 people aged between 60 and 84 years old (7 males and 12 females) were recruited from the local area, from a broad mixture of computer and DTV users and non-users.

Using a qualitative, 'Wizard of Oz' type approach participants were asked to simulate navigation of a real-time system, in order to give a realistic sense of how the interfaces would perform before further implementation and development. For this set of studies the investigator used a standard keyboard to mimic user reactions, based on the input selections made using the remote control. This was largely due to some technical difficulties in mapping between buttons and functions across the interfaces created.

Initially, pilot studies identified a number of issues in relation to users understanding the set-up procedure, and that users found the initial number of tasks rather overwhelming. Based on this feedback, aspects of the sessions were then amended before the main study.

During the main study, sessions were divided into three parts. Firstly, given their limited technological experience, older participants were shown four simple navigational examples and were guided through the process of how they would control the interactive content using the simplified remote control. This was done to allow them to get familiar with using the remote control handset and have an understanding of the different navigational concepts. Once participants felt comfortable with the tasks at hand, they were then presented with four prototypes, and asked to try to complete two tasks: i) record and send a new video message; ii) find and replay an 'old' (previously recorded) video message. To limit any bias of learning, the study counterbalanced the presentation order of interfaces across sessions. Once complete, each participant was asked to fill in a questionnaire summarizing their feedback on the different layouts used during the one hour session.

To replicate a real world system, the prototypes were iteratively developed in Adobe Actionscript 2/Flash 8, in conjunction with Flash Media Server (FMS) for real time video streaming. Earlier versions of Flash Player (5+), a standard for delivering web-based content are now increasingly supported on a number of commercial set-top box systems [1]. Information was displayed on a 26" LG widescreen LCD television connected to a single PC, using a Logitech Quickcam Pro 4000 web camera for audio and video messaging.

3.2 Results

Overall, users were highly engaged and intrigued by the prototypes used. In some cases, inexperienced participants were more apprehensive and/or uncertain in making screen selections, having asked for more confirmation in actions they were about to, or had undertaken. In other instances, users felt very comfortable in experimenting with the different layouts, and were confident in their actions made. Hesitancy, at times was dismissed with an expectation that understanding of the different layouts would be acquired through practice. However, it is difficult to assess the extent older users would persist with more difficult aspects of the layouts, were they at home in a more familiar setting. Based on the varying degrees of learnability, reflected in the ageing dynamics of the group, only six participants managed to finish all tasks within the one hour allocated.

In terms of prototype preferences, more users favored the elliptical carousel design (see figure 2), commenting on its simplicity, easy of use and ability to guide them through the various steps at hand. However, participants were largely positive about all the interfaces shown, despite the observations finding noticeable differences between what users' said they preferred, in comparison to what they could actually do. This was often complicated by the visual prompting necessary to remind users of the different layouts used at the end of a session.

With regards to constructive feedback, participants were less critical of the layout themselves, and praised the ease of use compared to more conventional computer-based systems. In particular, they were far more self critical for not understanding aspects of the layouts, rather than as a result of the designs implemented.

To illustrate some of the results, a selected summary of the questionnaire and qualitative study is given below.

- **The remote control**
The handset was rated very highly for being big and simple to use, with comments that the keys were easily distinguishable, particularly in comparison to more standard remote controls. In one case it was directly compared to a mobile crane control in its shape, design and functionality, while favorable remarks were made that it had the simplicity of something a young child could use.

Some mapping issues were observed in relation to the different on-screen layouts, particularly as the learning and unlearning of each prototype further complicated the direct manipulation of screen objects. The ambiguity of the 'in' and 'out' buttons, referred to as the 'positive' and 'negative' (see figure 1) and multi-functionality of the 'in' button, in comparison to the 'out' button which singularly operated navigation also caused some confusion, as one participant commented:

> *Every fiber of my being wants to press the out button, because it's going out... you're actually in the place, you're in the recording studio as it were, so to send the message you would be sending it out, or is that stupid?*

- **Video messaging**

Given the novelty of video messaging for many of the user group, some users were somewhat reluctant to see themselves for the first time on-screen. Noticeable problems with the four button video controls (record, play, stop and send) included a tendency for participants to repetitively repress buttons to stop functions, highlight but not select items, and more generally forget appropriate mappings, even after correct button sequences were made.

In terms of their understanding of video messaging, similar analogies were made to the use of more conventional technologies, with parallels to a video cassette running inside the system (to stop recording a message). Observations revealed intriguing patterns of behaviour, where for example, one participant would press play before the record button to create a new message. When asked why he did this, he explained that this is how he would record something on this stereo at home (pressing 'play' *and* 'record'). Such, variable differences in the ways technology can be perceived to work by older generations was well summarized by one person's remarks:

> *I was fourteen when I left school, and technology for me was when I learned how to use a pencil sharpener.*

- **On-screen navigation**

The studies found noticeable differences between the newly designed and more conventional layout. For example, most people liked and understood the techniques of slowly zooming in and out, and rotating through information, which in conjunction with 'real world' metaphors, such as the use of 'flipping', or turning over of graphical objects, (termed by one user as 'natural progression'), to reveal subsequent layers, were relatively easy navigation concepts to understand. In relation to these approaches, users commented on the visibility of information, which was purposefully limited to a minimal selection of items per screen.

In comparison, it was discovered that the more traditional linear drop-down boxes and menu lists of the *Standard* interface proved far more difficult to grasp, for unlike the other interfaces, information was largely concealed from view. Users often became flummoxed regarding where to find information, such as a specific contact (i.e. in an address book). For example, they were initially unaware (without advice) that they had to scroll down a list to find such information, despite at times seeing screen prompts like the directional arrow keys. Common assumptions were made that when a contact was not directly visible to view, that they would be available on a separate drop-down menu with the heading of *photographs*, (as each contact was visually represented as an image of that person, they were mistakenly thought of as a 'photograph'). In addition, navigational choices between the 'down' navigation button to open a drop-down menu box, and 'in' to select items were very confusing concepts to remember. At times, observations revealed users would select items, then (not realizing the item was selected) would attempt to re-select. In other instances, when the information was not directly available to view, users would select the 'press to go' (on-screen) button (sometimes referred to as the 'go' button), assuming this would help them in the process of finding the relevant information. However, this option was only designed to take them to the next screen in the application once all appropriate menu selections on that 'page' had been made. Consequentially, this only contributed to more navigational problems.

Alternatively, layouts that demonstrated aspects of continuity appeared to have clear strengths in aiding navigation. These included (although not always noticeable at first) the design of the 3D graphical history in the *Carousel* that perceptually illustrated the sequence of steps selected. In this case it was suggested that additional search facilities should be available in the navigational line, to find, for example, when a previous message was sent. A highly liked interface, the 3D motion of the *Carousel,* was favored due its fluidity and simplicity of movement in which information was sequentially presented (with related information still visible). Minor criticisms of this approach involved the slowness of the moving carousel to return back to previous screens. Consequentially, the speed of the carousel could easily be rectified in subsequent software development. However, this issue does highlight the complexity of adequately matching user with system requirements, given such variable needs. In addition, creative suggestions included the ability to hold down key presses to speed up transitions, with ideas from some computer users of an equivalent 'home button' as found on a typical web browser. As previously mentioned, other transitional aspects of turning and zooming in and out to reveal underlying information in the *Flipper* version, which was designed with a very real-world metaphor in mind similar to sorting through stacks of physical paper, was easily identified with, and thought useful in searching through larger amounts of data.

Visually similar in design to the *Flipper*, the use of semi-transparency overlays (in the *Transparency* version), while not the case for all participants, appeared an unnecessary distraction, causing users to overly hesitate in trying to select un-selectable items, and reposition themselves nearer the TV screen to read on-screen text. This noticeably caused more difficulties for those people with low vision. It is possible that altering the level of transparency may alleviate these difficulties, although it may also be that the overlay approach itself is not helpful for older adults. These issues warrant further investigation.

Given the diversity of older users, particular their inexperience with 'traditional' forms of digital technology, the research also identified more general issues governing successful interaction. For example, despite limiting menu choices to a selection of four items at any one time, individuals still made assumptions like, for example, the choice of 'pictures' instead of 'video messages' (to send a video message), as in one case the recipient of the message would perceive 'seeing' the incoming message, presumably like a picture. Examples like these, clearly demonstrate the inherent challenges in mapping 'appropriate' operations with functions in any interactive system, given differences in how some older people will 'perceive' the technology to work.

As a final example, the findings revealed an immediate expectation by a few individuals to automatically speak into the screen to record a message, without pressing any buttons or navigating to any specific point on screen. Although this may be accountable to initial nervousness in using the system, it does demonstrate another challenge presented by older users unfamiliar with even the basic concepts of video messaging.

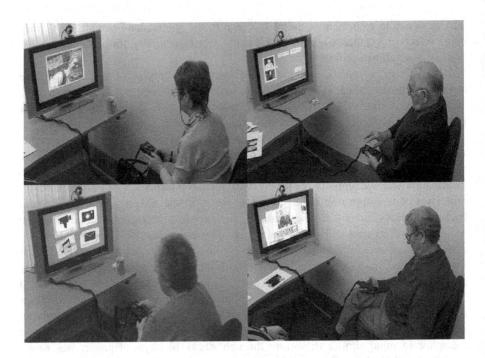

Fig. 6. Screenshots of participants interacting with some of the different interfaces presented

4   Conclusion and Further Work

Significant work is needed on the design of interfaces that can support the skills and abilities of a heterogeneous ageing population. As a result, more research is necessary to embrace the need for far more creative and useable interfaces for older adults - a significant challenge given the potentially widening gap of inclusivity for this largely emerging and developing technology.

Preliminary evaluations have found that the use of 'continuity' potentially offers more 'intuitive' approaches for people unfamiliar with associated interactive systems. In particular, the authors believe more dynamic navigational techniques that can mimic aspects of real world artifacts, in a manner individuals can quickly relate to, present possible new direction within DTV interface design. However, the success of such a system is dependent on user-centered research approaches, which can take into account the value of a 'dual interface' system, such as an appropriate inputting control, as well as on-screen interaction.

Our research in developing a simplified six-button remote control received high praise from older users, despite its rather early stage of development. In comparison, the study found a number of weaknesses in the design of more conventional layouts, which have drawn ideas from desktop metaphors, particular in their concealment of information using standard drop-down and scrolling menus

As an extension of this project, the research is now focused on more quantitative analysis of understanding more detailed aspects of continuity and interactive narrative with DTV, using a fully functional remote control. These include the visualization of potentially much larger and therefore complex sets of data that could be annotated and organized by audiences of older people. Given the objectives of this current research project, methodologies will continue to be applied which reflect the user-centered nature of this investigation.

References

1. Adobe Systems Incorporated.: Mobile and devices developer centre. (Retrieved 9th February 2007) http://www.adobe.com/devnet/devices/itv.html
2. Bederson, B., Meyer, J., and Good, L.: Jazz: an extensible zoomable user interface graphics toolkit in Java. Proceedings of the 13th annual ACM symposium on user interface and technology (2000) 171-180
3. Card, S.K., Robertson, G., and Mackinlay. J.D.: The information visualizer: An information workspace. Proceedings of the SIGCHI conference on Human factors in computing systems: Reaching through technology (1991) 181- 186
4. Carmichael, A., Rice, M., Sloan, S., and Gregor, P.: Digital switchover or digital divide: A prognosis for usable and accessible interactive digital television in the UK. Universal Access in the Information Society Journal 4(4) (2005) 400-416
5. Crabtree, A., Hemmings, T., and Rodden, T.: Supporting communication within domestic settings. Home Oriented Informatics and Telematics Conference (2003)
6. Eisma, R., Dickinson, A., Goodman, J., Mival, O., Syme, A. and Tiwari, L., 2003, Mutual inspiration in the development of new technology for older people. Include 2003 (2003) 252-259
7. Eisma, R., Dickinson, A., Goodman, J., Syme, A., Tiwari, L. and Newell, A.F.: Early user involvement in the development of information technology related products for older people. Universal Access in the Information Society 3(2) (2004) 131-140
8. Fisk, J., Rogers, W.A., Charness, N., Czaja, S.J., and Sharit, J.: Designing for older adults: principles and creative human factors approaches. London: CRC Press (2000)
9. Fry, B.: Computational information design. PhD thesis, MIT (2004)
10. Luyten, K., Thys, K., Huypens, S., Coninx, K.: Telebuddies: social stitching with interactive television. CHI 2006 extended abstracts on Human factors in computing systems. ACM Press (2006) 1049-1054
11. Ofcom.: Executive summary of report on media literacy amongst older people. (Retrieved 17th February 2007)
http://www.ofcom.org.uk/advice/media_literacy/medlitpub/medlitpubrss/older/older.pdf
12. Rice, M., Newell, A., and Morgan, M.: Forum Theatre as a requirements gathering methodology in the design of a home telecommunication system for older adults. Behaviour and Information Technology Journal (In press)
13. Rubin, A.M., and Rubin, R.B.: Older persons' TV viewing patterns and motivations. Communication Research, 9,(2), (1982) 287-313
14. Vanparijs, F., Coppens, T., Godon, M., Bouwen, J.: Social Television: Enabling Rich Communication and Community Support with AmigoTV. (Retrieved 24 February 2007) http://www.ist-ipmedianet.org/Alcatel_AmigoTV_paper_ICIN_2004_final-1.pdf

Psychological Backgrounds for Inducing Cooperation in Peer-to-Peer Television

Jenneke Fokker[1], Huib de Ridder[1], Piet Westendorp[1], and Johan Pouwelse[2]

[1] Faculty of Industrial Design Engineering,
[2] Faculty of Electrical Engineering, Mathematics and Computer Science,
Delft University of Technology
Delft, The Netherlands
{j.e.fokker,h.deridder,p.h.westendorp,j.a.pouwelse}@tudelft.nl

Abstract. Television and the Internet have proven to be a popular combination for both broadcasters and viewers. Because of this popularity they are increasingly facing the consequences of central bottlenecks, which could be overcome by taking a different approach: Peer-to-Peer (P2P) technology. P2P systems can only be successful with as much cooperation among as many users as possible. We explain how this cooperation is hard to enforce, and how inducing it might be more successful. This paper lists relevant psychological backgrounds that can be used to induce this cooperation, along with possible applications for our system called Peer-to-Peer Television (P2P-TV).

Keywords: Peer-to-peer technology, inducing cooperation, altruism, (social) psychological theories.

1 Introduction

The world of television is expanding its traditional broadcasts with flexible, nearly unlimited access to content and narrowcasting of niche content over the Internet. For many, YouTube.com has set the trend of massive injection and distribution of user-generated content. But the Internet is not only used for user-generated video content. The combination of television and the Internet gives broadcasters the chance to reach a much bigger and diverse audience. Users are no longer restricted to fixed broadcast schedules and have faster and more dynamic access to more content. However, central websites like YouTube have drawbacks. Client-server architectures are unfit for large amounts of users trying to access the same file at the same time, resulting in reduced quality-of-service (QoS) and availability of content, plus delays and increased download times. Large servers are needed to support this large community. By using Peer-to-Peer (P2P) technology it is possible to remove all central bottlenecks. However, the performance in a P2P system fully depends on the level of cooperation.

There are advantages as well as disadvantages to P2P technology. Both users and broadcasters benefit from P2P technology for the following reasons:

P. Cesar et al. (Eds.): EuroITV 2007, LNCS 4471, pp. 136–145, 2007.
© Springer-Verlag Berlin Heidelberg 2007

- P2P technology will have low cost of ownership for content, because it aggregates distributed resources through smart interoperability,
- One-click uploading and distribution to thousands of viewers of user generated content becomes possible with hardly any costs involved,
- Television broadcasters do not need an expensive and high maintenance central server. The existing infrastructure is used and any maintenance effort is distributed over the users,
- It is perfect for distributing large files among large amounts of viewers at the same time, because the more viewers, the faster the download will become.

This only holds if all users are prepared to contribute as much as possible. However, for online systems it has been found that only 1% of the users is responsible for almost all contributions, about 9% contributes every once in a while, and 90% only lurks and contributes nothing [1-3]. The latter want a high profit at no costs. In P2P networks there is an increased chance of social loafing, because people think it is less likely that they will be evaluated on an individual basis [4, 5]. P2P technology allows this kind of behavior because of one of its main characteristics, namely no central server with the following consequences:

- There is no central authority in charge to monitor the network, safeguard the technical and artistic quality of content, and metadata describing the files.
- The system can be misused deliberately or unintentionally. If users misbehave, they usually remain unseen.
- The system depends on the availability of distributed resources and good quality content. But P2P networks consist of diverse and anonymous users, and most of them usually do not feel responsible to contribute to the community, apart from the technically enforced tit-for-tat (t4t) mechanism as used in BitTorrent [6].

A technological solution would be regulation or enforcement of more cooperation. However, this is limited, because it would require complex distributed algorithms, in which decisions have to be made at each local peer, usually with little global knowledge [7]. An alternative is to look for means to *induce* massive, positive, and voluntary cooperation of users. For this, we need to know what could possibly motivate users – in particular the majority of 'lurkers' – to behave altruistically. The aim of this paper is to look for human motivations that can be used to induce cooperation in P2P networks. To this end (social) psychological literature was reviewed using keywords like altruism, cooperation, and prosocial behavior. In section 2 we reflect on cooperation in Peer-to-Peer Television (P2P-TV). In section 3 relevant psychological backgrounds are presented together with possible applications.

2   Cooperation in P2P-TV

P2P-TV [8] is one of the research vehicles of the I-Share project [9]. Within this project we will make our ideas about how human cooperation can be induced operational and tested in future versions of P2P-TV. Within this project we identified the following 4 aspects of cooperation that are essential for the success of P2P-TV:

1. **Peer uptime**. When a few peers stay online for a long period of time, the health and availability of content is improved.
2. **Donate bandwidth**. Users should donate their upload bandwidth even after their download(s) have finished.
3. **Injection**. It is vital that fresh content of good quality is available.
4. **Moderation**. With P2P networks there is no immediate certainty about what content is being distributed. It could contain viruses and possibly, copyrighted content. Moderation is quality control that consists of ensuring that both metadata and content is protected against intentional pollution and user mistakes.

These aspects are not easily enforced, but inducement of cooperation might be more successful. We believe P2P-TV users can be induced to cooperate voluntarily in an online environment where there are no real face-to-face encounters, nor a central authority to enforce this cooperation, because people *do* help others: next to selfish behavior, altruistic motives abound. The term altruism (a.k.a. prosocial behavior in social psychology) refers to all actions that provide benefit to others but that have no obvious benefits for the person who helps [10]. Altruism not only occurs in real life (e.g. donating blood), but also in virtual environments. Just look at Wikipedia.org or Flickr.com. Wikipedia is a web-based, free-content encyclopedia, written and moderated collaboratively by volunteers. Flickr is a photo sharing website. Users contribute not only by putting their pictures on the website, but also by annotating and moderating them. In previous work [11] we have made an inventory of mechanisms to induce massive and voluntary cooperation already used in state-of-the-art websites, among which Wikipedia and Flickr. In the next section some of these mechanisms are used as examples of how relevant psychological backgrounds could be applied in P2P-TV.

3   Relevant Psychological Backgrounds

People often behave seemingly less selfish in situations that involve or affect others than they would when it only affects themselves. What people decide in these situations sometimes seems hard to explain from a selfish point of view. This section explains the underlying rationale of what seems irrational at first sight. To reach this we should look at what theories can possibly explain altruism and how they can be applied to P2P-TV. We present a list of 13 theories and we discuss their usefulness in the context of P2P-TV. They are mostly taken from (social) psychology and evolutionary biology. We do not claim to be complete, but we do think that this list gives a good overview of human motivations that could underlie altruism. The theories are listed in order of their frequency of operationalizations in state-of-the-art websites.

Costly Signaling Theory
People provide large benefits to others even when they know this help will not be reciprocated, because this costly, altruistic act may benefit the altruist indirectly by gaining status [12,13]. McAndrew [13] states: "If one can afford to expend a great deal of money, energy, or time in a manner that seems to be irrelevant to one's selfish interests, then the resources that one has in reserve must be very great indeed." This is also called competitive altruism [14]; altruism, if publicly displayed, increases the reputation and status of the altruists, which makes them more attractive interaction partners. Mauss [15] found strong examples of competitive altruism amongst tribes

along the North Pacific coast of North America who, in a ceremony called Potlatch, give away valuable goods to display wealth and status. The other tribe is expected to reciprocate with interest. Not being able to reciprocate means a loss of rank or status.

Application: It is important to realize that this theory will only work in P2P-TV if people's *behavior is visible to others*, as this boosts their self-esteem and is beneficial to their status and reputation. Costly signaling can be found in almost all investigated websites and applications, among which SETI@Home (Fig. 1). Users make much personal information public, thus making themselves vulnerable to malicious others, but also making themselves more trustworthy and interesting to possible interaction partners. It is important to *allow users to stand out of the crowd.*

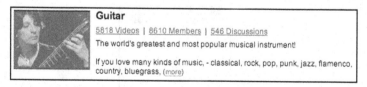

Fig. 1. A public SETI@Home user profile, often used to show off with in message boards

Social Impact Theory

This theory explains that the group influences the decisions that individual members make. The likelihood that a person will respond to social influence will increase with:

1. Strength: the power and status of the group,
2. Immediacy: how close the group is to you in space and time, and
3. Size: as group size increases, 'diffusion of responsibility' occurs more often: each member feels less and less responsible for the task, and puts less effort in it [10].

Application: The third point is especially important for P2P systems, in which people hardly ever feel responsible to contribute. To make sure that users take responsibility, it should be possible to start and join *small enough groups that are powerful and exclusive*. This way they will value belonging to that group much more and contribute more voluntarily. The *need to belong* is fundamental to a large part of the investigated websites and applications. For instance, MySpace, YouTube (Fig. 2), and Flickr all evolve around communities.

> **Guitar**
> 5818 Videos | 8610 Members | 546 Discussions
> The world's greatest and most popular musical instrument!
>
> If you love many kinds of music, - classical, rock, pop, punk, jazz, flamenco, country, bluegrass, (more)

Fig. 2. 'Guitar', one of the most productive and largest groups on YouTube

Social Exchange Theory

When people give something, they expect something in return. Social exchange theory explains that the goods that are exchanged need not be of the same type. Esteem is regarded as an exchangeable good as well [16]. The fear of loosing esteem could also make people try to compensate by helping more. The goods exchanged usually differ between exchange relationships (e.g. business relations) and communal relationships (e.g. close friends) [17]. Exchange relationships have a much shorter 'return-on-investment' time.

Application: The social exchange theory can be easily applied in P2P-TV by providing the means to *express approval or disapproval* in return for received help. This is very similar to eBay's user-to-user moderation involving a transaction between a buyer and a seller (Fig. 3).

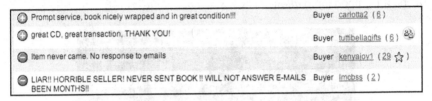

Fig. 3. Expressing approval or disapproval about a transaction in eBay

In P2P-TV we require immediate reciprocity of bandwidth (for which exchange relationships are ideal), and we should allow delayed reciprocity for communal relationships. In other words, *allow for different return-on-investment times for different relationship strengths.* To the best of our knowledge, this has never been built in any other application or website. It also implies that users must be able to *set the relationship type,* similar to for instance Orkut, which uses the types 'best friends', 'good friends', 'friends', 'acquaintances', and 'haven't met'.

Social Learning Theory

Most human behavior is learned observationally through modeling the behaviors, attitudes, and emotional reactions of others [18]. People observe others, form an idea of how new behaviors are performed, and use this information in later situations as a guide. People will adopt modeled behavior quicker if the model is similar to the observer or enjoys a high status and admiration from its peers.

Application: Translating the similarity principle into P2P-TV implies that we have to *show the similarity* between two users, for instance in their taste for TV-shows, like what Last.fm does with the similarity in taste for music (Fig. 4).

Fig. 4. Similarity in taste for music between two users of Last.fm

This is what we also recognize in Amazon's "Customers who bought this item also bought". Another application is, if we want users to set an example to others, that their altruistic behavior should be *as visible as possible* to others. The more visible someone's behavior is, the more likely someone else will follow his footsteps. Yet another option is to create a role model with a higher authority, who can set an example to newbies and explain the social norms.

Social Balance Theory
People seek balanced states in their relationships, called interpersonal consistency [19], both in the context of dyads as in a peer group. For instance, liking the person/group you are associated with, or disliking a person/group you are not associated with, are both states of balance. Imbalance will make people act, either by changing their sentiment about or their association with that person or group. These principles are quite similar to cognitive dissonance theory and social identity theory.

Application: Users should feel the *need to belong* to groups in P2P-TV. This is quite basic to social software, like Skype, Orkut, or MySpace. This need can be exploited if the *groups are formed around the 4 aspects of cooperation* in P2P-TV, for instance the 'injection' group. People will be allowed to join after they have injected fresh content. This is similar to the application of the social identity theory.

Group Selection Theory
The group selection theory states that selective forces can act on competing groups of individuals, not just competing individuals. Darwin himself was the first to suggest that altruism evolves by group selection. This theory suggests to account for behaviors observed in both human and animal societies that appear to benefit the group, even to the cost of individuals.

Application: Translating these principles P2P-TV implies that we should enable groups to form within the application, and that *users should be informed of the group's power and reputation*.

Social Identity Theory
Group membership contributes to establishment of a positive social identity [20]. The greater the number of prestigious, restrictive groups an individual is admitted to, the more his self-concept is reinforced. The value derived from joining a group can depend on the effort it took to become a member. A group that accepts anyone without any restrictions, won't boost the members' self esteem. People usually try to maintain positive views of the groups they are linked to, are positively biased in their judgments of other individuals in those groups, and negatively biased to those outside of the groups they belong to.

Application: As was said before in the social impact theory, people have a *need to belong*. If someone belongs to a group within P2P-TV, it is likely he will contribute to that group. Moreover, the groups should have *rules for admitting* people, like hacker communities in which newbies first have to prove their hack-skills before they get admitted. Another example is Orkut. People can only join if they were invited. We should *create a feeling of exclusiveness*. It is also important that it is *visible* to which groups a user belongs, because it boosts his self-esteem if he knows others can see he belongs to a very exclusive group.

Theory of Reciprocal Altruism

The theory of reciprocal altruism explains that cooperation is conditional: A cooperator will keep helping an unrelated individual, unless the latter refuses to reciprocate [21].

Application: The implications of this theory for P2P-TV are that if we want users to help each other repeatedly, it must be possible to *keep track of their given help / received help ratio* and *make it visible* to others. Another consequence is that *users must be able to rebuke each other* for not reciprocating help. Of course, the opposite is just as important: *show approval for reciprocating*.

Equity Theory

This theory emphasizes fairness. People expect a fair share of available resources that is appropriate to their status [22]. If not, they may experience cognitive dissonance.

Application: For P2P-TV we propose to use these principles by making transactions transparent: *Show how much others contribute in respect to their available resources.* This is more than the BitTorrent sharing ratio, which is based on the tit-for-tat principle: people must give as much as they have received.

Kin Selection Theory

This theory has its origin in Hamilton's theory of inclusive fitness [23]. It states that – given a cost/benefit ratio -altruism is more likely with higher relatedness. If two individuals are sufficiently closely related, altruism can benefit reproduction of a set of genes, despite losses to the individual altruist. The benefit of altruism decreases rapidly with declining relatedness [24].

Application: Kinship could be translated into *friendship*, as is done by many social networks, for instance in LinkedIn (Fig. 5). Instead of showing the relatedness between two peers, we should show the *degrees of separation* (1st degree = friend, 2nd = friend of a friend, and so on).

Your Network of Trusted Professionals

You are at the center of your network. Your connections can introduce you to 22.200+ professionals — here's how your network breaks down:

1 Your Connections Your trusted friends and colleagues		28
2 Two degrees away Friends of friends; each connected to one of your connections		500+
3 Three degrees away Reach these users through a friend and one of their friends		21,700+
Total users you can contact through an Introduction		22,200+

Fig. 5. Degrees of separation in LinkedIn

Theory of Group Cohesiveness

This theory explains how small, face-to-face informal social groups exert pressure on their members to uphold social norms. Cohesiveness is defined as the resultant of all the forces acting on members of a group to remain in the group [25]. The determinants of group cohesiveness are:

1. Attractiveness of the group to its members,
2. The mutual attraction of those members to each other as individuals, and
3. The mediation of individual goals by the group.

Application: Even though this theory was formulated for situations of face-to-face encounters, we can apply it to encounters in P2P-TV as well. The more users identify with a group and its members, the more they will feel obliged to uphold the social norms of that community. This means we should *make information about a group and its members as visible as possible.*

Cognitive Evaluation Theory

Faced with a task, people evaluate it in terms of how well it meets their needs for feeling competent and in control. If they think they will be able to complete the task, they are 'intrinsically motivated' and don't need further external motivation. The cognitive evaluation theory was formulated to explain effects of rewards, feedback, and other external events on intrinsic motivation [26]. In contrast to operant conditioning - where desired behavior can be reached by rewards and punishments - the cognitive evaluation theory states that extrinsic motivations can have a counter-productive effect on intrinsic motivation, because they conduce toward an external perceived locus of causality. Too much rewards or punishments will have a counter effect if participants perceive them to be controlling, rather than supportive [27, 28].

Application: The implication for P2P-TV is that we need to *find a balance between facilitating and enforcing cooperation.* However, it seems difficult to advice on applications of this principle.

Self-affirmation Theory

This theory explains how the overall goal of people is to protect their image of self-integrity, of their moral and adaptive adequacy [29]. When this image is threatened, people will respond in such a way that is least harmful to their self-worth. There are two ways to respond to such threats: 1) through defensive responses that directly reduce the threat, and 2) through the affirmation of alternative sources of self-integrity. An example: If you show me how I cannot sing, I'll go and play guitar even more, which I know I am better at.

Application: We should *make it possible for users to specialize in one of the 4 aspects of cooperation* in P2P-TV, for instance allow them to become 'top moderators'.

Summary

Social psychology literature on human cooperative behavior turns out to be a useful source for deriving motives to cooperate in P2P systems. The search resulted in a great number of proposed applications: show the similarity between users, make behavior publicly visible, make it possible for users to express approval or disapproval about each other, allow different return-on-investment times for different relationship types, show how much others contribute in respect to their total resources, exploit the need to belong, and make groups small, powerful and exclusive, allow users to stand out of the crowd, display information on friendship and the degrees of separation, let users specialize in one of the four aspects of cooperation, keep track of the given help/received help ratio, make information about a group and its members visible, and finally, make users feel intrinsically motivated to cooperate. This list points out the following general properties that always have to be taken into account when trying to induce cooperation in P2P systems:

- Exploit the need to make friends, belong to groups as well as the need to stand out of the crowd,
- Status and reputation are extremely powerful, and
- Use the fact that people seek balance and avoid imbalance.

The examples given in this paper suggest that these properties can be incorporated into technological systems.

4   Conclusions

P2P technology is vital to the Television in the future, with cooperation being the most challenging problem in P2P systems. We listed 13 theories, which provide fertile ground for solving that challenge. This publication is the first recipe for addressing cooperation in P2P systems with a profound theoretical background. It seeks to bridge theory and practice by applying all theories to the relevant context of use.

Acknowledgments. This research is carried out as part of the I-Share project [9].

References

[1]   Adar, E. and Huberman, B.A., Free riding on Gnutella. First Monday. 2000.
[2]   De Valck, K. Virtual Communities of Consumption: Networks of Consumer Knowledge and Companionship, Erasmus University Rotterdam, Rotterdam, 2005.
[3]   Participation Inequality: Encouraging More Users to Contribute, http://www.useit.com/alertbox/participation_inequality.html, October 10, 2006.
[4]   Harkins, S. and Szymanski, K., Social loafing and group evaluation. Journal of Personality and Social Psychology, 56. 934-941. 1989.
[5]   Goren, H., Kurzban, R. and Rapoport, A., Social loafing vs. social enhancement: Public goods provisioning in real-time with irrevocable commitments. Organizational Behavior and Human Decision Processes, 90. 277-290. 2003.
[6]   Pouwelse, J.A., Garbacki, P., Epema, D.H.J. and Sips, H.J., The BitTorrent p2p file-sharing system: Measurements and analysis. in 4th International Workshop on Peer-to-Peer Systems (IPTPS'05), Ithaca, New York, 24-25 February, 2004.
[7]   Milojicic, D.S., Kalogeraki, V., Lukose, R., Nagaraja, K., Pruyne, J., Richard, B., Rollins, S. and Xu, Z., Peer-to-Peer Computing. HP Laboratories Palo Alto, 2002, http://www.dps.uibk.ac.at/uploads/82/HPL-2002-57R1.pdf.
[8]   Wang, J., Pouwelse, J., Fokker, J., De Vries, A.P. and Reinders, M.J.T., Personalization on a peer-to-peer television system. Multimedia Tools and Applications, 32 (2). 2007.
[9]   Sharing resources in virtual communities for storage, communications, and processing of multimedia data, www.freeband.nl/project.cfm?id=520, December, 2006.
[10] Baron, R.A., Byrne, D. and Johnson, B.T., Exploring Social Psychology. Allyn and Bacon, Needham Heights, MA, 1998.
[11] Fokker, J., Buntine, W., Pouwelse, J., De Ridder, H. and Westendorp, P., Tagging in Peer-to-Peer Wikipedia: A method to induce cooperation. in Open Source Information Retrieval Workshop (OSIR'06), Seattle, WA, USA, August 6-11, 2006.

[12] Grafen, A., Biological Signals as Handicaps. Journal of Theoretical Biology, 144 (4). 517-546. 1990.

[13] McAndrew, F.T., New Evolutionary Perspectives on Altruism: Multilevel-Selection and Costly-Signaling Theories. Current Directions in Psychological Science, 11 (2). 79-82. 2002.

[14] Hardy, C.L. and Van Vugt, M., Nice guys finish first: The competitive altruism hypothesis. Personality and Social Psychology Bulletin, 32 (10). 1402-1413. 2006.

[15] Mauss, M., The gift: the form and reason for exchange in Archaic societies. Norton, New York, 2000.

[16] Homans, G.C., Social Behavior as Exchange. American Journal of Sociology, 63 (6). 597-606. 1958.

[17] Clark, M.S. and Mills, J., The difference between communal and exchange relationships: What it is and is not. Personality and Social Psychology Bulletin, 19. 684-691. 1993.

[18] Bandura, A., Social Learning Theory. General Learning Press, New York, 1971.

[19] Heider, F., The Pscychology of Interpersonal Relations. John Wiley & Sons, 1958.

[20] Tajfel, H. and Turner, J.C. The social identity theory of intergroup behavior. in Worchel, S. and Austin, W. eds. Psychology of Intergroup Relations, Nelson Hall, Chicago, 1986, 7-24.

[21] Trivers, R., The Evolution of Reciprocal Altruism. Quarterly Review of Biology, 46. 35-57. 1971.

[22] Greenberg, J. and Scott, K.S., Why do workers bite the hands that feed them? Employee theft as a social exchange process. . JAI Press, Greenwich, CT, 1996.

[23] Hamilton, W.D., The genetical evolution of social behaviour. I. Journal of Theoretical Biology, 7 (1). 1-16. 1964.

[24] Brembs, B. Hamilton's Theory. in Brenner, S. and Miller, J. eds. Encyclopedia of Genetics, Academic Press, London, New York, 2001, 906-910.

[25] Festinger, L., Schachter, S. and Back, K., Social pressures in informal groups: A study of human factors in housing. Harper & Brothers, New York, 1950.

[26] Ryan, R.M. and Deci, E.L., Self-Determination Theory and the Facilitation of Intrinsic Motivation, Social Development, and Well-Being. American Psychologist, 55 (1). 68-78. 2000.

[27] Frey, B. and Jegen, R., Motivation crowding theory: A survey of empirical evidence. Journal of Economic Surveys, 5 (5). 589-611. 2001.

[28] Ripeanu, M., Mowbray, M., Andrade, N. and Lima, A., Gifting technologies: A BitTorrent case study. First Monday, 11. 2006.

[29] Steele, C.M. The psychology of self-affirmation: Sustaining the integrity of the self. in Berkowitz, L. ed. Advances in experimental social psychology, Academic Press, New York, 1988, 261-301.

Trends in the Living Room and Beyond

Regina Bernhaupt, Marianna Obrist, Astrid Weiss,
Elke Beck, and Manfred Tscheligi

HCI & Usability Unit, ICT&S Center, University of Salzburg, Sigmund-Haffner-Gasse 18
5020 Salzburg, Austria
firstname.secondname@sbg.ac.at

Abstract. Investigating the context home becomes more and more necessary for future developments of interactive TV services and of new interaction techniques. In this paper, findings from two ethnographic studies are presented. In these studies a new methodological variation of cultural probing called creative cultural probing (CCP) was developed. The aim of our research was to investigate activities and interaction techniques in the living room and beyond. In this paper, the results of the studies are presented and some major trends for the home context are highlighted. The studies indicate that supporting social interaction and personal activities as well as personalization, security and communication needs have to be addressed in the future more thoroughly.

Keywords: context home, living room, ethnography, cultural probing, interactive television.

1 Introduction

Information and communication technologies (ICTs) and other technological innovations have a tremendous influence on and play a major role in people's daily life. Home studies are central to understand the process of domestication and consumption of domestic technologies [18]. Researchers from various fields started to investigate people's daily usage of technology in the context home by using and adapting various methods. Ethnographic studies and cultural probing [7, 11, 10] are used to obtain a more in depth perspective on today's trends in the living room.

To inform new forms of interactive television (iTV) services and interaction concepts, we investigated current trends in the living room and beyond. We conducted two ethnographic studies using a new methodological variation of cultural probing. This methodological variation enabled us to use and stimulate the creative potential of the study participants to invent, investigate, suggest or even produce new forms of ICTs they would like to have in their living rooms. The main research questions for the first study were: What kind of activities and interactions take place in the living room? and How can peoples' activities and interactions be supported by interactive TV services in their homes? The second study is also based on these questions but focuses more on the extended home context. In each study were addressed three different research topics. The first study aimed to better understand the living room as a main space for interactions. Moreover, people's activities in front of the TV as well as people's requirements regarding interaction techniques in the

P. Cesar et al. (Eds.): EuroITV 2007, LNCS 4471, pp. 146–155, 2007.
© Springer-Verlag Berlin Heidelberg 2007

context home were investigated. The second study should provide deeper insights in the areas of extended home, shared experience, and new interaction concepts.

2 The Method

We developed a variation of cultural probing called creative cultural probing (CCP). The developed CCP cards offer two main advantages: First, they are following a special topic for each week within the ethnographic studies, like *[sitting] in front of the TV*. This weekly topics were extended by semi-structured stimuli and increased users involvement into the studies and stimulated a creative idea generation process within the participating households. Second, the creative cards were supplemented by photo and video documentation facilities (disposable cameras and multi-functional video cameras). Moreover, a first visit and a final interview were conducted in the households in order to discuss the material produced by the household themselves.

Even though our studies might not be described as ethnographic studies in a classical ethnological or sociological sense as described by Fetterman [6], Atkinson [2] or Geertz [8] we analyzed our collected material like traditional field notes. "Writing descriptions is not merely a matter of accurately capturing as closely as possible observed reality, of 'putting into words' overheard talk and witnessed activities. [...] But, in fact, there is no single 'natural' or 'correct' way to record what one observes" [5]. We present our ethnographic field notes as an attempt to make sense and help interpret the material we collected from each topic we addressed[1]. The two reported studies were embedded in a larger project framework (iiTV@home and iTV 4 ALL), which will be described briefly in the following sections.

3 The Living Room Context

To explore people's activities and interactions in the living room we conducted an ethnographic study from May to June 2006. We recruited participants from an existing field trial of iTV in the Federal Province of Salzburg. The project called iiTV@home (information oriented interactive TV at home) mainly focused on the development of new forms of news and information oriented regional iTV services. Based on former studies [15, 4] we recruited households with elderly participants or with more than three family members. These households are more likely interested in the services offered during the three month field trial. From the 40 households within the iiTV@home project 16 participated in the ethnographic living room study.

Participants' media habits were explored in detail. The amount of TV sets ranges from one to four sets among the participating households, nearly half of the households own two TV sets. The primary TV set is usually placed in the living room. At the same time, the living room is, apart from the kitchen, one of the most important rooms for social interaction at home. Six households have also Internet access in the living room. The reasons for watching TV are rather divergent: from being entertained and receiving information to recreation. The participants were especially

---

[1] As the whole study was conducted in German, the quotations used in this paper are translated to English.

interested in news with local and national content, documentaries and sport reports. Many participants also identified watching TV as a major common activity, along with eating and playing games.

3.1 Set-Up of Study One

The ethnographic study conducted lasted three weeks. In the interview at the end of the study we discussed the results of the probing material with the most active participant in the household. Each of the 16 households received a package with several CCP cards for a three weeks period accompanied with a pre-questionnaire to capture demographic data and TV viewing behaviours. Figure 1 shows one of the packages. Participants were asked to store the package on the table of the living room to enable all family members to actively contribute during the whole week.

In addition, eight households got a multi-functional video camera and eight households a disposable camera to record their ideas and contributions. Within this first study we addressed the following topics: In the living room, in front of the TV and interaction techniques in the context home. These topics were selected based on previous findings in the field of iTV services [15].

Fig 1. Creative cultural probing package with disposable camera

3.2 The Living Room

We made efforts to gain a better understanding of the physical space of the living room and its contributions to the concept of home. Venkatesh [18] points out: "The physical space has both a functional and a symbolic value". To explore this context, we asked participants to use the probe package and mainly to fill out the creative cards. "In front of the TV" included sentences to be completed, for example: 'I have an idea...', 'I write down information about ...', 'I am working on ...'. Other questions included elements and symbols to engage individuals to encourage family collaboration during the study. We, for instance, asked participants to name five things they like to do in the living room, things they would like to change in the living room, to adopt it to their needs. The living room is still the main place for social interaction among family members. It is central for most of the family oriented activities – either technologically oriented like watching TV – or non-technological social activities like simple card playing. People described the living room as a recreational area. Most activities mentioned are related to watching TV, listening to music or simply playing with the kids or the pets. The living room is an important place for socializing with family members, friends, guests or neighbours. It is a place where people meet and discuss about everyday occurrences; they take care about their loved ones. The five most mentioned things people do in their living room were: socializing, watching TV, listening music/radio, reading and playing.

A participant (male, 46 years old, 2 children) summarized in an interview: *"I can watch TV, be lazy, read something, ... In the living room I have a lot of fluffy things which make me feel at home and comfortable. I spend my time there when all my work is finished – unfortunately only in the evening. But the living room is also the place where my son plays on the Play Station"*. One participant (male, 67 years old) said: *"We designed our own house as an open space, where the kitchen and the living room are one big room with different spaces. I can cook and serve the food or drinks to my guests in the same room, I can watch TV on my comfortable chair, I can listen to music and have some day dreams. I can read the newspaper, sort the advertising or read the daily mail... and I can change the look of the room, whenever I want. But, I have still to buy a new entertainment rack, as there is not enough space for all the technology (TV, DVD player, digital TV receiver, stereo system) in the living room."*

Roles and usage patterns in the living room are influenced by age, the number of family members and work as well as leisure activities, and last but not least by time. The living room is the place where people find the quietness, relaxing atmosphere and privacy they need. It is a personal and social space for relaxing and dwelling, but is also characterized as a technological space. People often do not realize the technology surrounding them, until they are asked for it. Technology is integrated into the physical environment and has become part of it (domestication process [9]).

3.3   In Front of the TV

In front of the TV people typically want to relax, but are interactive at the same time [13]. Interactivity is an integral component of the iTV user experience, presumed that interactivity is not understood in a technological sense, but defined as a psychological and emotional process. While watching TV people precede to do a lot of different activities, like changing the sound of the TV several times, depending on contextual influences (for example getting a call from a friend). A female participant (45 years old, living with her husband, three children and the grandparents) stated: *„Most of the time I talk to my family – but they normally tell me to be quiet [laughing] ... so I go on with my housework, like ironing, writing the shopping list or reading the newspaper. Late in the evening, I have more time to watch TV, as the others are sleeping and most of the work is finished, then I can watch TV, when I know that there is something interesting on the TV (I always check this in advance)... sometimes I'm upset because I missed or forgot a program. Therefore, I would really like to have a kind of time shifting, so I can watch the program when I've time, which is quite rare..."*

Other participants reported that they take notes while watching TV. They write down Internet addresses, telephone numbers, names of experts mentioned within a TV program. They also write down lottery results or compose their shopping list. Socializing, discussing and sharing information is also a main activity in front of the TV. This clearly demonstrates how active people are in front of the TV and that they do not only concentrate on the program, which is going on, but they complete different TV related and non-TV related activities. One of the main challenges for designers, especially for iTV designers will be to support such activities or to transform the above data into new ideas for home based technologies.

3.4 Interaction Techniques

In a first step we focused on the traditional way of interaction with the TV – the remote control. Some participants were quite creative when demonstrating their difficulties with today's interaction techniques in the living room. In one household the children draw their desired remote control (see Figure 2). *"... the remote control should have a funny and cool shape (like a pyramid), an integrated clock and a function to see what's going on in different channels. The remote control should be small and handy"* (2 girls, 11 and 13 years old).

Fig. 2. Design of a remote control with the shape of a pyramid, done by 2 girls

Some additional remarks can be made about the usage of the remote control. A participant (male, 42 years old, 6 household members) explained that: *"Our TV remote control is very old... we have fixed it several time with glue strip,... we have also bought a new one, but we still use the old one, because it is easier to use... we know where to press to get what we want. We use only selected buttons of our remote controls... some are really useless."* Five out of 16 households described to us, that they have replaced or changed their remote control because it was broken. Only two households reported that they bought a multifunctional remote control. Multifunctional remote controls were often too complicated to use for many of the household members (elderly or females), so that a coexistence of old and new remote controls can be found in such households. A more technical oriented participant (male, 45 years old, and engineer) described his idea for a remote control as follows: *"I need a multifunctional remote control, because I like to program it according to my preferences... define which button has a particular function and so on. In addition, it must have a simple interface, so that also my daughter can use it... I though about a LCD display and a kind of trackball on the remote control, with which I can navigate through the menu. Moreover, speech recognition – similar to mobile phones – could be used to choose a program or to select other functions."*

3.5 Findings: Study One

1. The living room is a social and individual space, where technology is an important but not recognized as an essential part. Technology becomes part of this personal space only when it supports the feeling of being at home, to be private and to relax.
2. TV viewing is strongly related with other activities, by doing other things in the background or doing things at the same time, like watching TV and talking to somebody on the phone. TV is perceived as a medium for recreation and information, depending on the context, including time as a major contextual factor.
3. Remote controls are often perceived as unusable and participants complain about the large number of multiple remote controls in their homes and their complexity. Some quite clear solutions have been elaborated and expressed by the participants: focusing on the most important buttons and supporting additional requirements through display or a menu on the remote control.

Inspired by the results of creative cultural probing, we developed the probe package further and used it in an even broader study by approaching three topics, emerged from the first research and based on current trends and developments (e.g. extended home concept).

4 The Living Room and Beyond

To investigate current usage trends of ICTs within the living room and beyond, we set up a second ethnographic study. We also used the CCP method within this study which was conducted as integral part of the ongoing project iTV4ALL. We investigated the concept of extended home, shared experience, and new forms of interaction techniques. The iTV4ALL project currently focuses on the development of new forms of interaction techniques within the context home, especially on new concepts of iTV services combined with intelligent remote controls. We recruited 40 participating households for this second ethnographic study. None of the households participated in any of the former studies. During the recruiting interview we classified 20 households as media-entertainment oriented, 20 other households were recruited representative for the population of Austria. We chose 14 households with more than three family members and six households with couples for each of the two groups. In a pre-questionnaire we investigated detailed characteristics about the participants' homes. People used several TV sets and most of them owned at least a VCR, DVD-player and a radio. The main activities participants mentioned for daily entertainment in their spare time were watching TV, radio, mobile phone telephony, reading and using the computer. Thus, using devices as entertainment seems to play an important role in the daily routines of the participating households.

4.1 Set-Up Study Two

During the study ten media-entertainment households tested a universal remote control. 20 households were equipped with a multi-functional video camera (Mustek DV5200 or Mustek DV 9300). The other households used a one way disposable camera. All households received a package with creative cards and some modelling clay. We additionally developed a card game to increase involvement of kids. Distribution of cameras and card games was counter-balanced between the two household-groups. Households testing the remote control were selected randomly. The researchers had requested that participants take a photo each time there is a symbol on the CCP card or they are on the road and in contact with technology (this activity was made clear to participants as it was important to obtain more information for the extended home concept).

4.2 Understanding the Extended Home Concept

Extended home (Xhome) can be defined as: "the family accessing communication elements, or media entertainment and consumption of personal objects, while they are away from home" [14]. The main idea of this concept is that smart and connected devices provide the background for ubiquitous connectivity and communication. Mainly Schotanus [17] worked on the topic extended home and stresses that "Xhome is a relatively open system: many users can make use of the Xhome, not only the inhabitants of Xhome make use of the network capabilities, but also many visitors"

[17]. Based on this definition we investigated entertainment, leisure and fun with respect to the concept of the extended home. Related to this topic, a participant (male 25 years old, student) mentioned: *"[This] technological invention simplifies my life... I have seen something on the TV, they have installed a central computer into a house in the foyer, which controls everything, means all technical devices, light, electricity, water, heating - everything; I thought something like this would be really convenient. That was simply a screen, a touch screen, which was installed into the wall."* This example shows that even though people do not really know the meaning of terms like "extended home" or "smart home" they do have a clear idea of how technology can simplify their daily lives.

Nowadays people use a lot of different technologies when they are on the go. Almost everybody uses a mobile phone to stay connected and to be reachable, but they also use MP3 players, iPods or CD players to enhance their daily routines and to overcome boredom, for instance, during waiting periods. Moreover, people are used to the ability of mobile phones and digital cameras to capture precious moments during holydays but also in everyday life. One mother noted: *"On the playground, it bothers me when the battery of my mobile phone or my digital camera is empty"*. This leads to the conclusion that people are currently more accustomed to the fact that technologies accompany them. Our research also highlighted ways in which people shared ideas how to make their life easier by using technology: *"To remotely switch on the coffee machine before I come home would be convenient or to program the video recorder, or to access the computer, or to pre-heat food, that would be nice, or to control the heating, that would be great"* (male, 24 years old, student). Another participant (female, 27 years old, student) stated: *My mother is afraid of burglar while we are on holidays, therefore a remote control for the house would be good to bluff burglars by controlling the curtains, switching on and of the lights; ...then grandma has not to come twice a week"*.

During the post interviews more ideas concerning smart homes were expressed. They were often related to storing information and knowledge. Participants had the following idea: *"It would be convenient to access personal data which is stored at home or when I've forgot something, e.g. addresses which are saved on my mobile phone which I forgot at home; or hearing music with my mobile phone which connects to my MP3-player at home"* (male, 28 years old, engineer). *„I can imagine to access my computer or server when I am on the move and to access my data"* (male, 24 years old, student). Similar wishes were stated on the creative cards: people would like to store addresses, telephone numbers, pictures and photographs at home and have access to this information when they are on the move. Additionally they would also like to have access to their e-mails.

4.3 Understanding Shared Experience

Agamanolis highlights that "Broadcasting is all about creating shared experiences" [1]. New technologies will enable new modes of awareness and communication among different groups of people that were not possible before. These new capabilities and ways of 'staying in touch' could serve a significant role in swift acceptance and deployment iTV technologies". Our understanding of shared experience was also related to Battarbee's [3] definition of co-experience, which "is the seamless blend of user experience of products and social interaction". We specifically approached the following questions: Which activities do people already share at home? Which technologies support shared experience at home? Which contents do people like to share?

A huge variety of technologies exist that participants of our study mentioned as being used together. The most frequently stated ones are TV, CD-player, radio, DVD-player and also the Internet, when they are not experienced users. TV was a medium which people like to use together with other persons because they like to discuss topics while watching TV. Thus, news and sport programs are often watched together. A feeling of community is often experienced while watching a quiz show. Many participants mentioned that they like to be engaged in guessing. Future ways of shared experiences were also envisioned by the participants; above all via video telephony like Skype. *„I already did that; it works with Skype Internet telephony, if you have a webcam. Philip and I, for instance, were in Linz and we watched soccer; Flo called us, so we installed the webcam, put the laptop next to it, ..., we put the microphone into the centre an turned the computer loud, ..."* (male, 25 years old, student).

For our participants, it seemed to be more important to see the face of the one she is talking to. They also expressed this idea with modelling clay in week 3 of our study. One household built a monitor which is connected to a computer and connectable to any mobile phone, so that it is possible to communicate with somebody while watching TV (see Figure 3).

Fig. 3. Idea of a screen connectable to any mobile phone and PC created with modelling clay

Nevertheless people do not want to share everything. On the question "Do you want to know what other people are doing at the moment, so that you do not bother them with a phone call", 17 participants answered that this is a violation of privacy and 14 expressed that this is not necessary, because they just ask if they disturb. On the other hand some participants answered that they could imagine this as beneficial for instance with a status message on the phone like "I am in a concert; I call you back in 30 minutes". Some technical scepticism can also be read between the lines. Probably that is the reason why people want to share selected private contents like photographs and films above all with their family and friends. Moreover they want to inform each other about urgent topics (car accidents, traffic jams, thunderstorms) or the daily news. Two technologies were also often mentioned as worse to use when somebody else is nearby: the telephone and the Internet.

4.4 Interaction Techniques in the (Future) Living Room

Like Knoche et al. pointed out: "Interaction spans devices" [12]. Users often combine multiple devices in their daily routines, but each device has a separate remote control, so the user has to face difficulties in interaction. Portolan et al. hypothesised for instance that voice control can support such an interaction problem: "in front of a table of channels, people prefer to speak out the channel's name instead of navigating through the table" [16]. Definitely interaction problems accompany people's daily routines with technologies and create their own support and prevention strategies.

On the question "Did you ever buy a device that you never really used?"...only 4 out of 40 households answered this question with "no". It seems that people believe that they can make life easier or more enjoyable by buying technologies. But what are the reasons that this strategy does not always work? A participant explained as follows: *"If I cannot understand just trough trying out how a new device works I need to read the manual; if the manual of a device which I do not necessarily need is too complicated, I stop trying and try it again later on"* (female, 25 years old, student). Eight households admitted that they became angry if the technical equipment in their homes did not work correctly. 27 out of 40 households noted on the creative card that they need to read the manual when a problem with a device occurs. On the other hand 18 households also wrote that they organize help for technical problems, for instance, 11 participants mentioned to ask a friend. A main statement from the participants was their intention to get context-dependent help and that they don't like to read instruction guides.

4.5 Findings: Study Two

1. The idea of a smart or extended home cannot be verbally expressed by the participants. They are used to be accompanied by technology in their daily life and have clear ideas how they would like to be connected with their home, for instance controlling their devices at home or experiencing a feeling of security when they can watch their home while they are on the move.
2. The main activity participants like to share is still watching TV, which they experienced as "doing something together". A special popular variation of this activity is guessing on TV-quiz shows. Another clear trend is video telephony as a way of spending an evening together over a distance. Privacy is an important topic and has to be considered in this context.
3. Almost all participating households bought at least one technical device, they never used. Participants would like to have easier manuals with pictures and personalized or phonetic support. Moreover, they would like to have one remote control to control everything.

5 Conclusion

In these two ethnographic studies we used a methodological variation of cultural probing called creative cultural probing (CCP). The CCP cards proved to gather a huge amount of qualitative data. The additional photo and video material was easy to analyse because of its connection to the creative cards. In general, a categorization of the gathered data according to the predefined research areas proofed to be valuable. The results of the two studies showed that people still want remote controls as input device, although remote controls are perceived as being too complex and difficult to use. Moreover, existing interaction techniques only little support shared experiences. New interaction techniques additionally raise questions regarding privacy and security issues especially for the extended home context. Based on the findings described and summarized in section 3.5 and 4.5 we begun to develop a new universal remote control, using only one button and integrated with a display to inform users about what they have to do. The manual is replaced by a video [19]. We are currently extending this concept by addressing issues of connectedness (talking to each other), personalization, and security based on the findings during the ethnographic studies.

References

1. Agamanolis, St.: At the intersection of broadband and broadcasting: How ITV technologies can support human connectedness. Proceedings of EuroiTV 2006, Athens, Greece, May 25-26, (2006) 17-22.
2. Atkinson, P. et al. (Eds.): Handbook of Ethnography. London: Sage (2001).
3. Battarbee, K. Defining Co-experience. In: proceedings of Conference on Designing Pleasurable Products and Interfaces, Pittsburgh, 23-26 June, ACM Press (2003), 109-113.
4. Bernhaupt, R., Obrist, M. and Tscheligi, M. Usability and Usage of iTV Services: Lessons learned in an Austrian Field Trial. Proceedings of EuroiTV 2006, Athens, Greece, May 25-26, (2006) 234-241.
5. Emerson, R. M., Fretz, R. I. and Shaw, L. Writing Ethnographic Fieldnotes. Chicago: University of Chicago Press (1995).
6. Fetterman, D. M.: Ethnography: step by step. 2. Edition. Thousand Oaks: Sage Publications (1998).
7. Gaver, B., Dunne, T. and Pacenti, E. Design: Cultural Probes. In Interactions 6, 1 (1999), 21-29.
8. Geertz, C.: Dichte Beschreibung: Beiträge zum Verstehen kultureller Systeme. Frankfurt a. M.: Suhrkamp (1987).
9. Haddon, L.: The Contribution of Domestication Research to In-Home Computing and Media Consumption. The Information Society Journal, 22 (2006) 195-203.
10. Hutchinson, H., Mackay, W., Westerlund, B., Bederson, B.B., Druin, A., Plaisant, C., Beaudouin-Lafon, M., Conversy, S., Evans, H., Hansen, H., Roussel, N., Eiderbäck, B., Lindquist, S. and Sundblad, Y. Technology Probes: Inspiring Design for and with Families. In Proceedings of the CHI'03, ACM Press (2003), 17-24.
11. Jääskö, V. and Mattelmäki, T. Observing and Probing. In Proceedings of the International Conference on Designing Pleasurable Products and Interfaces DPPI'03, ACM Press (2003), 126-131.
12. Knoche, H., McCarthy, J. D.: Design Requirements for Mobile TV. In Proceedings of Mobile HCI 2005, 19-22 September, Salzburg, Austria (2005), 69-76.
13. Lull, J.: Inside Family Viewing. Routhledge, 1990.
14. Nokia: Bringing Mobility to the Homes: Home Domain Short Paper. (2004). Retrieved 15 December 2006, from http://nokiapapers.techrepublic.com.com/whitepaper.aspx?docid=236041
15. Obrist, M., Bernhaupt, R. and Tscheligi, M.: Interactive Television for the Home: An ethnographic study on users requirements and experiences. Proceedings of EuroiTV 2006, Athens, Greece, May 25-26, (2006) 349-358.
16. Portolan, N., Nael, M., Renoullin, J. L., and Naudin, S.: Will we speak to our TV remote control in the future? In: Proceedings of HFT'99 (1999).
17. Schotanus, H. A. and Verkoelen C. A. A.; Extended home environment from a security perspective; X-home deliverable (2003).
18. Venkatesh, A.: Introduction to the Special Issue on "ICT in Everyday Life: Home and Personal Environments. The Information Society Journal, 22 (2006) 191-194.
19. Vexo: vexo.ruwido.com, Instruction Video (last visited: 11-12-2006).

SenSee Framework for Personalized Access to TV Content

Lora Aroyo[1,2], Pieter Bellekens[1], Martin Bjorkman[1], Geert-Jan Houben[1,3],
Paul Akkermans[1,4], and Annelies Kaptein[4]

[1] Eindhoven University of Technology (TU/e), Computer Science
{p.a.e.bellekens, m.bjorkman}@tue.nl
[2] Vrije Universiteit Amsterdam (VU), Computer Science
l.m.aroyo@cs.vu.nl
[3] Vrije Universiteit Brussels, Computer Science
Geert-Jan.Houben@vub.ac.be
[4] Stoneroos Digital Television, Hilversum
{annelies.kaptein, paul}@stoneroos.nl
http://www.stoneroos.nl

Abstract. In this paper we present our framework, SenSee, designed
to provide context-aware and personalized search that can be used to
support multimedia applications in making content recommendations.
Our primary demonstration application built upon the framework tar-
gets the growing digital television domain where we foresee an increasing
need for user-adaptive functionality to counter the looming content explosion which will make current television zapping inadequate. Via our
AJAX-based interface we show how different user contexts, such as location, time and audience, in combination with a standard user profile can
improve the multimedia (TV content) consumption experience. In modeling the user (profile and context) SenSee exploits ontologies to express
the semantics involved. We illustrate via experiments the influence of the
user's current context and demonstrate the difference when we dis/en-
able the inclusion of different ontologies describing time, geographical,
lexical and TV domain knowledge.

1 Introduction

While there already exist multiple strategies and approaches to find and recommend data like music, text, videos and images on the Web, television broadcasts
appears to be one of the last uncharted content resources. The main reason
arises from the fact that this content has not been made public nor annotated
in a computer-readable way. However, over the last years, with the appearance of multiple *connected home* scenarios [1], a convergence of content from
personal computers, PDAs, mobiles and television sets has emerged. This convergence now opens more possibilities for bringing personalization also to the
television environment in the home, although several differences in the domains
need to be taken into account. One of the main issues is the difference between

P. Cesar et al. (Eds.): EuroITV 2007, LNCS 4471, pp. 156–165, 2007.
© Springer-Verlag Berlin Heidelberg 2007

the inherently *personal* computer [2] and the more sharing-oriented television environment. In a computer environment, the system knows which user is currently logged in, can guess his native language, location and current time(zone), whereas a traditional television system has little of this knowledge. This relates in other words to *context*, which in a TV domain is very important because of the timed/regionalised nature of broadcasted content.

There is an increasing trend towards an integration that allows switching between the virtual (Web), mobile and physical (e.g. home, museum, clubs) spaces Figure 1.In the virtual Web space users are actively interacting with content and applications by searching, browsing and performing numerous information intensive tasks. In the mobile space, the use sessions are short in terms of time, where users aims at staying up-to-date and consuming small items from e.g. RSS feeds of news headlines and weather forecasts. It can also be used to quickly select interesting items that can later be consumed in full in the virtual space. Devices used here are limited in terms of bandwidth and screen size. Typically, in the physical space, the focus is on consumption of media and passive entertainment, where a push strategy for content is the typical pattern of user interaction with the devices. In order to provide a personalized experience to the user accross the three spaces we propose to integrate and use the tools, devices and the interaction abilities in a complementary way. In other words, our vision is that the Web environment could be used as a remote control to the physical space, where the mobile devices can be used as carriers of the information and services between the virtual and physical spaces. In this paper, through the SenSee framework, we present our engineering approach in realizing a smooth and complementary integration of those spaces.

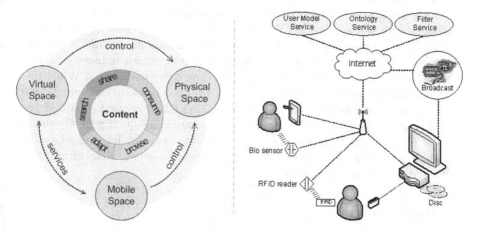

Fig. 1. Virtual, mobile and physical spaces, and instantiation in the SenSee framework

We describes a semantics-based framework, distributed over the three spaces, which can provide extra functionality for TV-related applications like searching and recommendation mounted within a connected home setting Figure 1. It enables amongst others personalization and context-based adaptation which utilizes domain ontologies and user models. Like previously mentioned, contextual information is of great importance to understand group interests[3] in different situations, social groups and age categories. Every user may have very different interests in the morning, the weekend or when together with friends. Therefore, adding a context that includes current time, geographical location, and/or audience, on top of content-based filtering[4] proves to be particularly valuable in this setting. Here, we describe the personalization functionality of the SenSee framework based on the background knowledge in terms of domain-related ontologies and user models. We give a short overview of related work in Section 2, the requirements for the design of the SenSee framework in Section 3, the architecture design in Section 4. Finally, we present the experimental test setting and conclusions from the results in Section 5.

2   Related Work

Tsinaraki et al. [5] follow an approach for the content modeling using TV-Anytime, MPEG7 and specific domain ontologies for enhanced semantics. However, they emphasize on the making of an ontology-based semantic indexing for retrieval of audiovisual content and boosting the retrieval effectiveness, whereas in SenSee we focus on the personalization of the search and recommendation of the retrieved content for a specific set of users in different contexts. Furthermore, Ardissono et al. [6] emphasizes that there is a need for personalization in dealing with vast amounts of multimedia content. We believe that personalizing the experience of the connected home is significant for the selection and enjoyment of this content abundance.

AVATAR [7] is an example of a TV recommender system which makes use of reasoning with semantics for TV content and user preferences to get valuable results. In that approach the authors make use of a combination of TV-Anytime metadata fields and a custom-made genre hierarchy, which induces a possible compatibility issue with the official TV-Anytime topic hierarchies. While their recommendation algorithm is an effective hybrid combination of content-based and collaborative filtering, there is no inclusion of user context. The different models constitute a necessary requirement for enabling intelligent filtering of content to make recommendations [8]. By this we mean finding and suggesting content that should be interesting for the current user(s), while filtering out unwanted or uninteresting information.

3   Requirements

For the design of the SenSee semantic-based framework for personalization and interaction in an ambient home media environment we have performed domain analysis in order to extract realistic requirements.

- Integrate search and retrieval of distributed heterogeneous content (e.g. public collections of audio, video and textual material) via diverse channels (e.g.

IP and broadcast) as well as from local storages and portable media. In this context we focus on providing uniform uniqueness for every content-element retrieved in a common content specification schema (e.g. TV-Anytime) by realizing on-the-fly conversion of content (e.g. from XMLTV, HTML to TV-Anytime). Further, we ensure context-aware retrieval of (1) existing TV-Anytime packages, (2) dynamically constructed packages, (3) payed or not payed services (e.g. iTunes) and user generated content, annotations and tagging.

- Integrated semantic content model to support mappings to multiple common vocabularies in different domains (e.g. ontologies, thesauri). Important aspects here are related to the extensibility of the pool of common vocabularies and mappings and the scalability of collections, vocabularies, users, contexts and devices.
- Personalized experience for individual and group users. In the context of multple users and multiple devices, where individual and group users can interact with several devices at the same time within one session, it is crucial to support heterogeneous input of user and context data (e.g. sensors, web interfaces, TV remote control), as well as tailored presentation generation for different users and devices. In order to realize a true cross-context personalization we need to also provide a domain independent modeling of users, devices and contexts.
- Open communication protocol to connect between the framework components and interoperability with third party applications
- Maintenance, sharing and retrieval policies of personal content (e.g. pictures, audio files, etc.) with peers (e.g. individual or groups)
- Creation/assigning of user privileges for individual and group users, devices

4   System Architecture

SenSee has been developed as part of a study on ontology-driven user adaptation for TV content handling in ambient home media centers. This has been carried out within the European ITEA-funded Passepartout project, with partners like Philips, Thomson, INRIA and ETRI. SenSee illustrates a connected home media environment enabling personalized access and interaction with multimedia content. It is a connecting point for home devices, such as shared (large) screens, personal (small) handhelds, hand-gesture recognition and biosensor-based interfaces. The result of the SenSee framework is realized in two applications for personalized program TV guide - a Web-based and a settop-box-based [9] in order to show the connection between the Virtual and Physical spaces.

In Figure 2 at the bottom various heterogeneous content sources like IP, broadcast, media (e.g. DVD, Blu-Ray) and local storage provide content. At the of the figure are the client applications using SenSee framework. The content is processed in the retrieval and personalization components in the middle part of the figure. To the right we see a list of external services:

- User Model Service (UMS): keeps and manages all the users' profiles including information like characteristics, interests, disabilities and preferences, while incorporating the proper context; user profiles and contexts are both maintained within a Sesame repository [10]. Thus, the UMS provides a general interface to access repositories with user related information and context data. All user statements are expressed here as contextualized statements, i.e. valid in 0 or more contexts. Realizing this user model repository as a shared external service makes it possible to access the user relevant data in a distributed environment.

- Ontology Service (OS): manages all vocabularies[1] needed to make the system 'understand' concept and term semantics when searching and filtering content. For example, extend search queries with synonyms, e.g. 'bike' = 'bicycle', and translate keywords to corresponding metadata, e.g. 'evening' = 'start 18:00:00, end 22:59:59'.
- Filter Service (FS): specifies different content filters to be used when searching or recommending content to a specific user or a group of users. It holds rule-based filters for different aspects of content and user data. We idenitify three categories of filter: (1) monitoring the consumption of content to update User Model (e.g. if the users watches a lot of action movies we can conclude that the user has a positive interest in action movies); (2) reasoning in the User Model to find new data (e.g. we can deduce which stereotypes a user belongs to, and how strong this correspondence is; (3) analysing the User Model to recommend content.
- CRID Authority: part of the TV-Anytime specification, responsible for assigning unique identifiers (CRIDs)[11] for every content element. It maintains information of where content is stored or broadcasted. It also creates new a CRID when new content is to be published by the user and make this publicly available. Since the CRID is a unique identifier, the CA either creates truly unique identifiers by itself or communicates with other CRID Authorities.
- Metadata Service: part of the TV-Anytime specification, responsible for providing the correct metadata given a CRID and for storing the metadata that describes content in TV-Anytime. It can also be used to publish new metadata if the user creates own content.

Currently we use a set of heterogeneous (publicly) available metadata sources which serve as the searchable content. If metadata is non TV-Anytime compliant, transformations are performed to obtain a consistent TV-Anytime data set. Our most frequently used sources are:

- BBC Backstage[2]: metadata in the TV-Anytime format
- XML-TV[3]: manage and retrieve TV listings stored in the XML-TV format
- Websites: for example IMDB[4] movie metadata

---

[1] http://wwwis.win.tue.nl/ ppartout/Blu-IS/Ontologies/
[2] http://backstage.bbc.co.uk/data/7DayListingData
[3] http://xmltv.org/wiki/
[4] http://imdb.com

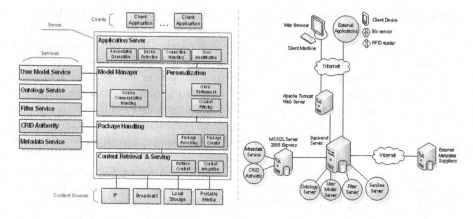

Fig. 2. SenSee architecture and implementation

The vocabularies and concepts used in SenSee are a user model schema; TV-Anytime and MPEG7[12] ontologies for description of incoming content; the OWL-Time[13] for time conceptualizations extended by us with a set of instances like 'afternoon', 'Wednesday' and 'weekend'; an RDF schema to model a country - province - city relation for a number of (European) countries; and WordNet[14] to provide synonyms, hyponyms and some other lexical relations.

An example of using this conceptualization is that if the current context includes currentTime:MondayMorning (reference to the Time ontology) and currentLocation:Amsterdam (reference to the Geo ontology), while the user model contains {user}interestIn{X}, {X}interestSubject{'Weather forecast'}, {X}interestValue{'HIGH'} for this context, it can be concluded that a recommendation of weather forecast content on a Monday morning in Amsterdam will be much appreciated.

Figure 2 shows that with SenSee we provide a set of functionalities which can be used by multiple, possibly very different, client applications, e.g. personalized search and recommendation[5]. The interface is an AJAX Web-application build via the Google Web Toolkit (GWT) framework and communicates to the SenSee server via the XML-RPC communication protocol. With this interface we enable two kinds of content retrieval. The user can either ask for a recommendation or engage in a user-driven content search. When a user enters some keywords, SenSee tries to exploit the conceptualization by trying to find ontological matches, similarities, synonyms and others, to help the user in his searching process.

5 Experiments

In order to test and evaluate the SenSee framework, a number of experiments were conducted. Here we explain some of the hypotheses and the experimental

---

[5] http://wwwis.win.tue.nl:8888/SenSee/

setting in terms of the test data, methodology and measurements. The hypotheses in this test were fourfold. (1) Analyzing the user input and automatically extending the input with related terms will increase the recall of content and put less demand on the user to use the exact same keywords that occur in the metadata. (2) Matching the user input to concepts in the domain models a higher precision can be obtained, due to translating ambiguous string input to precise terms suitable for the metadata formats used. (3) User preferences can be applied to personalize the search. (4) Personalization can be taken beyond general recommendations and adapt to the user's context of time, location and audience.

The test data used in the experiments comprises a set of TV program metadata describing titles, cast, synopsis etc. of these programs and their broadcast schedule. In total, this contained metadata for 1937 programs which were broadcasted on UK-based channels during one complete week in October 2006. Prior to the testing this data was investigated in order to verify that an even distribution of program types occurred. This was among other things done in terms of looking at the genre distribution. Moreover, six user profiles were constructed and given various interests and contexts. For the domain knowledge models as previously mentioned in the system architecture, the test was run using the TV genre classification, geographical, lexical (WordNet) and time ontologies. Keyword analysis was further done using the Lucene Java text search engine library from Apache[6].

The search and recommendation were tested by a set of constructed user input strings that covered terms from each one of the modeled domains, i.e. TV genre classification, time concepts, geographical as well as free-text keywords. The number of resulting TV programs that our application found was measured and in the result tables that illustrate the examples in the following chapter this value is shown in the column labeled *Found*. In order to judge the correctness of this number, a manual verification was done for each search, counting how many programs fit the search according to domain experts.

In the example tables this is labelled *Match*. A manual verification of how many of the programs shown in the result were irrelevant to the search was also made, labeled *False* as short for false positives. Based on this a recall measure was calculated, as the number of results that the application found divided by the number found in the manual control. Precision was calculated as the share of results that were not considered as false positives.

6   Results and Discussion

Several effects, benefits and shortcomings were observed in the experimental results. This chapter covers an analysis of each one of the techniques applied and a selection of the test results to be able to discuss strong and weak points that were found in the testing.

---

[6] http://lucene.apache.org/java/docs

6.1   Domain Ontologies

First, using an ontology to add more keywords for synonyms and closely related terms broadened the search and made it less dependent on the user to use the exact same words as in the program metadata.

Table 1. Results table with ontologies inclusion

Query	Query text	Match	Knowledge	Found	False	Recall	Precision
1a	"Friday"	284	-	0	0	0%	N/A
1b	"Friday"	284	O:time	284	0	100%	100%
2a	"news"	287	-	112	19	39%	83%
2b	"news"	287	O:TVA	248	19	86%	92%
3a	"england"	11	-	0	0	0%	N/A
3b	"england"	11	O:geo	11	0	100%	100%

Second, when ontology concepts were used, the appropriate translation to formats which suited the metadata could be applied. For example, the results in table 1 for queries 1a and 1b show the difference between when "Friday" is simply used as a string and on the other hand interpreted as a time concept by using the time ontology (shown as "O:time" in the table). The lack of interpretation constrains the search to a simple string matching between the keywords and the content metadata. However, when using the time ontology, "Friday" was identified as a time concept, which enabled a search for programs scheduled between 00:00 and 23:59 on the specific date of the next Friday. This translation helps the application in finding relevant content with matching metadata.

6.2   User Profile

The great benefit of applying user profiles lies in enabling personalizing the search and making sure that the most relevant content for the user is recommended. As we have demonstrated, the employment of domain ontologies finds more content whereas the improvement of user profiles on the other hand, is to narrow the results and arrange the presented results in a personalized order. This is realized by calculating a recommendation score for each program that was found and use this to sort the programs and filter out those that are below a certain score threshold. To give a simple yet illustrative example consider the results for queries 4a in table 2, which is a simple keyword search, and 4b, which applies the user profile (UP).

Without the notion of context, the interest values in the user profiles can only provide general recommendations, whereas in reality people may have very different TV interests.

6.3   User Context

The test results illustrate two different ways in which context can influence our search. Regard the results of queries 5a-5c in table 3, which shows a search for

Table 2. Results table with user profile inclusion

Query	Query text	Match	Knowledge	Found	False	Recall	Precision	User
4a	"marriage"	8	-	8	2	100%	75%	
4b	"marriage"	8	UP	6	0	75%	100%	Martin

"latest sport". In these examples the queries were run around 18 o'clock on a Friday, and thus the current context was in this case Friday evening. The first query is included for comparison and shows a search where no user context is known, which in SenSee means no consideration of current time. In query 5b the user John logged in. From his current context the application added "Friday evening" to the query which in the table is shown by "UC:'Fri. Eve'".

Table 3. Results table for user context inclusion

Query	Query text	Match	Knowledge	Found	False	Recall	Precision	User
5a	"latest sport"	256	O	256	0	100%	N/A	
5b	"latest sport"	10	O, UC:"Fri. Eve"	10	2	100%	80%	John
5c	"latest sport"	10	O, UC:"Fri. Eve", UP:"Fri:News:-4"	6	2	60%	67%	John
5d	"latest sport"	10	O, UC:"Fri. Eve", UP:"Fri:News:-4,+5"	10	1	100%	90%	John, Rocio

The second way concerns finding and applying user interests which are valid in a particular arbitrary context. For example, the user John does not like watching news on Friday evenings, say for reasons of relaxing. His interest in the genre "News" has therefore a strength of -4 in the context of "Friday evening". It makes the interest expression valid only when the user's current time is within that time interval (query 5c).

7   Conclusion

In this paper we have shown the SenSee framework for context-aware personalization in search and recommendation functionality. Exploiting ontological structures for domain knowledge, user profile and user context, SenSee offers services to include context effectively in the personalized search. Through experiments we were able to observe the advantages of the ontology-based approach used in SenSee and we could demonstrate the ontological engineering needed for linking the user model to background knowledge for effective personalized search.

Acknowledgements

This research is supported by the European ITEA program with national funding from Senter Novem. We would like to thank our Philips partners for the valuable discussion on the SenSee architecture.

References

1. de Ruyter, B., Aarts, E.: Ambient intelligence: visualizing the future. In: AVI '04: Proceedings of the working conference on Advanced visual interfaces, New York, NY, USA, ACM Press (2004) 203–208
2. Dobbelaar, A.: Televising cyberspace: and the web would never be the same. (1998)
3. Masthoff, J.: Group modeling: Selecting a sequence of television items to suit a group of viewers. User Model. User-Adapt. Interact. **14** (2004) 37–85
4. Balabanovic, M., Shoham, Y.: Fab: content-based, collaborative recommendation. Commun. ACM **40** (1997) 66–72
5. Tsinaraki, C., Polydoros, P., Christodoulakis, S.: Integration of owl ontologies in mpeg-7 and tv-anytime compliant semantic indexing. In: CAiSE. (2004) 398–413
6. Ardissono, L., Gena, C., Torasso, P., Bellifemine, F.: User modeling and recommendation techniques for personalized electronic program guides. Personalized Digital Television. Targeting programs to individual users (2004)
7. Blanco Fernndez, Y., Pazos Arias, J.J., Gil Solla, A., Ramos Cabrer, M., Lpez Nores, M.: Bringing together content-based methods, collaborative filtering and semantic inference to improve personalized tv. 4th European Conference on Interactive Television (EuroITV 2006), (2006)
8. van Setten, M.: Supporting people in finding information: Hybrid recommender systems and goal-based structuring. Telematica Instituut Fundamental Research Series, No.016 (TI/FRS/016). Universal Press. (2005)
9. Akkermans, P., Bellekens, P., Bjorkman, M., Aroyo, L.: ifanzy: Personalised filtering using semantically enriched tv-anytime content. In: EuroITV. (2005)
10. Broekstra, J., Kampman, A., van Harmelen, F.: Sesame: A generic architecture for storing and querying rdf and rdf schema. (2002)
11. Earnshaw, N.: The tv-anytime content reference identifier (crid) (2005)
12. IEEE: Mpeg-7: The generic multimedia content description standard, part 1. IEEE MultiMedia **9** (2002) 78–87
13. Hobbs, J.R., Pan, F.: An ontology of time for the semantic web. ACM Transactions on Asian Language Information Processing (TALIP) **3** (2004) 66–85
14. Miller, G.A.: Wordnet: a lexical database for english. Commun. ACM **38** (1995) 39–41

AIMED- A Personalized TV Recommendation System

Shang H. Hsu[1], Ming-Hui Wen[1], Hsin-Chieh Lin[1], Chun-Chia Lee[1],
and Chia-Hoang Lee[2]

[1] Department of Industrial Engineering and Management
[2] Department of Computer Science
National Chiao Tung University, 1001 Ta Hsueh Road, Hsinchu, Taiwan
shhsu@cc.nctu.edu.tw

Abstract. Previous personalized DTV recommendation systems focus only on viewers' historical viewing records or demographic data. This study proposes a new recommending mechanism from a user oriented perspective. The recommending mechanism is based on user properties such as Activities, Interests, Moods, Experiences, and Demographic information—AIMED. The AIMED data is fed into a neural network model to predict TV viewers' program preferences. Evaluation results indicate that the AIMED model significantly increases recommendation accuracy and decreases prediction errors compared to the conventional model.

Keywords: TV program recommendation system, predictor, personal information, lifestyle, activity, interest, mood.

1 Introduction

Digital TV (DTV) allows people to access numerous and varying kinds of TV programs without space-time constraints. Although electronic program guides (EPGs) can increase the accessibility of TV programs, they often overload users by providing too many program options. Therefore, the usefulness of EPG is an important issue in DTV design.

To enhance the usefulness of EPGs, researchers have begun to develop TV recommendation mechanisms (i.e., embedded assistance) to help users access the TV programs of their choice. Recommendation mechanisms operate by collecting viewing history data over a period of time, gleaning user viewing preferences from the data, mapping user preferences for TV program attributes, filtering non-interesting programs, and finally recommending an appropriate program [4, 7]. In general, these TV program recommendation mechanisms can be divided into two types—content-based filtering and collaborative filtering [3, 8].

Content-based filtering recommendation operates by automatically tracking each user's TV viewing patterns. Program descriptors, such as the program category, the name of the actor or actress, program keywords, viewing time period, and so on, and a set of similarity metrics of user profile are collected. Using these data, the recommender builds a user profile that represents the viewing preferences of each

P. Cesar et al. (Eds.): EuroITV 2007, LNCS 4471, pp. 166–174, 2007.
© Springer-Verlag Berlin Heidelberg 2007

user. After building a user profile, the recommender compares program attributes to user profiles and calculates the similarity between the two components. Based on similarities, the recommender then recommends suitable TV programs to the user [1, 5]. Examples of this kind of recommender include the 'User Modeling Component (UMC)' system developed by Ardissono et al., [4], and the recommendation system proposed by Zimmerman et al.[16].

Collaborative filtering recommendation is based on program appraisal by a group of viewers [6]. The recommendation system stores massive amounts of viewer preference data in a database. The system then recommends programs to users based on program ratings given by people with similar profiles. This system effectively forms a viewing community whose members share similar viewing preferences or similar viewing habits. In this virtual community, viewers can share information with each other or recommend programs to other viewers [5]. Examples of this kind of recommender include the TV-scout system developed by Baudisc and Brueckner [7] or the peer-to-peer (p2p) recommender system proposed by Wang et al. [14].

Although both types of recommenders can assist TV viewers with program selection, they both have some weaknesses. For example, a content-based filtering recommender only follows data from users' viewing histories and their viewing behavior. Therefore, it cannot extend to other types of programs or provide new programs to viewers. This problem causes over-specialization in recommended programs [5]. On the other hand, a collaborative filtering recommender depends on other viewers' suggestion data, without which the mechanism cannot make good recommendations [5].

This study therefore proposes a recommendation mechanism based on a user-oriented perspective, using the predictors of user Activity, Interest, Mood, Experience, and Demographic information—AIMED. The AIMED recommender is a hybrid recommendation system based on the content-based and collaborative filtering methods. It makes program suggestions using not only viewers' personal profile prediction criteria such as demographic, lifestyle, and explicit preference information, from conventional recommendation models, but also inputs users' viewing contextual information, such as mood and viewing behavior, into a prediction model. By doing so, it has two advantages. Firstly, the recommender can avoid the weaknesses of conventional content-based filtering and collaborative filtering while taking advantage of their strengths. At the initial use, program recommendation can be inferred from viewer group's preference when the information of user's viewing history is not available yet. As the system gathers more information about user's viewing context, adding viewing context into the prediction of program preference can fine-tune program recommendation to match personal preference of an individual user. Secondly, a well-trained AIMED recommender could suggest a suitable program to users by considering both long term program preferences and the particular viewing context. Therefore, an AIMED recommender is able to adapt to the viewing context. This paper describes in detail the mechanisms of the AIMED recommender, and discusses the evaluation of the AIMED system.

2 AIMED Recommendation System Development

2.1 AIMED Program Recommendation Predictor Definition

2.1.1 Activity and Interest—Two User Lifestyle Descriptors

Traditional program recommenders, which use demographic information, cannot accurately determine user requirements; they must also consider user lifestyles to generate an accurate picture of user requirements and provide the appropriate support [11]. Activity and interest are the two main predictors used to describe users' lifestyles [13]. Early studies report that user viewing preferences are related to their lifestyles. For example, Frank and Greenberg [9] surveyed 2476 TV viewers and clustered them into 14 lifestyle groups. Their study shows that the 14 lifestyle groups were significantly different in program selecting and viewing. Gena and Ardissono [10] reported similar results. They built a lifestyle knowledge model which offers personalized TV program recommendations to users. This model provides better recommendations to TV viewers by filtering information related to their interests.

2.1.2 Mood

Previous studies state that users' moods will influence their program selecting preferences. For example, Zillmann, Hezel, & Medoff [15] found that TV viewers' moods cause a selective exposure effect. Their research indicates that when TV viewers experience a negative emotional state, they tend to watch competition-style programs to experience excitement and happiness from the program. In contrast, viewers tend to choose action-style programs, and not competition-style programs, when they are in a positive mood. The study of Perse [12] proposes the same results. That is, user viewing preferences are related to user moods. This correlation might be a good predictor for program recommendation.

2.1.3 Experience

Many existing personal program recommenders use viewers' histories. To increase prediction accuracy, a database must collect viewing data over a long time period. These kinds of systems operate by recording viewing data, and then using a data mining technique to predict viewers' preferences [4, 16].

2.1.4 Demographic Information

Demographic data is also a factor can influence viewers' program preferences [2]. Currently, many program recommendation systems use this variable to predict users' program preferences [4, 16]. Demographic information classifies viewers into separate preference sets and then maps them to appropriate program styles. A demographic recommender can function before other types of predictors, such as a history trace or viewing behavior recommender. Therefore, this predictor is an important factor in developing a personalized program recommender.

2.2 The AIMED Recommendation System Framework

This module uses the artificial neural networks (ANN) technique to construct the recommendation prediction model and effectively predict user preferences. The ANN technique is appropriate for this study because its can be applied to solve linear or nonlinear mathematical problems. Specifically, this study uses the back-propagation neural network (BPN) method, one of the more commonly used neural network methods. The BPN model comprises three main layers: input, hidden, and output. Each layer is linked by a weighted connection that calculates the model. The model is established by importing data from the four modules. The system recommends user-preferred DTV programs when users request DTV program recommendations.

Specifically, the AIMED system comprises four modules: (1) user profiles and user stereotypes; (2) viewing communities; (3) program metadata; (4) viewing context module. The following sections describe these four modules in detail.

2.2.1 User Profiles and User Group Modeling

The user profile contains basic information about the user. User fills out a questionnaire when they register the TV program recommender. The questionnaire includes three parts: (1) demographic data, (2) lifestyle (interests and activities), and (3) program category preference. This user information is stored in the set-top box and sends the user profile to the program recommendation engine whenever the user requests program recommendations.

A hierarchical cluster analysis (with the K-means method) uses socio-demographic, activities, interests and preference data, to develop viewer group models. A set of key descriptors identifies each viewer group. Matching between the individual user profiles and the viewer group model is based on similarities in these key descriptors. Matching allows the system to recommend a set of candidate programs which are preferred by the viewing group, which share a similar profile.

2.2.2 Viewing Community

To prevent the over-specialization problem of conventional recommendation models, this study embeds the concept of collaborative filtering recommendation into the AIMED system. The collaborative filtering mechanism determines the match between an individual user and a viewing community according to similarities in key characteristics. In addition, the AIMED constantly updates the viewer group model and retrieves relevant program recommendation information from the community.

2.2.3 Program Metadata

The program metadata model stores program attributes. This study adopted the TV program categories defined by the National Communication Commission (NCC) of Taiwan, namely, Education, Drama, Shopping, Entertainment, Sports/Healthcare, Cartoons, Fashion, and News. The program attributes in this study include the channel number, name of program, language of program, and cast.

This study ran another artificial neural network to infer a recommendation set based on the mapping between viewer group data (demographic, activities, interests and program preferences) and program metadata.

2.2.4 Viewing Context Module

The viewing context module records a user's viewing behaviors under different moods. The module automatically records viewing behavior such as the channel number, the viewing time, and the duration of viewing on of each channel. Users provide mood information by pressing the "mood buttons" built into the remote control.

To identify viewing preferences for different moods, an artificial neural network models the relationship between different moods and different program categories. Based on the connected-weight of the neural network model, this study calculates the relative importance of viewing preferences for different moods. This information shows users' viewing preferences within different viewing contexts. Additionally, viewing behavior helps determine the program preference ranking under each mood.

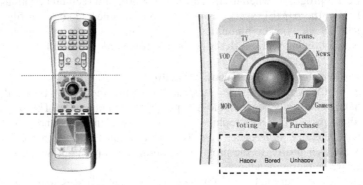

Fig. 1. Concept of remote control and mood input button

2.3 Use Scenario

To describe a real-world application of the AIMED system, consider the following scenario. All first-time users must fill out a questionnaire which gathers demographic data, lifestyle tendencies, and TV program preferences when they register for the AIMED system. The information will be stored as the user profile in the set-top box. The profile will be mapped to an appropriate viewer group model. The service provider constantly updates the viewer group model as new users join the viewing community.

During TV watching, users input their moods into the set-top box through the remote control. The system simultaneously records TV program metadata. Moreover,

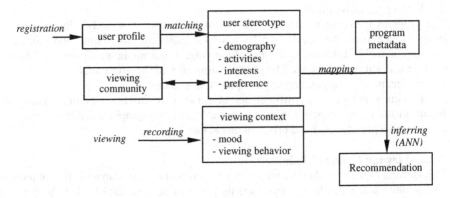

Fig. 2. AIMED recommendation system mechanism

the user can rate her or his preferences on the program being watched. The service provider sends these rating scores back to the viewing group model to form program recommendation rankings. Each user's program preference model is formed according to similarities between the user profile and the viewing group model. When a user presses the "mood" key on the remote control, the AIMED system recommends a program suitable to the viewing context.

3 System Evaluation

To evaluate the performance of AIMED system, this study attempts to simulate the operating process of an AIMED system in a set-top box and evaluate the quality of the AIMED recommendation model. Real-world user profiles and viewing behavior data were collected. The system then constructs viewer group models with the user profile data. Viewing behavior under different moods forms the basis for user's personal viewing context model. After the AIMED system is built, the evaluation process begins. The following paragraphs describe this process.

3.1 Data Collection

One hundred fifty five participants filled out user profile questionnaires. These questionnaires gathered user's socio-demographic, lifestyle (i.e., activities and interests), and program preferences. Specifically, "demographic information" includes a viewer's age, gender, family type, education, occupation, and monthly income. "Activities and interests" were collected by a questionnaire containing forty items, and users rated all items with a five-point Likert scale.

In addition, participants kept a viewing diary for two weeks. During those two weeks, participants recorded their "viewing behavior" and "mood" every time they watched TV. Viewing behavior includes the name of the program, channel number, day and viewing time, the length of viewing, and program preference level.

Seventy two percents of participants returned the questionnaires and diaries. Table 1 lists the data used for program recommendation.

Table 1. Input and output variables of the AIMED model

I/O	Descriptors	Levels
ANN input factors	Activities	40 activity factors
	Interests	40 interest factors
	Mood	3 states of mood (happy/bored/unhappy)
	Experiences	8 categories of program
		4 types of program languages
		5 levels of age (20~50 above)
		2 gender types (male/ female)
	Demography	5 types of family style
		4 levels of education
		6 levels of monthly income
		10 types of occupation
ANN output factors	Preference	5 levels of preference of programs
	Accuracy	Rate of accuracy = right hit (user likes and system recommended correct reject (user dislikes and system does not recommend)

3.2 Data Analysis

As for demographic information, the ages of participants ranged from 15 to 65, and the average age was 29.9 years. Among the participants, 41.1% were male, and 58.9% were female. Most participants were students. The average TV watching time was 2.75 hours on weekdays, and 6.76 hours on weekends.

Activities and Interests refer to users' activities, and the forty questions were extracted by principal component analysis with the varimax rotation method (Kaiser-Meyer-Olkin measure of sampling adequacy [KMO] = .70). This method extracted twelve factors: "Casual reading," "Sports," "Arts," "Leisure," "Visual-audio entertainment," "Formal learning," "Shopping," "Social drinking," "Social," "Fashion," "Daily lives," and "Outdoor activities." Users' interests were also extracted using principal component analysis with the varimax rotation method (KMO = .71), and eleven factors were extracted: "Arts," "Entertainment," "Gaming," "Learning," "Social activities," "Leisure," "Housekeeping," "Spirit," "Reading," "Sports," and "Travel."

Three lifestyle types were identified using cluster analysis: Type 1 (including 30 users), Type 2 (including 12 users), and Type 3 (including 70 users). ANOVA analysis was conducted to examine the differences between the three types. Results indicate that the activities and interests of the three lifestyle types were significantly different ($p<.05$).

The frequency distribution of viewer mood states during viewing revealed that viewers were most often happy (57.32%) and bored (41.76%). Only a few times did viewers claim that they were unhappy (0.009%). Therefore, the prediction model included viewing behaviors under the happy and bored mood states.

Preference distribution revealed that 13.69% of the programs received a "like very much" rating, 50.66% received a "like" rating, and 33.74% were neutral. Only a few programs were disliked (0.015%) and very much disliked (0.003%).

3.3 Evaluation Instruments and Validation Criteria

Based on the indicators mentioned above, this study compared the newly proposed AIMED model with the conventional model. This study used two evaluation indicators: *prediction errors for program preferences* and *recommendation accuracy*. The prediction errors for the program preferences indicator represent the root mean square error (RMSE) between the prediction value and actual value for the recommendation system. Lower scores in this indicator represent higher system prediction accuracy. The recommendation accuracy indicator represents the rate of successful recommendations (including right hit: user likes and system recommended, and correct reject: user dislikes and system does not recommend). High accuracy in this value signifies a powerful system classification capability.

3.4 Results

3.4.1 The AIMED System vs. the Conventional Model: Prediction Error Results

The number of hidden layers affects the model's prediction results. Thus, this study conducted a number of trials using different numbers of hidden layers, ranging from 5 to 12. Figure 3(A) shows the minimum prediction error (0.0956) when the AIMED prediction model had 10 hidden layers. The minimum prediction error was superior to that of the conventional model (0.1013). The average error of the AIMED model

(0.1021) at various hidden layers was lower than that of the conventional model (0.1082). In addition, a one-way analysis of variance (ANOVA) was conducted to examine the difference between the two models. This analysis showed that the RMS errors of the two models were significantly different ($F= 13.71, p< 0.01$). Post-hoc tests revealed that the AIMED prediction model was significantly superior to the conventional prediction model.

3.4.2 The AIMED Model vs. the Conventional Model: Recommendation Accuracy Results

Figure 3(B) shows that the AIMED model achieves its highest accuracy (76.6%) with 8 hidden layers, which is superior to the highest accuracy yielded by the conventional model (73.2%). Also, the average accuracy of the AIMED model (74.43%) at varying numbers of hidden layers was higher than the conventional model average accuracy (71.95%). One-way ANOVA analysis results indicates that the accuracy scores of the two models were significantly different ($F= 13.55, p < 0.005$). Post-hoc tests revealed that the AIMED prediction model was significantly superior to the conventional prediction model.

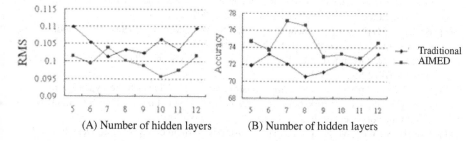

(A) Number of hidden layers   (B) Number of hidden layers

Fig. 3. Prediction error results (A) and Recommendation accuracy results (B)

4 Conclusions

This study proposes a hybrid program recommendation system accounts for both user viewing contexts and personal attributes. Evaluation results indicate that the AIMED model significantly increases recommendation accuracy and decreases prediction errors. Moreover, the artificial neural network results suggest that the user moods and lifestyles play important roles in deriving accurate DTV program recommendations. Therefore, users' emotional states should be considered in the development of DTV services.

The current version of the AIMED model assumes that TV viewing takes place at a fixed indoor location. Accordingly, the viewing context variables only include users' moods and viewing behavior under each mood state. In our future work, the viewing context should also consider viewing environment characteristics so that the AIMED model can be extended to the mobile TV environment.

Acknowledgement

This research is supported by MediaTek Research Center, National Chiao Tung University, Taiwan.

References

[1] Alspector, J., Kolez, A., and Karunanithi, N.: Comparing Feature-Based and Clique-Based User Models for Movie Selection. In Proceedings of the Third ACM Conference on Digital Libraries, Pittsburgh, PA, ACM (1998)

[2] Ang, I.: Living Room Wars. London: Routledge (1996)

[3] Ansari, A., Essegaier, S.,and Kohli, R.: Internet recommendation systems. Journal of Marketing Research, Vol. 37, No. 3. (2000) 363-375

[4] Ardissono, L., Gena, C., Torasso, P., Bellifemine, F., Difino, A., and Negro, B.: User modeling and recommendation techniques for personalized electronic program guides. In Ardissono, L., Kobsa, A., & Maybury, M. (eds.): Personalized Digital Television: Targeting Programs to Individual Viewers, Dordrecht, NL: Kluwer (2004) 3-26

[5] Balabanovic, M., & Shoham, Y.: FAB: Content-Based Collaborative Recommender, Communications of the ACM, Vol. 40, No. 3. ACM (1997) 66-72

[6] Basu, C., Hirsh, H., & Cohen, W.: Recommendation as classification: Using social and content-based information in recommendation. In Recommender System Workshop' 98. (1998) 11-15

[7] Baudisch, P. & Brueckner, L.: TV Scout: Guiding Users from Printed TV Program Guides to Personalized TV Recommendation. In Proceedings of the 2nd Workshop on Personalization in Future TV, Malaga, Spain, (2002) 157-166

[8] Burke, R.: Hybrid Recommender Systems: Survey and Experiments. User Modeling and User Adapted Interaction, Vol. 12, No. 4. (2002) 331-370

[9] Frank, R., & Greenberg, M.: The public's use of television: Who watches what and why. Beverly Hills: Sage (1980)

[10] Gena, C., & Ardissono, L.: On the Construction of TV Viewer Stereotypes Starting from Lifestyle Surveys. Workshop on Personalization in Future TV, 8th International Conference on User Modeling, Sonthofen, Germany (2001)

[11] Hsu, H. S., Wen, M. H., Lee, C. H.: An Activity-Oriented Approach to Designing a User Interface for Digital Television. In proceedings of the 4th Euro iTV conference, Athens, Greece (2006) 83-90

[12] Perse, E. M.: Implications of cognitive and affective involvement for channel changing. Journal of Communication, Vol. 48, No. 3. (1998) 49-68

[13] Reynolds, F. D., and Darden, W. R.: Constructing life style and psychographics. In W. D. Wells (eds.), Life style and Psychographics, Chicago: American Marketing Association, (1974) 71-96

[14] Wang, J. Polwelse, J., Fokker, J., & Reinders, M. J. T.: Personalization of a peer-to-peer television system. In proceedings of the 4th EuroiTV conference, Athens, Greece (2006) 147-155

[15] Zillmann, D., Hezel, R. T., & Medoff, N. J.: The effect of affective states on selective exposure to televised entertainment fare. Journal of Applied Social Psychology, Vol. 10, (1980) 323-339

[16] Zimmerman, J., Kurapati, K., Buczak, A., Schaffer, D., Gutta, S., & Martino, J.: TV Personalization system. Design of a TV Show Recommender Engine and Interface. In Ardissono, L., Kobsa, A., & Maybury, M. (eds.), Personalized Digital Television: Targeting Programs to Individual Viewers Dordrecht, NL: Kluwer (2004) 27-51

Fuzzy Clustering Based Ad Recommendation for TV Programs

Sudha Velusamy[1], Lakshmi Gopal[1], Sridhar V[1]., and Shalabh Bhatnagar[2]

[1] Applied Research Group,
Satyam Computer Services Limited, Bangalore 560012, India
{Sudha_V,Lakshmi_Gopal,Sridhar}@satyam.com
[2] Department of Computer Science and Automation
Indian Institute of Science, Bangalore 560012, India
Shalabh@csa.iisc.ernet.in

Abstract. Advertisements(Ads) are the main revenue earner for Television (TV) broadcasters. As TV reaches a large audience, it acts as the best media for advertisements of products and services. With the emergence of digital TV, it is important for the broadcasters to provide an intelligent service according to the various dimensions like program features, ad features, viewers' interest and sponsors' preference. We present an automatic ad recommendation algorithm that selects a set of ads by considering these dimensions and semantically match them with programs. Features of the ad video are captured interms of annotations and they are grouped into number of predefined semantic categories by using a categorization technique. Fuzzy categorical data clustering technique is applied on categorized data for selecting better suited ads for a particular program. Since the same ad can be recommended for more than one program depending upon multiple parameters, fuzzy clustering acts as the best suited method for ad recommendation. The relative fuzzy score called *"degree of membership"* calculated for each ad indicates the membership of a particular ad to different program clusters. Subjective evaluation of the algorithm is done by 10 different people and rated with a high success score.

Keywords: Ad Recommendation, Personalization, Fuzzy Clustering, Text Categorization.

1 Introduction

TV has become the most liked media for entertainment and information as there are a variety of channels catering to varied people interests. As TV reaches a large audience, it acts as the best media for advertisements of products and services. With the emergence of digital TV, it is important for the broadcasters to provide an intelligent service according to the viewer's preferences.

There are many research papers available on ad recommendation in the literature [1,2,3]. They mainly focus on ad selection for Web and personalized digital TV. The Web ad selectors personalizes advertisements for users based on the

P. Cesar et al. (Eds.): EuroITV 2007, LNCS 4471, pp. 175–184, 2007.

content of their preferred cites. For digital interactive TV system, ad selectors deliver the personalized interactive ads based on the learnt user profile. As the main revenue for TV channels is from the program sponsors, it is essential to capture the viewers' attention for their ads. There are systems like IndexTV [4] which personalizes the TV programs to individual viewers. Intent tracking of TV viewers studied in [5] also shows that viewers' interest is an important parameter for ad recommendation. At the same time, if the context of ads matches with the program context, it makes a better impact on the viewers. The studies in the literature for instance [6] suggest that when the content/theme of the ads shown are relevant to the aired programs, they make a better impact on viewers. So, there is a need for a technique that groups/clusters ads relevant to an on going program while considering the program content as well as external parameters like viewers' interest and sponsors' preference. We have present a fuzzy clustering based ad recommendation system, which recommends ads specific to broadcast TV programs.

Clustering is a technique which groups data points such that points within a single group/cluster have similar characteristics (or are close to each other) while points in different groups are dissimilar. Most previous work on clustering focus on numerical data whose attributes are represented by numerical values and exploit the typical dissimilarity measures like Euclidean distance measure. But, in case of ad database, which contains ad video descriptions that are mostly of textual data that are otherwise called as *nominal categorical data*, the ad attribute values cannot be totally ordered. For example, the shape descriptions like *circle, rectangle, square* cannot be ordered as numerical values can. So the traditional approach of converting the categorical data into numeric values, and use typical numerical data clustering techniques might not produce meaningful results for un-ordered categorical data. Hence the categorical data requires special method of clustering.

A few algorithms have been proposed in recent years for clustering the un-ordered categorical data. They belong to different types of clustering like hard partitioning, fuzzy partitioning or hierarchical method. Zengyou's [7] method called *squeezer* picks the data consecutively and hierarchically clusters it with any one of the existing clusters if it is similar, else forms a new cluster. A robust clustering algorithm($ROCK$) [8] works based on a link similarity measure for merging similar clusters. Huang [9] proposed a k-modes categorical data clustering by extending the k-means algorithm. It clusters categorical as well as numerical data and has been shown to provide efficient clustering performance in real world databases. Zengyou's [10] histogram based categorical clustering method differs from Huang's technique in terms of centroid calculation.

In case of ad recommendation, while clustering the ads for different programs, there exists some amount of fuzziness where one ad can be featured in two or more programs. Hence, our main objective is to *"cluster the un-ordered categorical ad data into predefined program categories, while each ad can belong to more than one program cluster with different likeliness"*. So, we have used Huang and Ng's [11] generalization hard partitioning method called fuzzy k-modes clustering algorithm. The fuzzy score called *"degree of membership"* calculated for each ad indicates the likeliness of a particular ad to different program clusters. The rest of the paper is organized as follows: Section 2 explains the functionality of fuzzy based clustering technique. It includes the details of ad annotation, experimental database creation and pre-processing of data. The system evaluation results are given in section 3 and section 4 concludes the paper.

2   Clustering of Ads

The pictorial representation of automatic ad recommendation framework is given in Fig. 1. Our objective is to suitably match ads to programs, taking into account of various parameters/features like ad profile, viewers' interest and sponsors' preference. The features of the ads are captured in terms of description/annotation keywords by video content creators or broadcasters, and placed in the database. As these annotation keywords are large in number and have wide variation in meanings, search engine based semantic categorization of keywords is done as a pre-processing step. Thus helps in improving the efficiency of the clustering also.

Fuzzy K-Modes clustering is applied on the pre-processed ad data and clustered into three main program clusters - Entertainment, Sports and News. The fuzzy score associated with each ad gives the membership of a particular ad belonging to the programs. The various steps are explained in detail in the following subsections.

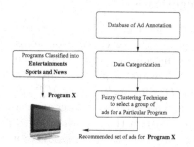

Fig. 1. Automatic Ad Recommendation Framework

2.1   Ad Annotation

The features of the ads in the database are represented using textual keywords called annotations. These annotations carry comments, explanations or external remarks describing the multi-modal information of an entity(ad). A relevant set of annotation keywords, which sufficiently describe the ads features like *context, people, famous persons, sponsors' detail* is selected with the help of media experts. These features are selected as per their importance studied in [4,6,5]. As ad creators generally involve people belonging to the targeted age group (audience), the audience information is derived from the *people* feature. The keywords are collected from 10 media experts watching various kind of TV programs that includes variety of ads from different channels that are aired all through the day and all days of the week. All the keywords collected under these features act as a training data and they are categorized semantically using a categorization technique, which is explained in section 2.2.

Experimental Database: As more number of ads only increase the database size and have nothing to do with increasing the accuracy of the ad selection, only 100 ads are collected and annotated by broadcasters. All the ads and their corresponding annotations are stored in the database. In the literature, the studies on the video features show classification as 'News', 'Sports' and 'Other program' classes. The 'Other program' class can be further categorized according to the available information in hand. So, we have classified all the available TV programs into only three different types - Entertainment, Sports and News. Each ad is clustered with any/all three programs with different degree of relevance.

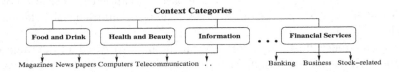

Fig. 2. Example - Context categories

2.2   Keywords Categorization

For clustering to be more effective, the keywords are pre-processed into a number of predefined categories. The categorization helps in clustering the *semantically similar* ads into same cluster and reduces the complexity of clustering large amount of data with wide variation. This is achieved with the help of search engines like *Open Directory Project(ODP)*[1], a web based categorization tool and *WordNet* [14], a synonym based categorization thesaurus. A variety of categorization techniques exist in the literature [12,13]. Typical approach is to categorize the total data into a certain number(A) of web related categories and map them to a number($B \leq A$) of desired categories. We have used a method of semantic categorization, which assists in increasing the clustering accuracy.

An initial set of N ads with their annotations forms the training data set. These keywords are collected for M ad features such as *context, people, famous persons etc.* Let the ad feature set be $A = \{A_1, A_2, .., A_m.., A_M\}$. Each feature, say A_m has N_m number of keywords associated with it. As these N_m keywords are large in number, they are semantically ordered or categorized into $'P'$ predefined categories. i.e., $A_m = \{a_{m1}, a_{m2}, .., a_{mp}.., a_{mP}\}$. The category $a_{mp}, \forall m, p$ is called the root attribute. For example the root attribute for the feature *"context"* are *"Food and Drinks"*, *"Beauty and Health"*, *"Financial Services"*, *"Education"* etc., (Refer Fig.2). These root attributes are selected by human experts

---

[1] http://dmoz.org/ , http://www.google.co.in/dirhp?hl=en

in the ad domain. The N_m keywords under A_m are distributed into the root attributes with the help of *ODP, WordNet* and *Hermatic Frequency Counter (HWFC)* (Refer Section 4). The keywords under each root attribute forms the adaptive reference dictionary to which any test keyword is automatically adapted to one of the root attributes. The adaptation procedure is given below.

Test Keyword Adaptation: Let $Y = [Y_1, Y_2, .., Y_m, .., Y_M]$ be a test keyword set having M attributes. Let $m = 1$ and $n = 1$ initially.

Step 0: Keywords under Y_m are given to *ODP* and *WordNet* and on the resultant pages *HWFC* is employed to sort the frequency of listed categories.

Step 1: The top 5 *HWFC* listed categories are taken in descending order and compared with A_m's root attributes $a_{m1}, a_{m2}, .., a_{mp}, .., a_{mP}$. If it matches with a_{mp} root attribute, it is added to a_{mp} category and the process is stopped else if there are no matches Step 2 is executed.

Step 2: Let the child attributes of a_{mp} be $q_{mpr}, m = 1, .., M$, $p = 1, .., P$, $r = 1, ..., R$ where R is the number of child attributes under a_{mp}. Y_m is compared with $q_{mpr} |_{r=1}$ for all $p = 1, ..., P$. If there is a match, the process is stopped else the next child attributes $q_{mpr} |_{r=2}$ for all $p = 1, ..., P$ is considered and the same process is repeated for all with increasing r until a match is found. Once the matching attribute is found, keywords under Y_m are appended with their matching root attribute.

Step 3: The Steps $0 - 2$ are repeated for $m = 2, ..., M$. ie for all the keywords of the data.

Step 4: All the above listed Steps are repeated for $n = 2$ to $n = N$. i.e., for all the ads in the data set. The categorized data set is stored in the database.

2.3   Fuzzy K-Modes Clustering

The fuzzy clustering algorithms are well known for clustering the patterns to all the clusters with different degrees of membership. Though the application of fuzzy clustering analysis to pure text partition is successful, it is rarely applied for semi-structured data classification such as XML documents. The k-means based fuzzy clustering technique is proven as one of the best methods of clustering. However, it performs well only on numerical data sets. This limitation is overcome in the Fuzzy K-Modes clustering algorithm that efficiently handles the categorical data sets. As the ad data set is un-ordered, the Fuzzy K-Modes clustering [15] is the best suited method to classify an ad into various program clusters with a different membership.

Let $X = \{X_1, X_2, .., X_n, .., X_N\}$ be a set of N categorized data stored in the database. Each data point $X_n, \forall n$ is defined by the set of features $\{A_1, A_2 ... A_m ... A_M\}$ where, each A_m has set of root attributes $\{a_{m1}, a_{m2}, . . . a_{mk} . . . , a_{mK}\}$ and their corresponding child attributes. Let X_n be denoted as $[\mu^{(1)} x_{n1}, \mu^{(2)} x_{n2}, . . . , \mu^{(m)} x_{nm}, . . . , \mu^{(M)} x_{nM}]$, where μ^m, $\forall m$ are the weightages given to the ad data features with the constraint $\sum_m \mu^{(m)} = 1$. These weights are decided according to the degree of importance of the features of the data.

The objective of the fuzzy k-modes is to minimize the cost function,

$$J_f = \sum_{n=1}^{N}\sum_{k=1}^{K}\omega_{nk}^{\gamma}d(V_k, X_n) \quad 0 \leq \omega \leq 1, \quad 1 \leq k \leq K, \quad 1 \leq n \leq N \quad (1)$$

subject to the constraints,

$$\sum_{k=1}^{K}\omega_{nk} = 1, \forall n \quad , \quad 0 < \sum_{n=1}^{N}\omega_{nk} < N, \forall k. \quad (2)$$

where, N is the number of ads in the database and K is the number of clusters. ω_{nk} in some sense represents the possibility of nth ad being assigned to the kth cluster. This results in the first constraint in equation 2. The second constraint in the equation 2 essentially implies that there is at least one element in each cluster and not all the elements are clustered into single cluster. $d(V_k, X_n)$ is defined as in equation 3 given below.

Generally, selecting an optimal value of K plays a crucial role in the clustering accuracy and there is no hard and fast rules to decide on this. We have fixed the number of clusters as $K = 3$ and labeled as Entertainment, Sports and News. ω_{nk} is the degree of membership for an ad x_n belonging to k^{th} cluster, γ takes the value greater than 1 and $V_k = [v_{k1}, v_{k2}, ..v_{km}, .., v_{kM}]$, is the center of kth cluster.

In order to minimize the cost function, we use the k-modes algorithm with a simple distance measure between the centers and datum, and updating the data cluster centers [9]. The hamming dissimilarity measure $d(V_k, X_n)$ between the centroid V_k and a data X_n is defined as,

$$d(V_k, X_n) = \sum_{m=1}^{M} \psi(v_{km}, x_{nm}), where \quad (3)$$

$$\psi(v_{km}, x_{nm}) = \begin{cases} 0, & v_{km} = x_{nm} \\ 1, & v_{km} \neq x_{nm} \end{cases} \quad (4)$$

Here, $\psi(v_{km}, x_{nm})$ is actually $1 - \delta(v_{km}, x_{nm})$, where $\delta(v_{km}, x_{nm})$ is the Dirac delta function. The implementation steps of the algorithm is given below.

Algorithm:

1. Let iteration index $\tau = 1$ and $V^{(\tau)} = \{V_1, V_2, .., V_k, ..V_K\}$ be a set of clusters. Select K initial modes, one for each cluster.
2. Calculate the membership values $W^{(\tau)} = \{\omega_{kn}\}$ for all $1 \leq k \leq K, 1 \leq n \leq N$ such that J_f is minimized. i.e, compare all the categorical ad data points with the initial K modes selected, using the similarity metric equation 3 and calculated membership values $W^{(\tau)}$. ω_{kn} is the fuzzy membership value of n_{th} ad belonging to k_{th} cluster.
3. Set iteration index $\tau : \tau + 1$. Update all K modes of the clusters using the membership value of each data point. i.e.,$V^{(\tau)} \rightarrow V^{(\tau+1)}$. Update $W^{(\tau)}$ using $V^{(\tau+1)}$.

4. Continue iterating the above step until the difference between $W^{(\tau)}$ and $W^{(\tau+1)}$ is less than the threshold ϵ.

As the performance of the algorithm depends upon the initial modes, the domain knowledge is used to select the initial modes that can be a better representatives of the classes Entertainment, Sports and News. The modes are updated using the procedure as in [9]. The broad idea of updating the modes is as follows. The cluster center V_k is defined as $[v_{k1}, v_{k2}, \ldots, v_{km}, \ldots, v_{kM}]$, $\forall m$. The cost function J_f is minimized if and only if $v_{km} \in \{A_m\}$. ie,

$$\sum_{n, x_{nm}=a_{mr}} \omega_{kn}^{\gamma} \geq \sum_{n, x_{nm}=a_{mt}} \omega_{kn}^{\gamma}, \quad 1 \leq n \leq N, 1 \leq m \leq M \qquad (5)$$

Refer [9] for the proof of fuzzy k-modes update method. The below given examples show how the various ad attributes and their relevancy are exploited in the clustering algorithm.

- "Beauty and Health" related items under the feature "context" gets more preference to "Entertainment" and "Sports" program than "News".
- If the "people" information is "family", the ad is recommended for "Entertainment".
- If an ad has "famous person", say a "sports star" in a "Car" ad, then the ad gets better weightage for "Sports" program.
- The external "sponsor details" attached with each ad directly gives the sponsors' preference for their ads with various programs. say, a "real-estate" advertiser would prefer their ads for "News" programs.

Refer Table 1 for some more examples. In the table, the ad features are shown in the order of, Ad Context/People in the ads/Famous person appearing the ad/Sponsors' preference. None indicates the absence of a particular feature.

Table 1. Performance of fuzzy k-modes clustering for ad selection

	Clustering Results		
	Degree of Membership $[0, 1]$		
Annotation	**Entertainment**	**Sports**	**News**
Paint/Adult/None/Ent	**0.62**	0.06	0.32
SoftDrink/Adult/Spt/Ent-Spt	0.40	**0.56**	0.04
Icecream/Kids/None/Ent	**0.70**	0.30	0.00
Footwear/Youth/Spt/Ent-Spt	0.25	**0.65**	0.10
Magazine/Adult/Nws/Ent-Nws	0.35	0.10	**0.55**

Note: Ent - Entertainment, Spt - Sports, Nws - News

3   Experiments and Results

The ad recommendation framework involves different experimental phases like keyword categorization, fuzzy k-modes clustering for selecting a set of ads for different types of programs. The categorization technique is tested using 1000 test keywords, which are different from the training set of keywords available in the dictionary. The categorization results are evaluated using the typical parameters called Precision and Recall (Refer section 4). These values were found to be 80% and 75% respectively.

Table 2. Comparison results of clustering

Effect of Categorization on Clustering						
	Without-C			With-C		
Keywords	Ent	Spt	Nws	Ent	Spt	Nws
Soap,Young girl,Film star,Ent	0.55	0.25	0.20	0.85	0.15	0.00
Shoe,Youth,Sport star,Spt	0.20	0.65	0.15	0.15	0.73	0.12
Magazine,Adult,None,Nws	0.35	0.25	0.40	0.25	0.05	0.70

Note: Ent - Entertainment, Spt - Sports, Nws - News, C-Categorization

The fuzzy k-modes clustering of categorized ad data are compared with the clustering results without categorization of data. It was found that the clustering accuracy was improved in case of clustering the categorized data. Table 2 shows the comparison results. The overall system accuracy is directly dependent on the robustness of the categorization and clustering. The algorithm clustered a high number of ads into its correctly relevant program type and only few ads into wrong program cluster. The ads recommended by fuzzy k-modes clustering technique are subjectively evaluated by 10 different people. They were asked to rate the relevance of ordered set of ads shown along with a program. Table 3 shows the over all performance result of automatic ad recommendation algorithm. The rating of the system was done by calculating the mean opinion score (MOS) with a maximum of 5. The system achieves an MOS of 4.5.

Table 3. Performance of Automatic Ad Recommendation Algorithm

Recommendation Results				
	No.of Ads Recommended			
Program Type	Manual	Automatic		
		Correct	Miss	False
Entertainment	45	40	6	1
Sports	35	32	1	2
News	20	18	2	0

4   Conclusions and Future Work

We have proposed an Automatic Ad Recommendation framework which efficiently clusters the categorized ads for three different programs - Entertainment, Sports and News. It takes into consideration the various parameters of the ads for matching them with the program context. Ads can thus have a better impact on the viewers and also increase the Return on Investment (ROI) for the sponsors. The categorized annotations of the ads are clustered using Fuzzy K-Modes clustering to belong to the three different classes of programs. Our procedure involving adaptive categorization, fuzzy clustering technique for grouping the relevant ads resulted in good performance. It must be noted that even though there are several works on the above mentioned areas, to the best of our knowledge, there is no prior work that uses this combination for recommendation.

The sequence of steps followed and the algorithms applied resulted in ad recommendations that were similar to the manual ad selection by human experts. The research issues that need to be addressed in future include considering more program features like mood, event, etc. Consideration of more sub-groups within the three main program classes is an another enhancement that could be done. Further, the extraction of features from ads and programs, automatically, resulting in less time spent on annotation by humans would provide a means to obtain ads for a given program in real-time and would be a step towards a fully automated system.

References

1. Sung Min Bae and Sang Chan Park, *"Fuzzy Web Ad Selector Based On Web Usage Mining"*, IEEE conference on Intelligent Systems, 2003.
2. Kurapati.K, Gutta.S, Schaffer.D, Martino.J and Zimmerman.J, *"A multi-agent TV recommender"*, Workshop on Personalization In Future TV workshop, Sonthofen, Germany, 2001.
3. Lekokas.G et al, *"A Lifestyle-Based Approach for Delivering Personalised Advertisements in Digital iTV"*, Jrl.of Computer Mediated Communications, Jan 2004
4. Marc Rovira et al, *"IndexTV: A MPEG-7 based Personlised Recommentation System for Digital TV "*,Proc.of IEEE International Conf.on Multimedia and Expo,2004
5. Amit.T, Srividya.G and Sridhar.V *"ITV Application for Intent Tracking"*, Proc. of Second European Conference on Interactive Television, 2004.
6. Kosala.R and Blockeel.H, *"Web Mining Research - A Survey"*, SIGKDD Explorations, Vol.2, Page.No 1 − 15, 2000.
7. He.Z, Xu.X and Deng.S, *"Squeezer: An Efficient Clustering Algorithm for Categorical Data"*, Jl.of Computer Science and Technology, Vol.17, pp.611 − 624, 2002.
8. Guha.S et al, *"ROCK: A Robust Clustering Algorithm for Categorical Attributes"*, Proc.of Internation Conf.on Data Engineering, pp.512 − 521, Mar.1999.
9. Huang.Z, *"Extensions to the K-Means Algorithm for Clustering Large Datasets with Categorical Values"*, Data Mining Knowledge Discovery, vol.2, Sept.1998.
10. He.Z, Xu.X, Deng.S and Dong.B, *"K-Histograms: An Efficient Clustering Algorithm for Categorical Dataset"*, Technical Report, 2003.
11. Huang.Z, *"A Fuzzy K-Modes Algorithm for Clustering Categorical Data"*, IEEE Transaction on Fuzzy Systems, Vol.7, No.4, Aug.1999.
12. Chen.H and Dumais, *"Bringing Order to the Web: Automatically categorizing search results"*, In CHI'00 Proceedings of the SIGCHI conference on Human factors in computing systems. ACM press, 2000.
13. Shen.D, Pan.R, Sun.J.T, Pan.J.J, Wu.K, Yin.J and Yang.Q *"Our Winning Solution to Query Classification in KDDCUP2005"*, SIGKDD Explore Newsletter, 2005.

14. Miller.G, Backwith.R, Fellbuam.C, Gross.D and Miller.K, *"Introduction to Word-Net - An Online Lexical Database"*, International Journal on Lexicography.
15. Frank.H, Frank.K, Rudolf.K and Thomas.R, *"Fuzzy Cluster Analysis: Methods for Classification, Data Analysis and Image Recognition"*, Wiley Publications, July.1999

Appendix

ODP is a web based categorization tool. Given a keyword, it lists its relevant categories. *WordNet* is a thesaurus which gives the synonyms and related words of a keyword. *HWFC* is a software tool, which ranks the frequency of words in a given page. It also provides the flexibility of searching for only relevant matching words. Precision and recall are defined as follows:

$$Precision \; = \; \frac{\sum_k \; No. \; of \; keywords \; correctly \; categorized \; as \; C_k}{\sum_k \; No. \; of \; keywords \; categoried \; as \; C_k}$$

$$Recall \; = \; \frac{\sum_k \; No. \; of \; keywords \; whose \; manual \; category \; is \; C_k}{\sum_k \; No. \; of \; categories \; retrieved}$$

Towards Content-Aware Coding: User Study

Nele Van den Ende[1,2], Huub de Hesselle[2], and Lydia Meesters[2]

[1] Philips Research Europe, HTC 31, 5656 AE Eindhoven, Netherlands
[2] Eindhoven University of Technology, HTI, Den Dolech 2, 5612 AZ Eindhoven, Netherlands
nele.van.den.ende@philips.com

Abstract. Developing a content-aware coding scheme that delivers ensured QoE for end-users includes finding out which content information will be most needed; especially when wireless networks are used to send video information. Wireless in-home networks suffer from interference which creates variable throughput, which causes problems when sending video material from one device to another. Temporal and quality scaling provide classes for video adaptation methods that can handle this variable throughput. Presented research concerns the effect of temporal scaling versus quality scaling on different kinds of video content. We looked at the difference in perceived video quality between I-Frame Delay (temporal scaling) and TransCoding (quality scaling). Results show that I-Frame Delay scored better for video content without a lot of background movement, while TransCoding was scored better for scenes with lot of background movement. There are also indications that information about scene changes can be helpful to create content-aware coding.

Keywords: user preferences, perceived video quality, video adaptation methods, QoE.

1 Introduction

Services offered via television are subject to the limits of the network to which the television set is connected. An underlying and supporting framework for interactive television has to be aware of issues that are connected to sending multimedia from one device to another. Furthermore, users might not be aware of possible issues and simply expect an always-accessible service, independent of where and what they are watching. When wireless networks are used to offer multimedia-rich services, it is important to keep in mind that wireless networks often suffer from disturbances. Such disturbances are usually caused by other networks, or consumer electronic devices such as microwaves and blue-tooth telephones, which probably is one of the reasons that disturbance often occurs in bursts, or clusters [1]. The result of disturbances in a wireless network with devices sending multimedia is an unpredictable bandwidth capacity. The unpredictability of the bandwidth will prevent flawless transmission of video and an ensured Quality of Experience (QoE) [2]. So, it is necessary to provide robust adaptive video encoding and transmission techniques that take unpredictable bandwidth into account.

P. Cesar et al. (Eds.): EuroITV 2007, LNCS 4471, pp. 185–194, 2007.

There is a wealth of research into such adaptation methods, and most of those can be placed into 3 different categories: spatial, temporal and quality scaling [3]. Only methods from temporal and quality scaling categories are used, so those two are discussed here (with the methods themselves discussed in Section 2). Temporal scaling provides a class of video adaptation methods in which frames are dropped when bandwidth decreases [3].The order in which frames are dropped depends on their relative importance. This relative importance is usually automatically determined by source coding of the multimedia material. Resulting video sequences show jerkiness, i.e. smoothness of video sequences is disturbed and observers perceive jerky motion. Note that spatial artifacts, such as blocking or blurring, hardly ever occur. Quality scaling is another class of video adaptation methods, where video material is degraded through dropping chrominance levels and/or changes in compression coefficients, such as quantization level [3]. Visual results of this degradation can be less color-saturated video material when chrominance levels are dropped. Requantization of video material can introduce blurriness and blockiness. (further details on visible artifacts can be found in [4]).

Perceived video quality is influenced by many components, such as image content, scene characteristics, image distortions, user preference, judgment strategy, methodology, the human visual system, platform …. Characteristics and properties of the human visual system (HVS), for example, are used in video coding (e.g. MPEG). Judgment strategy and methodology influences the way image material is rated [5]. From earlier experiments and existing theories it is possible to state that choosing the right video adaptation method to maximize QoE and perceived video quality also partially depends on shown video characteristics, such as scene changes [6] and motion of the video content [3]. Motion can come from background or foreground in-scene movement, but also from camera movement. Additionally, movement is probably not the only important and quantifiable factor that can be sent over with content information. Components such as scene changes and category of the video (e.g. sports, or more specialized, football) can also be determined and used for content-aware coding. Developing a content-aware coding scheme that delivers ensured QoE for end-users includes finding out which content information will be most efficient in determining when to use which video adaptation method.

Our research question concerns the effect of temporal scaling versus quality scaling. We also look at the effect of longer versus shorter disturbance, where a longer disturbance lasts 5 seconds and a shorter one 1 second, to find out whether there is an effect for duration. The last influence discussed is the effect of scene characteristics, such as scene changes, in-scene motion and camera movement. Once it is known which video adaptation method is best used for longer or shorter disturbance, or scene characteristics, another part of the puzzle to work towards content-aware coding is solved. Before moving on to the experiment, some background material concerning perceived video quality, MPEG, I-Frame Delay en TransCoding will be covered in Section 2. Section 3 gives an overview of the hypotheses and the used methodology, and Section 4 continues with a description and discussion of the results. Section 5 ends this paper with some conclusions and suggestions for future work.

2 Background

MPEG encoding is designed to compress video material, and to allow playback of compressed video material on different types of platforms. It works by introducing three different kinds of frames in the video stream. Intra-coded or I-frames are independent of each other and do not contain references to other frames. Predictive-coded or P-frames are dependent on the previous I or P-frame in the stream, while bi-directionally predictive coded or B-frames depend on both the previous I- or P-frame and the subsequent I- or P-frame. B-frames, consequentially, are seen as least important. In MPEG encoding, frames are grouped together in so-called 'Groups of Pictures' (GOP), with the usual display order being something along the lines of IBBPBBPBBPBB. Consequently, GOPs are encoded and sent in a different order than they are displayed, because the P-frames need to be sent over before the B-frames.

In MPEG coding, several HVS properties are exploited. Research into temporal and quality scaling methods has shown that the HVS is less sensitive to quantization noise for fast-motion video. The HVS is also less sensitive for frame-skipping in a slow-motion video [3,7,8]. However, there is also contradicting research, which shows that it is not always necessary to have a high frame rate when showing a high motion video sequence, depending on user interest and category of the content [9,10].

Considering the research question, two adaptation methods were selected to be able to look at the effect of temporal versus quality scaling. I-Frame Delay (IFD) is a type of temporal scaling, implemented for MPEG-2 coding. It works by dropping less important frames once it notices that its send buffer is getting full. IFD guarantees that, given enough effective bandwidth, the most important frames (i.e. I- and P-frames) will get through. The decoder receiving the adapted video sequence will repeat the previous frame when there is a notification that it did not receive the next frame [13]. TransCoding (TC) is an example of quality scaling, also implemented for MPEG-2. TC works via on-the-fly bitrate adjustment of the video sequence that is being transmitted. Video sequences are transcoded to a lower bitrate, which is done by re-quantizing the discreet cosine transform-components in MPEG-2 frames[14]. This can be visible through artifacts such as blockiness and blurriness.

Previous research concerning perceived video quality has shown that sustained blockiness or blurriness in a video has a negative impact on the perceived video quality [15]. It was also shown that the optimal frame rate, according to observers, depends on the type of motion displayed in the video. Video sequences that already show jerky motion are perceived as better quality when the spatial quality is enhanced for lower frame rates. The perceived video quality of video sequences portraying smoother motion seems rather unaffected when the frame rate is changed [15]. Results from experiments reported by [8] show that artifacts from quantization errors (e.g. blocking, false contouring) are rated lower on perceived video quality than either jerkiness or image blurring. [9] showed that their observers appeared more sensible to reductions in frame quality than in frame rate for videos shown on small screens (325x288 and 176x144 pixels). Note that these experiments were done with small displays and a CIF format (325x288), so it is difficult to say how easily these results can be transferred to larger video formats and screens. Further research done by [16] shows that less and longer quality drops are better received by observers than frequent but short-lived and more severe quality drops. Of course, this might only apply for larger screens, since earlier research also shows that observers prefer a lower frame rate for smaller screens [9]. Previous research also showed that the lowest perceived video quality (maximum distortion) was one of the most determining effects for the viewers' perceived video quality rating [17].

3   Methodology

The methodological section starts with the hypotheses we devised for this experiment and the implementation of the direct comparison method chosen to test the hypotheses. It then continues with describing the original video sequences and the stimulus set made with the video sequences. Lab-equipment is then discussed, followed by an overview of observer demographics and the procedure.

3.1   Hypotheses

I.   Observers will score video sequences modified with TC worse than video sequences modified with IFD on perceived video quality.
II. Observers will score perceived video quality for disturbances lasting 5 seconds worse than disturbances lasting 1 second.
III. Observers will be influenced by scene characteristics when scoring the video sequences on perceived video quality. Video sequences with more scene changes are more likely to mask modifications [6]; IFD and TC will be scored equal for such video sequences.

3.2   Direct Comparison Method

To compare two video sequences directly, ITU-R BT.500-11 (2002) recommends a direct comparison method (DC). This assures that the relation between combinations is assessed. We opted for the adjectival categorical judgement method, with the semantic comparison scale as seen in Fig. 1. One trial consisted of showing observers a pair of video sequences. Each video sequence is 10 seconds long, and is shown once in each pair. Before each video sequence, a 3-second grey field will be shown with a letter indicating which of the two videos will be shown. The letter 'A' is shown before the first video sequence, and the letter 'B' is shown before the second video sequence. Observers were asked to rate the second video sequence with respect to the first video sequence on a scale ranging from much better to much worse, while being shown a gray field that lasted 10 seconds, with 'vote now, please' (see Fig. 1 for full details). Sessions consist of several trials after each other, with a maximum duration of half an hour per session.

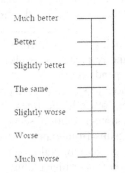

Fig. 1. Direct comparison scale

3.3 Original Video Sequences

Five video sequences were chosen to represent five categories: action, sports, animation, documentary and (soap)series. For the action video sequence, a video sequence from Hero was taken. The sports video sequence came from a soccer game, the animation video sequence from Chicken Little, the documentary video sequence from a piece of film about penguins and the (soap) series video sequence is taken from a Gilmore Girls episode. The chosen video sequences will be referred to as *Hero, Soccer, Chicken Little, Penguins* and *Gilmore Girls*. These video sequences were scored on three characteristics property categories: number of scene changes, amount of movement of the primary content, and the amount of camera or background movement, shown in Table 1. Only the number of scene changes is determined in an exact manner, hence the precise number in parentheses.

Table 1. Content property categories: number of scene changes and amount of content and camera movement in each scene. High: +++, medium: ++ and low: +.

Video sequences Content properties	Chicken Little	Penguins	Soccer	Gilmore Girls	Hero
Camera / background movement	+++	+++	++	+	+
Primary content movement	++	+	+++	+	+++
Scene changes	++ (3)	+ (1)	+(0)	+++(5)	+++ (7)

Hero, Chicken Little and *Gilmore Girls* were extracted from retail PAL region 2 DVDs. *Penguins* was taken from a Philips PAL DVD. *Soccer* was, due to availability, taken from a website offering a 7.5 Megabit MPEG-2 encoded version of a soccer match [Delos, 2006]. The original resolution was 608x480 pixels, which was scaled up using the lanzcos3 algorithm to 720x576 pixels.

3.4 Stimulus Set

The video sequences were all re-encoded with a simulation platform [18] to 4 Mbps, YUV 4:2:0 colour-space. Then the video sequences were encoded for each condition. For IFD, every second B-frame was dropped for the length of the disturbance. For TC, the bitrate was reduced from 4 Mbps to 2 Mbps for the length of the disturbance.

In this experiment, comparisons are made between IFD and TC, for losses caused by a disturbance which lasts either 5 seconds or 1 second. Hence, there are four combinations that have to be compared to each other: IFD with 1 sec loss, IFD with 5 sec loss, TC with 1 sec loss and TC with 5 sec loss. Losses were always introduced in the middle of a modified video sequence. Within each genre, all possible non-identical pairwise comparisons were used. Note that we did not compare any video sequences against themselves, and also did not use control combinations (i.e., compare a reference video sequence against a modified video sequence). This means that there are 6 combinations for each video sequence, and 30 combinations in total for observers to judge.

3.5 Apparatus

The lab used for the experiment was a living-room environment. The observers were seated on a sofa standing 2.5 meters (five times the height of the display) from the display. There was also a separate room to set up further equipment, with one-way windows so experimenters could monitor observers without disturbing them.

We set up a Philips 42" plasma display (model 42PF9966-12) in the living-room environment to show the stimulus set. In the experimenter room, a PC was connected to the display through DVI, with the stimulus sets placed on an external hard drive for convenience. The stimulus set was displayed on a resolution of 800x600, instead of the plasma display's native resolution of 1024x1024.

Observers were asked to rate during the 'voting' time using a slider with the graphical annotation shown in Fig. 1. These sliders were connected to the PC and measured ratings on a 1000-point scale. Observers were not expected to rate on a 1000-point scale, they were expected to use the categories provided with the direct comparison method. However, to be able to pick up all ratings around the borders of the categories, a 1000-point scale was programmed for the sliders. Measurements were recorded in a text-file and contained a time-stamp, a vote-index and the measured vote on each line. Note that it is possible for two observers to rate video sequences simultaneously. Observers were asked to set the slider to the desired position and then use the button on the device to indicate their vote.

3.6 Observers

In total, there were 28 observers: 16 males and 12 females. Observers were, at the time of testing, between 20 and 52 years old, with a mean age of 26. Most were naïve observers (i.e., without experience in the field of perceived video quality) and either students at a Dutch university or part of the work-force. No observers suffered from colour-deficiencies, as tested with the Ishihara test. Observers were tested for visus with the Landolt chart. Two observers scored a (corrected) visus of 1/0.8 (left/right), the other 26 showed a normal or corrected to normal visus of 1/1.

3.7 Procedure

Observers were scheduled to come to the laboratory alone or in pairs. On entering the living-room environment, they were tested for visual acuity and colour-deficiencies and asked several questions to ensure that they had not participated in an experiment concerning perceived video quality over the last six months. Next they were given instructions, telling them about the rating scale and the video sequence order they would encounter. Observers were given 1 training session, in which they were shown the 5 video sequences they would encounter in the other 30 trials. During the training the experiment leader was present to assist, should any difficulties arise. Observers were asked not to talk to each other during the sessions.

The experiment itself consisted of two sessions with a break in between (the break lasted as long as observers wished it to be but was rarely longer than 15 minutes). During each session, 15 video-pairs were presented. After finishing the training, the experimenter started the first session, and left the lab. The second session was started after the break, and again the experimenter left the lab. After the experiment, observers were asked to write down comments. Any questions observers had about the experiment were answered and they were given a business-gift (from Philips) for their participation.

4   Results

To look at the results, data were first assigned to the categorical scale on which observers had rated the video sequences. However, this only gives an overview of observer ratings' of TC or IFD with respect to TC or IFD. To look at the influence of TC or IFD separately, data were transformed based on Thurstone's Law of Comparative Judgment [19]. Thurstone's Law of Comparative Judgment assumes that the attribute strength of each stimulus is measured on an internal psychological scale - i.e. an interval scale - with Gaussian noise distribution. The transformation of the data was done by using data analysis tool DifScal to obtain a stimulus configuration per scene [20]. DifScal is a tool based on Thurstone's Law of comparative judgement, to analyze categorical comparison data. For each scene a frequency file is generated. This file contains seven 4x4 lower triangle matrices representing the seven judgment categories and the four pairwise combined versions of the original. Each cell in a matrix indicates the frequency with which an image pair is judged in that category, summed over all subjects.

4.1   Categorical Scale Results

A general overview shows that when IFD-1 sec is compared to IFD-5 sec and TC-1sec to TC-5sec, observers always prefer the 1 sec modified video sequence. This confirms our hypothesis "Observers will score disturbances lasting 5 seconds worse than disturbances lasting 1 second on perceived video quality".

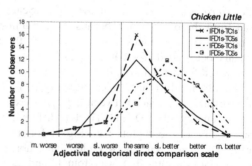

Fig. 2. Results for *Chicken Little*, showing observers' preference for all combinations where IFD is compared to TC

Results for *Chicken Little* show that observers have a preference for TC under all combinations where TC and IFD are compared to each other (see Fig. 2). Results for *Penguins* show that, when IFD and TC are compared for equal disturbances (IFD-1 sec vs. TC-1sec and IFD-5sec vs. TC-5 sec), observers also rated TC better. When asked to rate TC-5sec with respect to IFD-1 sec, observers did not show a preference, but when asked to rate TC-1sec with respect to IFD-5 sec, there was a preference towards TC again. It is not really possible, though, to rule out that this is also a preference for a 1 second disturbance.

Results for *Soccer* show that, when IFD and TC are compared for equal disturbances (IFD-1 sec vs. TC-1sec and IFD-5sec vs. TC-5 sec), observers rated IFD better. When asked to rate TC-5sec with respect to IFD-1 sec and TC-1sec with respect to IFD-5 sec, observers rated 1 sec modified video sequences as better (see Fig. 3). Results for *Gilmore Girls* show that, when observers were asked to rate IFD-5sec with respect to TC-5 sec, they rated IFD better. Observers did not show a preference when the disturbance was only 1

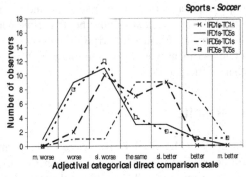

Fig. 3. Results for *Chicken Little*, showing observers' preference for all conditions where IFD is compared to TC

second long. When observers were asked to rate TC-5sec with respect to IFD-1 sec and TC-1sec with respect to IFD-5 sec, they again rated 1 sec modified video sequences as better.

Results for *Hero* show that, when observers were asked to rate IFD-5sec with respect to TC-5 sec, IFD was rated as better. But, when observers were asked to rate IFD-1 sec with respect to TC-1 sec, TC was rated as better. And again, when observers were asked to rate TC-5sec with respect to IFD-1 sec and TC-1sec with respect to IFD-5 sec, they rated 1 sec modified video sequences as better.

4.2 Difscal Results

For *Hero*, the action video sequence, DifScal reported a poor model fit. *Hero* stands out from the other scenes because of the number of scene changes it contains. The first part of *Hero* takes 2.5 seconds, with the rest of the scene showing one scene change per second. The data for *Hero* was not processed further with DifScal.

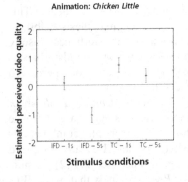

Results for the other scenes show that there is a distinct difference between the perceived video quality of IFD and TC for different scenes. From these plots (see Fig. 4 for an example), a difference between long and short disturbances using IFD was found, and is statistically significant as the confidence bars do not overlap, except for *Gilmore Girls*. There is no difference between long and short disturbances when using TC in *Penguins* and *Chicken Little*, as the confidence bars overlap. TC scored significantly better in those two scenes compared to IFD, while IFD scored better in *Soccer*, and a preference for IFD is noticeable in *Gilmore Girls*.

Fig. 4. Results for *Chicken Little*, showing mean and error-bars

Video sequences *Penguins* and *Chicken Little* in the 5 second disturbance condition show that there is a preference for TC (despite the bitrate advantage of IFD) whilst in *Soccer* there is a preference for IFD. The two scenes with the TC preference happen to be the two scenes with a high amount of camera movement, which might be a reason for this difference. In summary, whether IFD scores better or worse than TC is dependent on scene characteristics.

5 Discussion and Conclusion

The results point to a difference in perceived video quality between the four scenes. This confirms previous experiments done by [3,8,9], in which motion characteristics effects were also shown. As pointed out in the previous section, the amount of camera movement may be the reason for the difference in perceived video quality of IFD and TC between these four scenes. *Penguins* and *Chicken Little* both have relatively high amounts of camera movement, as opposed to the medium amount for *Soccer* and little amount for *Gilmore Girls*. The high amount of camera movement probably causes the jerkiness induced by IFD to be more detectable and disturbing than the loss of bitrate induced by TC. Our results confirm those of [9], because for *Soccer*, IFD is preferred over TransCoding, even though it contains a lot of movement. Details are also of importance here, and this may even be more so for bigger displays. One problem for motion determination is that, when extracting information about motion from the motion vectors in the video, it is currently not possible to distinguish whether it concerns camera movement, foreground movement or background movement. According to our results it is important to be able to make this distinction, but it is unclear how this should be accomplished and which part of the information is most necessary to include in content-aware coding.

Another influence on the results might be that a high amount of scene changes blurs the effect of the adaptive technologies under study. It is known that the HVS is less sensitive for video quality changes when those come right after a scene change [6]. So if there are a lot of scene changes, it is possible that video quality changes are less, or even not, noticed. In summary, the length of the disturbances influences perceived video quality negatively. In some scenes, the effects of the two techniques were less noticeable for the observers. I-Frame Delay scored better for video content without a lot of background or camera movement (*Soccer* and *Gilmore Girls*), while TransCoding was scored better for scenes with lot of background or camera movement (*Chicken Little* and *Penguins*).

As our study has shown, there is a lot of potential for video characteristics information to help with determining when to use which video adaptation method. Another potential avenue is how to incorporate this information in content-aware coding. Video characteristics information could be sent together with the video material, or be generated on the fly. Future work could include looking further into motion in video material and the influence of scene changes.

References

1. Aldridge, R., Ghanbari, M.: Bursty error model for digital transmission channels. Electronics Letters, 31. (1995) 2144-2145
2. Siller, M., Woods, J. C.: QoS arbitration for improving the QoE in multimedia transmission. (2003) 238-241
3. Tripathi, A., Claypool, M.: Improving Multimedia Streaming with Content-Aware Video Scaling. Proceedings of the Second International Workshop on Intelligent Multimedia Computing and Networking (IMMCN). (2002)
4. Yuen, M., Wu, H. R.: A survey of hybrid MC/DPCM/DCT video coding distortions. Signal Processing, 70. (30-11-1998) 247-278
5. Meesters, L. M. J. and Martens, J-B.: Influence of processing method, bit-rate, and scene content on perceived and predicted image quality. 3959. (2000) 45-55
6. Seyler, A., Budrikis, Z.: Detail perception after scene changes in television image presentations. Information Theory, IEEE Transactions on, 11. (1965) 31-43
7. Jae, C. K., Jae-kyoon, K., Woongshik, Y.: Adaptive video coding rate control for better perceived picture quality in time-varying channels. 2. (2003) 521-525
8. Wang, D., Speranza, F., Vincent, A., Martin, T., Blanchfield, P.: Toward optimal rate control: a study of the impact of spatial resolution, frame rate, and quantization on subjective video quality and bit rate. 5150. (2003) 198-209
9. McCarthy, J. D., Sasse, A., Miras, D.: Sharp or smooth?: comparing the effects of quantization vs. frame rate for streamed video. CHI 2004. (2004) 535-542
10. Hauske, G., Stockhammer, T., Hofmaier, R.: Subjective image quality of low-rate and low-resolution video sequences. (2003) 1-6
11. Haakma, R., Jarnikov, D., van der Stok, P.: Perceived quality of wirelessly transported videos. 1st. (2005) 213-239
12. Van den Ende, N., Haakma, R., Meesters, L. M. J.: Effect of MPEG-2 Compression Parameters on Perceived Video Image Quality. Society for Information Display, International Symposium, Seminar and Exhibition. (2006)
13. Kozlov, S., van der Stok, P., Lukkien, J.: Adaptive scheduling of MPEG video frames during real-time wireless video streaming. Sixth IEEE International Symposium on a World of Wireless Mobile and Multimedia Networks (WoWMoM'05). (2005)
14. Brouwers, C. J. J.: A real-time SNR scalable transcoder for MPEG-2 video streams. Eindhoven University of Technology (2006)
15. Masry, M., Hemami, S. S., Osberger, W. M., Rohaly, A. M.: Subjective quality evaluation of low-bit-rate video. 4299. (2001) 102-113
16. Zink, M., Künzel, O., Schmitt, J., Steinmetz, R.: Subjective impression of variations in layer encoded videos. (2003) 137-154
17. Hands, D. S.,Avons, S. E.: Recency and duration neglect in subjective assessment of television picture quality. Applied Cognitive Psychology, 15. (2001) 639-657
18. de Hesselle, H.: Toolkit for perception experiments: development, implementation and evaluation. Eindhoven University of Technology (2006)
19. Thurstone, L. L.: A law of comparative judgement. Psychological Review, 34. (1927) 273-286
20. Boschman, M. C.: DifScal: A tool for analyzing difference ratins on an ordinal category scale. Behaviour Research Methods, Instruments, & Computers, 33. (2001) 10-20

Personal TV: A Qualitative Study of Mobile TV Users

Yanqing Cui[1], Jan Chipchase[2], and Younghee Jung[2]

[1] Nokia Research Center Helsinki, Ruoholahti, 11-13 Itämerenkatu, Helsinki 00180, Finland
[2] Nokia Design Tokyo, Shimomeguro 1-8-1 Meguro-ku, Tokyo 153-0064, Japan
{yanqing.cui,jan.chipchase,younghee.jung}@nokia.com

Abstract. This paper describes a qualitative user study of mobile phone TV usage undertaken during September 2005 and centered on the real world Mobile TV usage of paying subscribers of live Mobile TV service in Seoul, South Korea. The study identified four primary use cases: at home; during the evening commute (both likely to be significantly culturally dependent); macro-breaks; and secret use. Barriers to use include: battery life; screen size; lack of compelling content; poor coverage and design implications are discussed. The study suggests that if the current barriers to use can be overcome Mobile TV is a viable competitor to existing forms of entertainment and media consumption. Actual usage suggests that Personal TV is a more accurate description for this kind of service than Mobile TV.

Keywords: Mobile TV, Personal TV, Radio, South Korea, Seoul.

1 Introduction

Digital Mobile TV is currently being hyped as the 'next big thing' for mobile phones. Given the difference between the mostly stationary television viewing habits and the inherent portability of mobile phone use what kind of user experience is possible? To answer this question a research team conducted a field study of Mobile TV service subscribers. Seoul was selected as a destination for the study because TU Media, the South Korean telecommunications operator launched the first commercial live Mobile TV service in May 2005.

1.1 Background

Seoul has an official population of approximately 10.3 million; however when proximate satellite cities are factored in the size is closer to 48 million. The subway system is the easiest and fastest way to move around the city. The Seoul subway has good cellular connectivity and use of mobile phones is a common sight. These factors suggest this to be a prime location to understand the potential of Mobile TV.

Consumers in South Korea have a number of ways to watch TV on their mobile phones: downloading via PC; streamed via web sites; video-on-demand; and via broadcast. Many conventional TV programs are widely available for live streaming and downloading from the internet shortly after being broadcast. From the user's

P. Cesar et al. (Eds.): EuroITV 2007, LNCS 4471, pp. 195–204, 2007.
© Springer-Verlag Berlin Heidelberg 2007

perspective the digital broadcast of live Mobile TV is similar to conventional TV prior to the personal video recorder (PVR) [1]. Once switched on a TV channel, the user can switch channels but the pausing of content is not available [2]. Mobile TV refers to live Mobile TV broadcast in this paper.

1.2 Prior Research

The literature was surveyed including: the VTT Mobile TV trial [1], MobiTV, DVB-H trials [3] and a few prototype systems [2, 5]. In a VTT Mobile-TV project, a prototype system was setup in 4 WLAN hot-spot areas. The user research found out: (i) Mobile TV was considered similar to television, rather than wireless multimedia; (ii) users normally watch short programs or segments from long programs. (iii) it was used generally as a replacement for reading the newspaper; and (iv) watching Mobile TV was a serial-solitary activity [1].

DVB Mobile TV trials showed that: (i) familiar conventional TV programs were the most popular content, followed by sports and news channels; (ii) that the primary context where Mobile TV was watched was traveling on public transport; an that it was also a popular compliment to home TV watching [3].

Knoche ran a series of experimental studies to explore questions of image resolution, video bit rate, and text legibility [5]. He proposed that Mobile TV viewing was transient, involving low user commitment; that users were worried about being too absorbed and becoming distracted from other tasks [2].

The prior studies observed participants who were recruited to use the service for the duration of the study. In our understanding, this is the first study of actual subscribers of the commercial service [1].

1.3 South Korea Mobile TV Field Study

The aim of the South Korea Mobile TV study was to explore the range of factors that would affect the Mobile TV viewing experience from understanding whether it changes mobile phone use, and consider the aspects of the South Korean experience would apply to the broader context.

2 Research Design

The research study was conducted in Seoul, South Korea, in September 2005, 4 months after TU Media launched their mobile TV service.

2.1 Methodology

A major study in South Korea had already collected extensive quantitative data [6].We therefore decided to conduct contextual interviews and observations such as on public transport and combine these with home based in-depth interviews. All interviews were conducted in Korean by a native speaker and later transcribed, and translated into English.

2.2 Study Participants

4 male and 4 female participants were recruited. The mean age was 24.1years old. 7 participants were not married, 6 participants shared their apartment with their parents. 5 did not have a TV set in their personal bedroom. Device ownership for all but one participant was from 2 to 3 months. One participant [F1] had used live streaming services for two years, and was included to provide a comparison. The average weekly use was 375.5 minutes.

3   Drivers for Using Mobile TV

3.1 A Desire to Kill Boredom

Given the long commuting times public transportation and the widespread cellular coverage it is no surprise that Mobile TV was used at these times as tool to kill boredom. Situations included extended waiting periods in a car whilst girlfriend is having a hospital appointment (Figure 1), waiting for friends in bars, plus use in the bathroom and whilst sitting on the toilet.

M4: "... wanted to watch real time TV programs when waiting for someone (having a hospital appointment), so I started to use mobile TV...

Fig. 1. Watching to kill time whilst waiting

3.2 Novelty, a Desire to Be First

The commercial Mobile TV service had been available for 4 months at the time of the study. All participants were early adopters of technology. As well as the service, the sliding keypad in the SKY IMB - 1000 was the first of its kind on the market. To some extent Mobile TV was considered just another gadget they had to try. Whilst novelty is enough to draw people into using a service it may become the reason for the same user to reject that service later on.

3.3 Staying Up to Date with Popular Events

As with prior studies [1, 2] a driver for adoption was that it enabled users to stay up to date with popular events, in particular via music and sports and game shows. However news was not mentioned by our participants as being a popular content type. One possible reason for lack of interest in news content was that our participants were relatively young, preferring entertainment over more weighty content types. On the other hand participants may have preferred to access news via other channels such as browsing the web at one of the many popular and oft frequented internet cafes. As

M1 "I can know the popular songs faster than others by listening to the audio channels of Mobile TV"

3.4 Other Motivations

TV channels that broadcast games such as Star Craft are especially popular with the younger generation of South Koreans and were noted by users as popular content. The game channel is available in the current Mobile TV offering.

M3. "After buying this Mobile TV phone, I only watched the game channel through the Mobile TV. I stopped the subscription to a paid Internet game site."

4 Context of Use

The research team noted four main use contexts for Mobile TV: at home; during the evening commute; during macro breaks; and lastly secret use. We also note that the shared watching of Mobile TV content and lending the device for watching were not uncommon.

4.1 Home

Amongst our participants, home use was the most prevalent context for Mobile TV watching which is somewhat surprising given the alternative forms of entertainment that were available in the home. Although larger televisions may be available in the home space participants had micro control over what was watched without the need to negotiate with other family members. Another explanation for the popularity of home use is that the user can control where content is watched. Our participants mentioned watching from their bedroom suggesting that convenience (conducting other activities in the same space, having access to a power source), comfort and privacy to being important part of the experience. These factors are amplified when the rest of the home is under the control of parents. None of the participants in our study mentioned viewing very personal media and we note that the bedroom is also conducive to its use. In addition to the above issues home use is different to other contexts in that it supports a variety of viewing styles – such as lean back, lean forward and ambient viewing.

M1. "... When my parents are in home, I cannot watch game channel from ordinary TV as they do not like me to watch it. This is the reason why I watch the game program on the mobile TV."

Fig. 2. Watching Mobile TV in home while lying on bed

4.2 Commuting

Mobile TV was used during the commute via bus and train (figure 3), in particular during the evenings. The need to maintain eye contact with the road restricted use whilst driving. It should be noted however that experience of watching Mobile TV during the commute can vary considerably influenced by factors such as: the predictability of journey times, whether seating is available; the need to switch seats; whether morning and evening commuting, the weather and carrying, traffic and road conditions, lighting and noise conditions, and lastly the density of the commuting space and whether other passengers can see what is viewed.

*F4: "When walking in the street, I usually
listen to the radio channels.
But I usually watch mobile TV in a subway on
the way to home"*

Fig. 3. Watching Mobile TV while commuting on a subway

4.3 Micro and Marco Breaks

We use the term micro and macro breaks to refer to moments of time between planned activities and tasks such as waiting for elevators to arrive, for friends to turn up, a few minutes at the end of a lunch break, plus cigarette and toilet breaks.

Whilst the term micro break is commonly used we extend this to macro breaks to draw reader's attention to the length of time required to setup Mobile TV. This includes the time it takes to select a TV channel, for the device to receive the signals, channel changing and subsequent delays, the need to locate and use a headset. Mobile TV is more suited to longer, that is, macro breaks. Furthermore the user may be required to engage in other status information tasks during these breaks – including keeping an eye out for friends or the arrival of public transport.

4.4 Secret Use

Our younger participants (F2, M1) detailed situations where watching TV was not socially acceptable but was never-the-less carried out – situations we refer to as secret use. Secret use was carried out in the classroom during classes (hidden in pencil or glasses case), in the library and supposed to be doing homework. We extrapolate from this that secret use is likely to extend to other contexts such as sitting through a boring meeting. Secret use may occur in any context where viewed content is not socially or legally acceptable (including during home, commuting or macro-breaks). In societies with high theft risk such as the UK or Brazil, the user may also wish to minimize the visible exposure an expensive device. Also watching TV implies that less of the user's senses are devoted to watching over other valuables, thereby possibly putting other objects at a higher risk of theft.

> *M1: "... a skill to watch mobile TV in class without being noticed....a long press of a special key, and the screen becomes dark as the phone is turned off when mobile TV is still running..."*

4.5 Shared Mobile TV Viewing

Contrary to prior research reports our study participants mentioned a number of situations where Mobile TV viewing was shared for co-viewing. As M1 commented: *"during the school lunch time I share my mobile TV with friends, usually up to four people"*. Involuntary or passive sharing is also possible - for example being overlooked by other passengers on a bus. Within our study sharing occurred amongst members of the same close social circle, but its possible that televised event such as sports are likely to be triggers for sharing with a broader range of people. Shared use implies a close physical proximity – dictated by the size of the screen and the angle at which viewing is possible and this echoes similar findings from a Finnish study [1].

The need for close physical contact may support or hinder use depending on the context. A flirting couple might enjoy the need to brush up against one another, but rivelous siblings may not. The shared experience may not include audio content if the context inhibits audio output. When a headset is required the opportunities for sharing are further restricted.

4.6 Device Lending

Our participants also noted situations where devices were lent to others – for example to watch a particular sport event or to have a trial on the mobile TV feature. Device lending is limited to an even a closer social circle than shared viewing. Our findings show that device lending has a strong influence on Mobile TV penetration. 3 participants claimed lending device enticed other people to purchase mobile TV.

> *M3:"Sometimes my sister borrows my phone to watches Mobile TV, but I have never shared it with her because the LCD is too small to share"*

5   Barriers to Adoption

5.1 Lack of Decent Content

None of participants in our study talked enthusiastically about Mobile TV contents which is unsurprising since popular content from other TV channels were not available via Mobile TV. However radio channels available through the same application were considered popular and widely used. What makes content compelling is subjective, and in part down to alternatives sources of the same medium (downloaded TV programmes, terrestrial, cable & satellite TV, video rentals, video on demand, etc) and alternative media (web access, newspapers, music, gaming, people, etc).

5.2 Battery Life

Watching Mobile TV is a significant drain the phone's battery. Whilst out and about the user may be forced to choose between viewing TV and staying connected. A number of our participants carried spare batteries, but their use is far from straight forward – spares need to be kept charged, if a spare has been carried for a while, they need to be taken out for charging and remember to place the battery back in the bag. Battery life is less of an issue in the home context where the device can either be docked in a charging cradle or connected to the nearest available power socket.

5.3 Phone Size

With the exception of one model, the Mobile TV phones were considerably bulkier than more regular handsets on the market. Prior research suggests that a majority of potential Mobile TV users are willing to compromise on phone size in order to have Mobile TV functionality. However even if the relatively bulky device is carried the issue is where it is carried. Numerous research studies on where people carry phones, [7] suggest that women are far more likely to carry phones in bags, and men in front pockets. The bulk of the current crop of devices is not well suited for pockets suggesting that men are more likely to have to switch to using bags.

5.4 Other Barriers

Whilst the rapid changing of TV channels is desirable [3] the situation for our participants was far from perfect – and they complained that channel changing was too slow – delays of up to 10 seconds were not uncommon. Whilst participants acknowledged that the antenna accessory improved signal quality, none carried the antenna outside the home – it was considered too bulky to take on the off-chance that Mobile TV would be watched and that reception improvement was required.

6 Discussion

6.1 The Future of Mobile TV

Motivations and barriers to use. The motivations why our participants tried mobile TV yielded few surprises beyond existing research. We noted that in some instances it could take up to a minute to connect to a TV signal after having selecting a channel to watch. This may be still acceptable for macro breaks but on a micro-break someone is going to have to be pretty sure that the content is desirable to watch before taking the effort to switch on.

Compelling content. Unique content was available for our participants but none considered it compelling must-watch TV. One bench-mark for compelling content is whether it is a stimulus for water-cooler conversations. The quality of the programmes available via TU Media was described by a local member of the research team as 3rd rate programmes available on free channels. Even if unique content is available there is unlikely to be sufficient market penetration for it to be a topic of communication. At this point the Mobile TV device is more a conversation starter than its access to content. We surmise that to be a success Mobile TV will require both popular content from other medium and content generated specifically for this service.

Alternative forms of entertainment. As flash memory and hard disk capacities become cheaper and components smaller the ability to transfer content from other content stores e.g. PC or home server will be in the hands of more people. Whether Digital Rights Management tools will allow user's to transfer content of their choosing is a separate issue.

6.2 Ubiquitous Mobile TV Viewing

Home users. A number of studies have shown it is relatively common to charge a mobile phone close to the bed [7, 8]. Satisfactory viewing of a Mobile TV screen may require a longer cable than if phone was being used for other tasks such as an alarm clock and any charging indicator light should be muted or disabled when the Mobile TV is on. The variety of viewing postures and the need to find and maintain a good reception somewhere in a room suggests support for multiple viewing angles. Multi-tasking needs to be supported, mostly to cope with communication requirements than tasks related to active mobility.

The biggest design opportunities are likely to be in the synergies between existing phone features and TV programmes. Visual radio programmers can provide links to programmes about to start on TV, SMSs can notify users of upcoming content and can be saved as reminders in the phone's calendar and audience participation can be extended via SMS voting.

Out and about. Prior research suggests that mobile phones are carried and often used from waking in the morning to going to bed at night and all situations in between [8]. Mobile TV can be watched when actively mobile – walking or moving around. But the small screen size makes most content too difficult to watch and the sensory engagement required to watch conflicts too much with the task of walking to be enjoyable. Another reason is the weight and the bulk of the device – a posture for continued viewing whilst walking would require the phone to be held out arm slightly raised in front of the body. An arm outstretched it simply too much of a strain [5].

Outside the home Mobile TV use was very much a lean forward experience. Leaning forward is driven by: the need to multi-task e.g. text messaging, channel switching, minimal screen size, the need to physically support the device. There are opportunities for lean back use in the home – where the device is placed in a cradle and watched.

Secret use. Secret use may be better supported through: the ability to quickly turn off the screen; tools to narrow down the viewing cone/angle; directional sound so that the audio only encompasses the user; a remote control making interaction less obvious; small wireless headsets for the same reason; minimizing the possibility of accidentally turning on the TV; and enabling quick recovery if the device is accidentally switched on by having dedicated volume control keys. A possible consequence of this behaviour is that when Mobile TV functionality becomes more mainstream users may wish to highlight that they are not watching TV but are actually engaged in more 'productive' tasks.

Sharing and lending. Sharing can be facilitated by use of a remote control to maintain a degree of control and distance during the sharing experience; allowing the user to silo personal content on the device – perhaps disabling features when the device is in TV watching mode; applying battery limits so that the TV cannot be watched when the battery runs 'too low'. Traditional TV is viewed in a domestic environment and often involves social sharing [9]. But the size of mobile phone and its nature as personal devices might create new practices of sociability while watching mobile TV. The proximity of the device and the cheek to cheek nature of the viewing experience means that it is not something you are likely to do with your colleague or an annoying younger brother. The upside is that close proximity might spur an occasional romance.

6.3 Immersion vs. Distraction

During the study we wondered whether an immersive experience was possible with Mobile TV, and if so, was it desirable? Our conclusion was that it is possible – 'all' it takes is wearing sound headphones and a reasonably moderate storyline, and in all but a few contexts desirable if the duration of the immersion is accounted for. Immersed watching risks leading to: personal danger to the user e.g. risk of theft or and associated assault; minor inconveniences such as missing a bus stop; awkward transitions between the immersed experience and the reality of the user's context in particular in pubic environments, etc.

Not all TV requires the user's undivided attention to be enjoyed and ambient watching, for example with the volume turned down is possible both at work and at home. But something more immersive will be desirable when lying in the warmth of a bed on a cold day. Given our desire to offer the user the best possible user experience how can we support immersion whilst keeping the user in control in these situations? One simple measure is the option to ensure the time is visible at all times. Another is to be able to prioritize device based interruptions – a user may want to know about a low battery warning but cares less for SMS notifications until after a programme has finished. We note that time-shifting capabilities put the user in control of when content is watched even if the pausing content is limited to a few minutes.

6.4 Cultural Differences

It is easy to understand that TV content is often targeted and segmented according to geographic territories and languages. But the cultural difference is also reflected in usage context. In cultures such as the US people are more likely to have a TV in their bedroom and in these instances Mobile TV will need to compete more directly with regular TV offerings. Commuting habits also vary significantly between cultures – both in terms of the time it takes to commute, and the mode of transport. Approximately 75% of US commuting done in single occupancy cars so the opportunity to watch Mobile TV at this time will be considerably less that in Korea. That cars are considered a viable source to charge mobile devices enables longer viewing in other contexts. In the study, the popularity of TV sharing and device lending very common in Korea can be partially explained by Korean collectivism culture. We may not be expecting it happens so often in individualism cultures such as Finland or Japan [10].

7 Conclusion

One consequence of having TV functionality on a mobile phone is that the device may be considered by peers to be more of a tool for sharing than a personal communication device. Watching broadcast TV is non-exclusive activity – and (with the exception of battery use) having 1 person or 3 people watching a programme makes no difference to the subscriber's cost. In this sense the mobile phone loses gains some of the characteristics of TV which in turn changes what it is as a device.

What does the future hold for Mobile TV? As with any service it depends on the user's expectation of what is encompassed by that service. If, as in South Korea, Mobile TV includes radio use then it's probably already considered a success. One of the primary benefits of Mobile TV is that it provides the user with a choice of content in a setting of the user's choosing. These and related findings have led us to believe that Mobile TV is more about personal experiences, than the need for mobility itself and we therefore consider Personal TV to be a better descriptor of this service. We note that personal experience is not necessarily solitary, and the fact that Mobile TV is consumed on a device with a myriad of communications options suggests a direction for further investigation.

Acknowledgement

Our thanks to Yonsei university HCI lab researchers for their help in gathering user data from Seoul: Jinwoo Kim, Boreum Choi, Inseong Lee, and Jieun Yoon.

References

1. Södergård, C. Mobile television - technology and user experiences Report on the Mobile-TV project (Rep. No. P506) VTT Information Technology, 2003
2. Knoche, H. and McCarthy J Design Requirements for Mobile TV. In Proceedings of MobileHCI'05. (Salzburg, Austria). ACM Press, New York, USA. 69-76, 2005
3. Mobile TV Forum. Now's the time to create the future. www.mobiletv.nokia.com/pilots
4. Taylor, A. & Harper, R. Switching on to switch off: An analysis of routine TV watching habits and their implications for electronic programme guide design. usableiTV, 1 (3), 7-13, 2002
5. Knoche H, McCarthy J, and Sasse M. Can Small Be Beautiful? Assessing Image Size Requirements for Mobile TV. In Proceedings of ACM Multimedia 6-12, 2005 November 2005, Singapore
6. NOP world. Mobile TV: Learnings from South Korea. 2005
7. Ichikawa, F., Chipchase J., & Grignani R. Where's the phone? A study of Mobile Phone Location in Public Spaces. In Proceedings of the IEE Mobility Conference 2005 (Mobility '05) (Guangzhou, China), 3-2B-2, 2005
8. Chipchase, J., Persson, P., Aarras, M., Piippo, P., & Yamamoto, T. Mobile Essentials: Field Study and Concepting. In proceedings of Designing the User Experience (DUX'05), 2005
9. Oehlberg, L.; Ducheneaut, N.; Thornton, J. D.; Moore, R. J.; Nickell, E. Social TV: Designing for distributed, sociable television viewing. EuroITV; 2006 May 25-26; Athens; Greece
10. Choi, B. Lee, I. Kim, J. and, Jeon Y. A qualitative cross-national study of cultural influences on mobile data service design. In Proceedings of CHI'05 (Portland, Oregon, USA) ACM Press, New York, USA, 661-170, 2005

"I Just Want to See the News" – Interactivity in Mobile Environments

Anne-Katrin Hübel, Johannes Theilmann, and Ulrich Theilmann

Visual.labs GmbH, Bleichgartenstr. 11,
63607 Wächtersbach, Germany
huebel@uni-leipzig.de, {jtheilmann,utheilmann}@visuallabs.de

Abstract. Mobile TV marketers are announcing mobile TV as a new interactive medium, however users seemingly "just want to see news" but cannot imagine using interactivity. This paper deals with the challenge of enabling and encouraging users to understand the benefits and potentials of interactivity. Specific interactive applications as well as strategies to set them up in the first phase of mobile TV will be presented. The market development of interactive mobile TV applications is described as a process of mutual learning involving all stakeholder of the new technology.

Keywords: interactive, interactivity, mobile, TV, television, learning, user, usability, content, DVB-H, IP Datacast.

1 Introduction

In recent years mobile phones have developed into mobile multimedia terminals incorporating diverse communication channels and media. The newest feature is a tuner to receive broadcasting signals that bring the TV world out of our living rooms onto mobile devices. Digital broadcast standards like Digital Video Broadcasting - Handhelds (DVB-H) provide high transmission capacity, effective mass communication and distribution of rich multimedia content. They complement the mobile telecom networks which make available interactive one-to-one secure communication as well as many-to-many communication on cell phones and permit individual authentication, billing and internet connection [1].

The synthesis of wireless broadcasting and communication technologies like Universal Mobile Telecommunications System (UMTS) in one device technically supports to offer interactive multimedia content to large numbers of mobile users. However, currently mobile TV propositions in Germany are based on a mixture of scheduled and on-demand services while the combination of mobile TV with interactive applications is hard to find [2].

However, the feasibility of mobile interactivity begs a couple of questions especially with respect to user behaviour and expectations. Does the traditional lean back medium TV actually leave space for an activation and "leaning forward" of the viewer? What features are imaginable? Do they have the potential to be used in a truly interactive manner and how could customers be encouraged to apply them?

P. Cesar et al. (Eds.): EuroITV 2007, LNCS 4471, pp. 205–214, 2007.
© Springer-Verlag Berlin Heidelberg 2007

In order to start finding answers to those questions we will first give a short theoretical overview over the concept of interactivity in order to afterwards test its applicability to specific mobile multimedia services. Users surprising the industry and possible strategies to canalize or at least be prepared for such surprises will conclude this paper.

2   Mobile Interactivity Theory

„[...] interactivity and its derivatives are used to represent so many different meanings that the word rather muddles rather than clarifies the speaker's intent". [3]

"Interactivity" is one of the buzzwords in the discourse on New Media and especially marketers trying to upvalue their digital lifestyle-products are using the term in an inflationary manner. Furnished with diffuse meanings "interactivity" serves as a projection screen for diverse hopes on activating the mobile user and thus opening up new sources of revenues. Interactive mobile and broadcast services are expected to add a whole new dimension to the usage of mobile phones [4]. To fully grasp the complexities as well as the potentials of interactive mobile features the following section examines earlier theoretical works on interactivity.

With regard to interactive television Höing [5], presented in Beckert [6], developed a five level model embracing very basic interactions like turning the TV on/off and switching channels as well as the highest level when users are able to communicate, create own content and distribute it through the medium. However, in contrast to the internet (especially to recent developments in the field of the participatory web) the interactive potentials of the TV set in the living room have never been fully realized [7]. Today, with telecommunications, internet and broadcasting technologies converging within the tiny mobile phone the idea of rendering a passive TV audience in active and media-savvy users is being reanimated.

Searching for further definitions of "interactivity" one soon can accumulate a collection of diverse ideas and understandings from various fields of practice and science [8]. Designers often use "interactivity" as synonym for navigation or to describe good design while in a sociological sense „interaction occurs as soon as the actions of two or more individuals are observed to be mutually interdependent." [9] Contrasting a strand of communication science focuses on interactivity as a feature of specific communication channels. For instance Rockley Miller regards "interactivity" as a „reciprocal dialogue between the user and the system" and concludes that interactive media are „media which involves [sinc!] the viewer as a source of input to determine the content and the duration of a message, which permits individualized program material." [10] Although more appropriate to the context discussed in this paper, the definition remains too closely bound to specific technologies (computer and video) and does not allow to differentiate forms and levels of interactivity. The latter shortcoming can be corrected by concentrating on the communication setting instead of only the channel. In this respect Everett Rogers describes interactivity as „the capability of new media communication systems (usually containing a computer as one component) to 'talk back' to the user, almost like an individual participating in a conversation." [11] Nevertheless, he also concentrates too strongly onto the actual technologies of his time [12]. To overcome such restrictions it is necessary to regard interactivity as a multidimensional phenomenon and combine the distinct dimensions into one theoretical framework. For instance McMillan and E. Downes split the concept of interactivity into the factors "sense of place", "direction of communication", "timing", "level of control" and "responsiveness and aim of communication" in order to receive two types of interactivity: the „perception-based" und „feature-based models of interactivity" [13].

As different as the diverse definitions in communication sciences may be, comparing them one can discover several parallels and commonalities. In this respect potential two-way-communication forms the minimum consensus of all researchers [14]. Furthermore, exchanges during the communication/interaction should be coherent and related to one another while their timing is widely regarded as flexible. Last but not least interactive options of a technology are often classified on a continuum ranging from high to low interactivity [15].

Nevertheless, due to the incongruity of definitions and in order to include new technologies, it is necessary to establish an understanding of "interactivity" that is more comprehensive than those commonly used. Kiousis [16] extracted fundamental definitions and elaborated the conclusion that:

"Interactivity can be defined as the degree to which a communication technology can create a mediated environment in which participants can communicate (one-to-one, one-to-many, many-to-many), both synchronously and asynchronously, and participate in reciprocal message exchanges (third-order dependency). With regard to human users, it additionally refers to their ability to perceive the experience as a simulation of interpersonal communication and increase their awareness of telepresence."

The definition allows for three different dimensions of interactivity and several *actants* interacting with each other to be included within the concept. Following it, "interactivity" can be observed empirically, if 1) at least two *actants* (human or technology) participate in the exchange, 2) a technology is present that facilitates the exchange and 3) users have the possibility to modify the mediated environment, e.g. through making inputs and creating texts.

At first glance the mobile seems like the ideal channel for incorporating interactive features in connection with broadcasting. The corresponding applications are technologically feasible and could already be included within the device [17]. Additionally people are already accustomed to engage actively with their mobile phone by using it as the primary connection with their social network, having it constantly nearby and employing it as complement or even substitute for calendar, watch, mp3-player, alarm clock, camera and gaming device. Feedback channels, the prerequisite for installing interactive applications, are the bottom of the idea of telephoning – two-way-technologies like IP Datacast over DVB-H add further bandwidth thus permitting for multimedia and advanced communication channels to be mobilized.

Therefore, in a purely technical sense mobile TV applications could meet the criteria of Kiousis` definition of interactivity bringing along all the advantages of the phenomenon like more control over TV consumption and further related activities with the medium. By giving the user a feeling of autonomy with regard to their communicative experience they might leave behind the couch potato as role model and become more dynamically involved in the process of consuming and shaping media [18]. In this respect research on interactivity in the world wide web has shown that more opportunities for interactivity correlate with higher levels of satisfaction, users having a stronger feeling of self-efficacy, better retention of contents, deeper involvement and a sense of belonging [19].

However, usability and simplicity of the services are must haves to spur user interest in interactive exchanges. Technically the respective applications might be limited by lacking bandwidth of mobile networks or a low performance of the end device. In addition to the assumed user expectation of "real TV" (see chapter 3 of this paper) on the mobile phone this might explain the lacking offer of interactivity in the field of mobile broadcasting. These factors show that one has to consider the range and design of offers as well as the perspective of the user to understand the whole picture of mobile interactivity. In the following chapters those aspects will be discussed.

3   Mobile Interactivity – Applications: Are They Truly Interactive?

The combination of mobile telecom networks and broadcast networks in one mobile end device opens up the opportunity of a range of innovative interactive digital services [20]. Not only the transfer of applications from the stationary internet world to mobile terminals is imaginable but also the development of entirely new services that exploit the possibilities and factor in the limitations of mobile phones as well as the specific mobile usage situations. Besides the small size of the display, limited battery-life and restricted input possibilities the experience of mobile TV is characterized by short intervals of media consumptions (compared to stationary TV), more sequential and a less intensive usage due to environmental influences [21].

Having this in mind, interactive applications shouldn't be simply transferred from one medium to the other but be developed for or adapted to mobile environments. In this respect several concrete applications could call for an activated user: An enhanced EPG (Electronic Program Guide) could support interactivity by providing not only comprehensive data on programs (individually compiled time schedules of linear programs, on-demand offers and previews) but also user evaluations and recommendations as well as the capacity to mark programs of interest and receive reminders. Additionally, the EPG could render possible direct and remote recording (PVR – Personal Video Recorder), allow users to instantaneously watch linear on-demand, streamed or pre-recorded programs and function as an interface for features like voting, sending requests, messaging, chatting and shopping.

From the perspective of marketers new personalized forms of advertising via a broadcast channel in connection with the straight occasion to make a purchase over the respective 2.5G/3G channel are especially appealing. In this regard they could take advantage of the characteristics of mobile networks which enable them to securely authenticate the end users, track their usage behaviour, location and personal characteristics. In a trial of so-called "personalized mobile TV advertising" Ericsson has been testing those new possibilities in Norway since December 2006 [22]. Via a Java client customers are enabled to watch mobile TV, interact for instance with talk show hosts through voting or chatting and contribute content by uploading photos and video clips. Advertisements in this environment are supposed to be tailored to the user's age, gender, location and personal interests.

Another offer which tried to integrate and activate its users was VIVA+ "Get the Clip" (now MTV), a music show that counted as one of the msot attractive formats during a German DVB-H trial [23]. Viewers were enabled to vote for new video clips, download the actual clip and purchase ring tones while at the same time following the program.

The question remains whether such applications potentiate true interactivity in a sense that fits Kiousis` definition of the term. The first two empirical conditions – participation of at least two, human or technological, *actants* as well as the presence of a facilitating technology – are fulfilled by all means. Indeed, whether this is holding true for the third condition – the chance to modify the mediated environment – has to be tested for every application separately through a structural analysis. Even though such an analysis would lead to the conclusion that the explained features do not fullfill all of Kiousis` prerequisites they potentially foster a more personalized and active viewing experience than traditional TV. The mobile screen has more to offer than pure "lean back" reception by at least opening up the possibility for the user to communicate with other users and/or the producer respectively provider. Whether they offer the chance for true interactivity and will be used in an interactive manner remains to be seen.

4 Mobile Interactivity: The User

4.1 The User as "the big Unknown"

The current range of mobile TV programs reveals a certain image and usage behaviour content and network providers ascribe to their customers. Supported by findings of IBM [24], it seems to be common knowledge that users mainly demand familiar programs and TV brands on their mobiles. 80% of the participants in the study stated they expect to see "classic TV"-shows in full length while interactive applications apparently do not play any major role in the range of formats customers wish to use while on the move.

Admittedly, such outcomes have to be taken with a pinch of salt. Asked several years ago whether they would like to use their cell phone as a camera, most customers would have responded "no". Yet, with increasingly better cameras being integrated into the mobile the function has become standard in most devices and today 29% of German mobile phone owners regularly shoot photos [25]. This shows that asking for expectations with regard to a service people could not test might produce biased outcomes that prove false as soon as the new application is widely available.

Similarly, Short Message Service (SMS) has been a surprising success for the mobile industry. Originally designed for business users a whole culture and even a new language has evolved around the service – meantime 81% of all German mobile users communicate via SMS at least once a week [25]. In contrast, the market launch of Wireless Application Protocol (WAP) had been accompanied by high expectations on the part of the industry – expectations the service never could meet [26].

Those experiences of earlier mobile technologies point to the fact of the user being "the dark horse" since the adoption and use of technology take place as a process of social appropriation. Mackay and Gillespie [27] describe technology as "a product of three conceptually distinct spheres: 1) conception, invention, development and design; 2) marketing; and 3) appropriation by users." Customers may surprise the industry by rejecting a certain technology, redefine its purpose or discover new personal symbolic meanings in it. Simultaneously one has to bear in mind that „technologies can be designed... to open certain options, and to close others" [28]. With regard to mobile TV and related interactive applications industrial players can influence the acceptance and adoption of the services through factors like scope and type of content, the pricing structure, usability of the services and end devices, technical functionality and reliabilty of the networks as well as marketing communication.

However, Mackays and Gillespies findings imply that even if sophisticated mobile services are provided it seems like kind of a gamble whether and how users will apply them. This holds especially true for mobile multimedia applications because the more interactive a technology, the more options consumers have to become producers with regard to the actual uses.

4.2 Educating Users Towards Exploiting Interactive Options

Bearing in mind the costs of developing, launching and marketing new mobile services to a broad customer base, strategies of "trial and error" to test new applications are financially risky. Rather, approaches are needed that first of all render user acceptance more predictable and minimize the danger of them ignoring or rejecting a specific technology while secondly leaving users the freedom to discover the medium and develop new usage patterns which in turn could benefit the popularity of the original service.

In order to advance the usage of interactive services on the mobile it is necessary to connect those new variables with known ones. "Anchors" have to be etsablished to create a familiar environment for the users where they easily can orient and sequentially discover the innovative features their mobile has to offer.

European studies on user demand for mobile TV reveal news as the most relevant content (Breunig, p.560 [2], Knoche & McCarthy [29]). A German survey also shows interest in mobile TV as being driven by the audience's desire for information: 91% of the participants regard news as essential content, followed by traffic information (71%) and live sports (61%) [30]. A Finnish mobile TV trial additionally revealed domestic brands as channels with the highest audience share pointing to the fact that mobile TV viewers expect well-known brands on their mobile screen [31]. Catering those expectations induces customer confidence into the new service and forms one of the "anchors" users might need to appropriate it.

Once users have discovered the linear mobile TV program the level of interactivity can be increased step by step bringing along an evolutionary change of usage patterns. Initially, complexity of such interactive applications should be rather low while maintaining a familiar viewing experience. Gradually the level of interactivity and with this the complexity of the services can be increased.

However, in case such changes happen over time during the general product lifecycle, one might loose more savvy users of the technology who probably know what is technologically feasible and consequently want to test and autonomously use all interactive features up from the beginning. This means, while not overburden the "average customer" who basically expects a traditional viewing experience, operators also need to satisfy advanced needs of interested and experienced consumers of mobile applications. Serving such different segments (the examples forming just to extremes of a continuum) requires a balanced approach towards the design of the mobile TV application.

One solution would be the provision of a basic and an advanced mobile TV client, the first operating at lower levels of interactivity with basic search functions, program reminders inserted in the calendar of the device and the gradual integration of amendments like detailed program information, "tell-a-friend"-functions or a feature to write and send evaluations of the program. Such options constitute successive steps on an individual learning curve accelerating the transition to more interactive applications. In this respect, a supporting "anchor" could be the introduction of a service that is known from other media or technological environments. With regard to user generated content mobile network operator Vodafone announced a cooperation with online video portal YouTube to realize the service on the mobile by transferring the brand and the portals basic functions from one medium to another [32].

The more comprehensive, advanced version of the mobile TV client is far more complex with regard to the number of possible choices and actions requiring a higher "mobile media literacy" from its users. Concrete features could be PVR - and Video on Demand-offers that are interrelated with the free as well as the paid linear program and allow for autonomous compiling of programs and and independent viewing experiences. Sophisticated "social applications" like chats or whole communities require even higher levels of user involvement but offer the chance to create a base for orientation in the mobile TV environment, further information transmission to and among the customers and program-related transactions[1] From a theoretical point of view, such comprehensive offers come closer to Kiousis´definition of interactivity since also the third condition – modification of the mediated environment – can be fullfilled because users can influence the content (e.g. by uploading own videos or reviews) and/or the design and structure of the mediated environment (e.g. by compiling a personal program overview).

In short, the first step towards exploiting all the options interactive mobile TV applications offer is to encourage users to change their passive consumption behaviour and signal them where and how they can get active. The challenge here is to educate users by showing them similarities to known media and let them transfer this literacy to mobile TV. Parallely, techno-savvy users should be given the chance to discover the interactive options up from the beginning. Their experiences and patterns of use might give insights into the processes of appropriation and adaptation of the respective applications and serve as an early indicator of rejection or redefinition of distinct features.

---

[1] For purposes of virtual communities see Porter, Constanze Elise [33] and: Ridings, Catherine M./ Gefen, David [34].

212   A.-K. Hübel, J. Theilmann, and U. Theilmann

5 Conclusion

For business purposes mobile phones seem to be a predestined platform for interactive applications in connection with mobile broadcasting. But are users also determined to use interactive services as they are set up by the industry? For now, the answer has to remain open since such features are hardly available yet. This lack may be explained by factors like the immaturity of the market in general as well as by users expecting traditional TV firsthand and companies avoiding the risk of developing, launching and marketing such services. Besides the risks and complexities, interactivity potentially benefits all participants along the value chain, from designers to producers, content aggregators, providers and customers – always provided that the system scores high on usability, its contents are of relevance to the user and the arising costs are transparent to those paying. In order to solve the problem of: "who was first? hen or egg?" users should be enabled to experience and learn how to use interactivity gradually since a sequential approach can promote a substantial change of usage patterns with users leaving their position as passive TV audience and becoming active and strongly involved in order to exploit all the possibilities of converging networks, media and mobile communication channels. Not everything that is technologically feasible will be used – the final decision over success or failure of the transition from "lean back" to an active and participatory use remains with the customer.

Based on experiences made with earlier innovations, users and industry have to establish a setting to learn from each other to develop effective and usable interactive mobile services. This may end up in a so called "virtuous" cycle with all actors involved in mobile TV benefiting from each other and creating an environment of reciprocal influence.

Services with high turnover rates but highly complex applications will barely convince a majority of users, especially not in the starting phase. The same holds true for the simple transmission of "traditional" TV. For service providers this means working closely together with costumers to capture user interests. Technically, interactive services can be provided – whether users will accept them and how much they are willing to pay has to be discovered during the development of the market. The process may be spurred by providing applications with different levels of complexity allowing users to learn progressively how to interact with and through their mobile TV application. The aim is not to endeavour persuading customers but to present them possibilities for the enhancement of their mobile TV experience by using interactive services.

References

1. See Pangalos, Paul: Interactive Mobile TV: An interworking architecture. Presentation held at Mobile VCE. November 22nd, 2005. (2005).
2. See Breunig, Christian: Mobiles Fernsehen in Deutschland. In: Media Perspektiven. NR. 11/2006. p.552 ff. (2006).
3. Heeter, Carrie: Interactivity in the Context of Designed Experiences. In: Journal of Interactive Advertizing, Vol.1., Fall 2000. 04.12.2006 Available at: http://www.jiad.org/vol1/no1/heeter/index.html. (2000).

4. Kaumanns, Ralf/Siegenheim, Veit: Handy-TV - Faktoren einer erfolgreichen Markteinführung. Ergebnisse einer repräsentativen Primärstudie. In: Media Perspektiven. No. 10/2006. p. 498. (2006).

5. Höing, Michael & Tremplin, Daniel: Marktübersicht Interaktives Fersehen. 25 in- und ausländische Systeme im Vergleich. Eine Analyse. Kommunikations-Kompendium Bd. 1. MGM: Unterföhring (1994).

6. Beckert, Bernd: Medienpolitische Stratgien für das interactive Fernsehen. Westdeutscher Verlag: Heidelberg (2002).

7. Beckert, Bernd: Interaktives Fernsehen im Kontext staatlicher Programme für die Informationsgesellschaft. Eine vergleichende Implementationsstudie von Info 2000 und NII. Doctoral Thesis. Institute for Social Sciences. Technical Univerity Munich.. p. 290. (2001)

8. Huebel, Anne-Katrin: Der virtuelle Wahlkampf. Interaktivität und politische Partizipation auf Kandidatenwebsites. VDM Verlag Dr. Mueller. p. 9 ff. (2007)

9. Duncan, Starkey Jr.: Interaction, Face-to-Face. In: International Encyclopedia of Communications. New York: Oxford University Press (1989). p. 325 cited in Jensen, F.J. : „Interactivity" – Tracking a new concept in media and communication studies. In: Mayer, Paul A. (Ed.): Computer, Media and Communication. Oxford: Oxford University Press, p. 165. (1999)

10. See Jensen, F.J.: „Interactivity" – Tracking a new concept in media and communication studies. In: Mayer, Paul A. (Hrsg.): Computer, Media and Communication. Oxford: Oxford University Press.. p. 170. (1999),

11. Rogers (1986) cited in Jensen, F.J.: „Interactivity" – Tracking a new concept in media and communication studies. In: Mayer, Paul A. (Hrsg.): Computer, Media and Communication. Oxford: Oxford University Press.. p. 172. (1999)

12. See Jensen, F.J.: „Interactivity" – Tracking a new concept in media and communication studies. In: Mayer, Paul A. (Hrsg.): Computer, Media and Communication. Oxford: Oxford University Press. p. 173. (1999)

13. Kiousis, Spiro: Interactivity: a concept explication. In: new media & society. Vol. 4 (3). p. 362. (2002).

14. Kiousis, Spiro: Interactivity: a concept explication. In: new media & society. Vol. 4 (3). p. 368. (2002).

15. See Huebel, Anne-Katrin: Der virtuelle Wahlkampf. Interaktivität und politische Partizipation auf Kandidatenwebsites. VDM Verlag Dr. Mueller.. p. 32. (2007).

16. Kiousis, Spiro: Interactivity: a concept explication. In: new media & society. Vol. 4 (3). p. 355-383. (2002).

17. See Ferré, Serge F. : DVB-H – Time to commercialize. Presentation held at 15. Symposium of Deutsche TV-Plattform. 16.02.2006. Charts: http://www.tv-plattform.de/download/symp06/charts/0_Ferre_keynote.pdf. (2006)

18. See Weare Christopher/ Lin Wang-Yin: Content analysis of the world wide web: opportunities and challenges. In: Social Science Computer Review, No. 18 (3).. p. 275. (2000)

19. See Sundar, Shyam S./ Kalyanaraman, Sriram/ Brown, Justin: Explicating Web Site Interactivity. Impression Formation Effects in Political Campaign Sites. In: Communication Research. No. 30 (1).. p. 35. (2003)

20. N.N.: Das Handy der Zukunft wird zum Multimedia-Center. Online since: 05.12.2006. Retrieved: 06.12.2006. http://www.inside-handy.de/news/pdf/7414/. (2006)

21. Huebel, Anne-Katrin/Steinmetz, Ruediger/Witschas, Stephan: Auf der Suche nach Fernseh-Mobilität. Zwischenbericht einer Leipziger Begleitstudie zum Handy-TV. In: Fernsehinformationen. Nr. 08/2006. p. 10. (2006)

214   A.-K. Hübel, J. Theilmann, and U. Theilmann

22. Erricson: Ericsson and NRK launch world first - customized mobile TV advertising. 06.12.2006: avilabe at: http://www.ericsson.com/ericsson/press/releases/20061206-1091729.shtml. (2006).

23. Sattler, Claus: Konvergenz von Mobilfunk und digitalem Fernsehen", presentation Potsdamer Multimedia Konferenz. (2004).

24. IBM Global Business Services: Konvergenz oder Divergenz. Erwartungen und Präferenzen der Konsumenten an die Telekommunikations- und Medienangebote von morgen. 04.12.2006. available at http://www-935.ibm.com/services/de/bcs/pdf/2006/konvergenz_divergenz_062006.pdf. (2006).

25. n.n.: Deutsche bei innovativen Handyfunktionen eher verhalten. Preise weiter zu hoch. 05.12.2006. available at: http://de.internet.com/index.php?id=2046586. (2006)

26. Teo, Thompson./Pok, Siau Heong: Adoption of WAP-enabled Mobile Phones Among Internet Users. Omega, Nr. 31. p. 483-498. (2003).

27. Mackay, Hughie & Gillespie, Gareth: Extending the Social Shaping of Technology Approach: Ideology and Appropriation. Social Studies of Science, Nr. 22. p. 685-715. (1992).

28. MacKenzie, D./Wajcman, J. (Hrsg.): The Social Shaping of Technology. Milton Keynes: Open University Press. p. 7. (1985) In: Mackay, Hughie & Gillespie, Gareth: Extending the Social Shaping of Technology Approach: Ideology and Appropriation. Social Studies of Science, Nr. 22. p. 685-715. (1992).

29. Knoche, Hendrik & McCarthy, John: Users' Needs and Expectations of Future Multimedia Services in Proceedings of the WWRF12, 05.12.2006 available at http://scholar.google.com/url?sa=U&q=http://www.cs.ucl.ac.uk/staff/H.Knoche/Hendrik%2520Knoche%2520-%2520Home_files/wwrf12-HOK,JDM.pdf (2004).

30. Schmidt, Claudia et al.: Mobiles Fernsehen: Interessen, potenzielle Nutzungskontexte und Einstellungen der Bevölkerung. In: Media Perspektiven. No. 1/2007. p. 14 (2007).

31. Kronlund, Jonas: Developing Advanced Interactive opportunities to develop new revenue streams. Presentation held at IST 2006. Conference Session on "Convergence of Interactive Mobile and Broadcast services". Helsinki, 23.11.2006. (2006).

32. Vodafone: Vodafone announces agreement to launch YouTube Mobile. Onlien since: 09.02.2007. Retrieved: 10.02.2007. http://www.vodafone.com/article_with_thumbnail/0,3038,OPCO%253D41000%2526CATEGORY_ID%253D20201%2526MT_ID%253Dpr%2526LANGUAGE_ID%253D1%2526CONTENT_ID%253D294557,00.html. (2007).

33. Porter, Constanze Elise: A Typology of Virtual Communities. A Multi-Disciplinary Foundation for Future Research. In: Journal of Computer-mediated Communication. Nr. 10 (1). http://jcmc.indiana.edu/vol10/issue1/porter.html#fourth. (2004).

34. Ridings, Catherine M./ Gefen, David: Virtual Community Attraction: Why People Hang Out Online. In: Journal of Computer-mediated Communication. No. 10 (1). Online since: January 2004. Retrieved: 20.10.2005. http://jcmc.indiana.edu/vol10/issue1/ridings_gefen.html. (2004)

Mobile TV in Everyday Life Contexts – Individual Entertainment or Shared Experiences?

Virpi Oksman[1,*], Elina Noppari[2], Antti Tammela[1],
Maarit Mäkinen[2], and Ville Ollikainen[3]

[1] VTT Technical Research Centre of Finland, Sinitaival 6, Tampere, Finland
[2] University of Tampere, Tampere, Finland
[3] VTT, Espoo, Finland
virpi.oksman@vtt.fi

Abstract. TV has often been regarded primarily as a traditional family medium [8], because it is mainly watched at home and used as a basis for interaction with others. Now that the mobile phone, which people seem to experience as a personal communication device, has developed functionalities peculiar to mass media, including a TV feature, it is interesting to know how these functionalities will be used throughout the day and in different everyday life contexts. Will mobile TV used mostly on the go or as an additional media at home? Will it become as a highly individualized media format or will the watching experience typically be shared with others?

This paper examines the users' mobile TV choices in different everyday life contexts. The data is based on ongoing empirical research in Finland in 2006. The tested mobile TV services included both news and entertainment contents, and were tested in 3G and DVB-H networks.

Keywords: Mobile TV, mobile news, mobile media, use contexts, user experiences.

1 Introduction

Being able to view news and other media contents such as your favourite soap operas on the go on a wireless handset has a value in many situations. On public transportation a mobile TV service offers a way to keep up-to-date all the time. The same goes for other public spaces like coffee shops, shopping malls, bus stops, entrance halls, queues in supermarkets and waiting rooms. Also in private spaces, there is a need for mobile media. Even in your own living rooms, at work, at a summer house, in a taxi or a private car, the opportunity to use mobile TV is interesting. Some family members may even wish to have their own *personal* mobile media service at home [13]. However, it is not yet clear, in which extent people will value the functional blending of mobile telephony and mass media broadcasting and how valuable the mobile TV service would be for users [9]. Therefore, it is important to find out in what kind of situations and for what purposes people would like to use

---

* Corresponding author.

P. Cesar et al. (Eds.): EuroITV 2007, LNCS 4471, pp. 215–225, 2007.

mobile TV. On balance, we will next take a closer look on some earlier findings of mobile TV user studies.

1.1 Some Earlier Experiences on Mobile TV Use Contexts

The usage of mobile phones evolves in the three general user spheres of home, work and public. Quite typically, mobile phones are regarded as devices for use in the public sphere for example while waiting or commuting. They are used kill dead moments and to keep their users entertained or up-to-date. [1]

Whereas the public sphere is going to remain an important area for mobile television usage, some studies have shown that mobile services are measurably used in the private area. For example mobile television pilot in Oxford, UK, revealed that about 50 percent of the test users viewed mobile television at home and didn't move anywhere while viewing. Typical time for using mobile television was late night, in bed, just before one was falling asleep. [1]

According to a Finnish mobile television pilot, people use different content types in different locations. News and information services are used everywhere throughout the day, and the mobile phone is considered as a valuable channel especially when something newsworthy suddenly happens. Live broadcasts of sports are watched anywhere if there is no conventional TV available. Series and entertainment services are viewed in short periods during waiting periods, for example on public transportation. Music is also listened to when on a move. Films and longer programs are only watched when the conventional TV is not available. Users may start watching a movie via the mobile phone and continue watching on their main TV when they get home. Mobile TV is often viewed during the daytime, which differs from the peak viewing times viewing of traditional television. [9]

The use of mobiles in the public sphere has certain limitations. For example users have been worried about becoming absorbed in mobile multimedia content, which requires their visual attention. They fear increased risks of accidents and lapses. The possibility of listening to music or the radio while on the move is thus highly valued, because it doesn't need visual attention. Also text legibility may be difficult when on a move. [5]

1.2 From News to User Generated Contents

The findings of a number of studies made on mobile TV show that the most popular content is news. [13, 6, 9] Different mobile television content types listed by their popularity are: 1. news 2. music 3. sports 4. cartoons 5. movies 6. soap operas 7. sitcoms. [6]

News is well suited to mobile phones, because the use of mobile TV bursts often lasts less than 10 minutes[2]. News channels are also quite easily re-broadcasted over

---

[1] According to a Finnish mobile television pilot, 43 % of test users used mobile television for killing time and 40 % to stay up-to-date while on a move.

[2] In a Finnish mobile television pilot an average use time of mobile television was 5-20 minutes daily. Only very active users viewed mobile television more than that – up to maximum 40 minutes per day.

the mobile phone, because the content of the channel is continually news: if the user selects the mobile news channel (s)he is most likely to get what (s)he expected. Other channels may have to think how well their broadcasting is fitting to the mobile environment. For example, if a mobile TV user selects a music channel, it's disappointing if there isn't music in the agenda during her/his short period of viewing. The limited time of mobile television use has ramifications for both on the type of content and the way that people consume it. [13, 4, 9] Most likely, customized services which address specific interests of the individual user will probably become more important. [3]

Digital music is one of the most popular form of mobile entertainment and it is supposed to be a key driver for customer adoption of new 3G services. The market for music-capable phones is expected to grow quickly. [7] According to a Siemens survey, the most attractive applications for American consumers are mobile email, mobile music and mobile TV. [12]

User generated podcasting – audio and video file sharing to a portable device – is also a significant phenomenon and regarded as one of the most important content types for mobile TV. There are plenty of amateur podcasters all over the world, which is seen for example in the enormous success of Youtube. There are sites for podsafe-music[3], where podcasters are able to download free background music for their shows. Other services are also created for podcasters, like podcast editing and voice offering services. The whole podcasting or mobcasting[4] phenomenon may affect the forms of present media supply. For example the Finnish Broadcasting Company, YLE, which started its podcasting experiment in autumn 2005, has recounted that one of the most wished-for podcast contents is a radio play.[5] The popularity of podcasting certainly challenges traditional media and their business models. The first open source radio station, based on podcasting, started in April 2005, in San Francisco.[6] The channel is moderated and quality controlled for unacceptable material. Overall, user-generated contents multiplies the whole media supply, and users have countless of channels to get contents just to their likings.

Clearly, user choices and preferences will determine the success of mobile TV services. Indeed, for media companies and consumers, mobile media is nothing new. Print media such as newspapers or magazines are mobile; the same holds true for media such as the car radio, or Walkman. [2] Thus, if new mobile broadcast services are to be successful, questions regarding the relevance of the service to consumers need to be asked. The research needs to ask questions such as: How does the service improve users' lives or help them? Why it is valuable to them? It is also important to consider the issues of when and where the usage will take place, as the mobile broadcasting services will most likely be used in different locations and times than the fixed media and information technologies. [10] Taking all the above points into consideration, the paper will next present the findings of a user study.

---

[3] http://music.podshow.com
[4] mobcasting is podcasting to a mobile phone.
[5] http://blogit.yle.fi/podcasting
[6] www.kyoradio.com

1.3 Research Questions

To find out how people would like to use mobile TV services, this article focuses on three main research themes based on empirical research:

- *In what kind of contexts and situations people would like to use mobile TV? Is it used as an individualized media device or in social situations, in fixed locations or mainly when the user on the move?*

- *When is the mobile prime time? Is it the same as television prime time, or perhaps a little bit earlier?*

- *What kind of contents people would choose to watch on mobile TV?*

2 Research Methods

The focus of our research is on developing mobile TV technologies and usability of the services. With our methodological approach, we hope to gain new insights into users' requirements and expectations of mobile television.

The purpose of the first field study was to explore users' media choices in different situations. The tested media service prototype combined text, audio and video and included solely news contents. Qualitative and quantitative methods are combined to make sure that adequate data is collected. Semi-structured interviews and media diaries help us understand users' media habits and how they voice their expectations and preferences. Log data reveals the time and duration of actual occurrences of service use. We asked the users to take some photos with the camera phone about the situations in which they used the mobile news service, and of other places, things or contexts that are important to them. This helps us gain an understanding about the role of media in the users' everyday lives.

The first field test started in March 2006 with users who used the service with 3G phones (Nokia 6630 and N70) for one month with Elisa subscription. Before the test period, the users were interviewed and they received information concerning the test. Demographic data and media user profiles were gathered from the users. The ages of the users ranged from 23 to 56. All of them worked at least part time. During the test period, the informants reported their user experiences in a test diary. After the test, the users were asked to fill in a usability evaluation form and they were interviewed again. The usability form covered questions such as the navigation and the ease with which the different functions could be utilized. The testers were also asked to assess how enjoyable they found watching the news and other media on the screen of the mobile phone. The log data of the service use was collected and analyzed statistically. The similar kinds of methods were used in the second field test, which started in October 2006 and ended in December; with the exception that the log data was not possible to collect from these applications. The main aims of the second test were to examine the user choices when different, more varied media contents were available and to estimate the quality difference between 3G TV and DVB-H TV as well as the usability of the services. Ten families tested 3G TV and DVB-H TV with Nokia N92 for a period of one month. The tested mobile TV services consisted of a wide range of different kinds of contents: from all the main TV channels to sports, news channels and from fashion TV to user generated contents.

The both of the test groups consisted of persons who have been using mobile phones and mobile services actively during the last few years. They were also keen news and media followers but had different kind of media user profiles each. Some of them were very loyal newspaper readers, while others regarded the Internet or TV as the best news or entertainment source. The test users had different kinds of hobbies, lifestyles and interests. During the test, they carried the test phone as their primary mobile, using it for both professional and personal communication. They did not have pay for using the developed services. Of course, the price of using the mobile TV services, when they are finally finished products on the market, is also a significant factor that will affect the use. Naturally, creating good technology and services and profitable business models are all difficult activities and if mobile broadcasting services are to become successful commercial activities, companies offering services have to devote significant attention to consumers and the market. [10, 3]

3 The Contexts of Use

- *What I appreciated most was the mobility of the service. Situations where you're travelling from one place to another and you have some time to spare; it's perfect for that. I watched a lot of news. I usually don't have much time for TV.* (Woman, 34)

The test users reported on their diaries about their media habits, expectations and preferences. It appeared that they valued greatly the possibility to watch mobile TV on the go. It was often used for just killing time but it obviously also possesses some novelty value which was present in the usage situations. It aroused curiosity also in situations with friends or colleagues. It was the most used media type in social situations when the device was tested with others.

- *TV was the most interesting to me. The thing I used the most was TV news during my coffee break at work. That way I came to show my friends that I had a TV in my mobile. Some thought, well, you always have to have the most latest gadget. Others said, ok, that's interesting, but the screen is very small. The size of the screen caused a little doubt about whether or not it's worth it.* (Man, 56)

The test users considered the service most useful while they are on the move and not at home or in situations where they are unattainable by regular media. However they used it also at home for mainly quick check ups and as a personal media device if they were not close to a TV-set. Users appreciated the ability to watch news any time they liked to.

It is very handy indeed that you are able to watch the news whenever it is suitable for you. You don't have to care about times. (Woman, 43)

The ability to select the media format suited for the situation at hand was considered important. Audio was perceived as suitable for situations where the user was mobile him/herself, e.g. while walking, cycling or roller skating. For situations when the user was sitting or standing still, the media form selected was more likely to be illustrated news, text or video.

> "The media format (text, video, audio) has more significance when it associated with situations you find yourself in. If you need to know the contents of a specific item of news, then I'd opt for a moving image, kind of like news broadcasts on TV, that's condensed information. If you want a more in-depth view, you read from the paper or an electronic service."
> (Man, 42)

The use of the mobile TV raised discussion in the immediate circle of the testers. The general view was that its use was best suited to situations where other media were not available or where people found themselves with time on their hands. They could use the service while waiting for someone, during their break from work, or while travelling on public transportation. Users described it as a nice way of passing the time.

The mobile TV service was mainly used as an individualized, personal media format. However, while watching TV, the device became occasionally more social, but after the demonstration phase it was mostly used by one person only.

> At work and where I study I would be with others, at home and in the bus I would use it on my own. It generated a lot of discussion about how it would work, what you could use it for and how nice it would be. For us mature students coming from different parts of Finland this would be really good as we tend to travel a lot from place to place. For when you're sitting on a train or in a bus or for lonely nights in student housing when you don't feel like going out. (Woman, 34)

Mobile TV was obviously not used while driving. Users mentioned that in noisy environments, like in a bus or in traffic, other media type than TV might be easier to use. The use of earpieces in a public place was seen as less awkward than it perhaps would have been before [see 11]; however, mobile TV would not be often used without earpieces for example in a bus, and sometimes it would be an extra effort to find and attach them to the phone.

Fig. 1. The mobile prime place. The mobile TV was used often when moving from one place to another.

3. 1 Mobile Primetime

The average viewing time for mobile TV news video was relatively short, clearly under 5 minutes (a median for video duration was 1 min 43 sec). The mobile media service use spread relatively evenly for the whole day, although use was more frequent during the mornings (from 8 to 10) and before the noon (from 10 to 12) and early in the evenings (from 16 to 18).

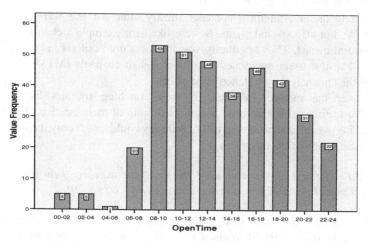

Fig. 2. The prime time of a mobile news service

The service use was most active in the beginning of the week. The usage tended to become less active during the weekends – it was remarkably low on Sundays, probably because people were at home watching regular TV broadcasts.

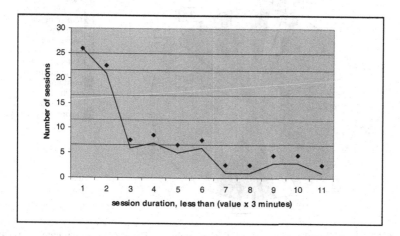

Fig. 3. The development of mobile TV sessions. It seems that the sessions tended to become shorter during the test. In this chart the first two testing days are ignored, as the usage activity tends to be especially high during the first couple of days.

3.2 The Most Interesting Media Contents in Mobiles

Clearly, as the earlier studies show, news was considered as one of the most interesting media contents in mobiles. The categories of domestic (25%), sports (15%) and foreign news (9%) attracted the most interest. Also the TV-program guide was checked quite often (11%). The local news and children's sections were read more randomly. There was high demand only for the latest news – the older news from the archive were barely read at all.

Regarding the entertainment contents, mostly same contents were watched as on regular TV, but also special channels were liked for example a channel focusing on local cultural events. Thus familiarity was the most used criteria in choosing the TV channel. The test users mentioned the major Finish channels (MTV3, Nelonen and YLE) as the channels they watched most often.

Moreover the mobile TV changed their watching routines by offering the possibility to follow their favorite programs despite of their location. The time used for watching was also shorter than usual, and they could watch only the most essential or interesting parts of the programs.

I could not finish the movies until the end, but watched them about 15 to 20 minutes. I think I watched news more than usually. (Woman, 29)

Video watching durations were considerably longer than on the news field trial, approximately from 5 to 10 minutes (according the testers' own report) and also longer durations up till 20 to 40 minutes were reported. Besides the new contents, also 3G and DVB-H reception difference may have an influence on session durations.

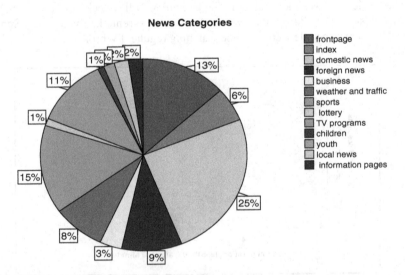

Fig. 4. The most popular news categories in mobiles. The regular news categories such as domestic news, sports and foreign news attracted the most interest in mobiles.

Also certain reality TV series that the users want to keep up with real time were mentioned as interesting contents. During the test period an obvious example of this was the reality TV show Big Brother, which in addition to television, was followed also through other media. The most avid follower was a 27-year old female student, who explained that it was essential daily to follow the events at the house from mobile TV while she was away from home.

The comments about interactive services of the mobile TV were most varying. Some users expected the mobile TV to include some kind of interactive services, while others didn't. The test users were mainly interested in applications for instance to buy or reserve concert tickets.

There could be interactivity in some channels, but too much of it would disturb. TV is for relaxing, and it requires some kind of passiveness. (Woman, 50)

The test users estimated that mobile TV would increase their media consuming from 5 to 10 percent or from 30 minutes to two hours per day. The extra time would include watching TV on the way to work, at the office, and in situations they don't have TV available.

Fig. 5. New contents for mobile TV? On mobile TV, mostly the same entertainment contents were watched as on regular TV, but also new special channels were liked for example a channel focusing on local cultural events

4 Conclusions

Although the field tests were constructed around testing a service in its early stage with a quite small test group, they yielded certain interesting results on the uses of mobile TV services in different contexts of people's daily lives. The empirical research shows that a device optimised for voice and text communication can offer users an interesting visual experience such as fresh TV news and entertaining contents.

The mobile phone as media is suitable for many different situations. Mobility, diversity and real time effect are considered to be the most important characteristics of the service and that combination distinguishes the use of the news service from other media use. Users appreciated updated information and information-rich media forms for mobile news delivery as well as the ability to select the media format suited for the situation. There was high demand for the latest news in mobiles. Users also appreciated fast functions and easy usability.

The mobile TV service was mainly used as an individualized, personal media format. As personal communication devices are turning into multimedia communication devices delivering news and other mass media content, new questions about user experience challenges will emerge. Two users interestingly pointed out that they would expect the user interface to display a new functional or visual idea. They had recently started using a text-based syndicated news browser (Kanavat) that has its own "smooth" scroll implementation which they found pleasant. For these users, the new scrolling implementation signified the service providers' investment and commitment to developing a good service, and this increased the users' positive attitude towards the service.

Users appreciated condensed information and media forms for mobile TV and news delivery. Most users looked the headlines or followed news several times a day – much more often than the traditional TV and news prime times would allow. It would be interesting to find the causes behind this as well – do we crave for news because we fear catastrophes or is it just some kind of ritual?

Thus usability issues regarding the small screen user interfaces will be particularly important and the quality of reception is crucial. In the long run, it will also be crucial to discover what kind of existing and new media formats and distribution channels will best suit mobile media.

References

1. Dowell B. (2006) Viewing habits shift into the bedroom.
   http://technology.guardian.co.uk/print/0,,329451221-117802,00.htm
2. Feldmann, V. (2005) Leveraging Mobile Media: Cross-media Strategy and Innovation Policy for Mobile Media Communication. New York: Physica- Verlag.
3. Grobel, J. (2006) Mobile Mass Media: A New Age for Consumers, Business, and Society? In Groebel, J., Noel, E., Feldmann, V. (eds.) Mobile Media. Lawrence Erlbaum Publishers.
4. Knoche, H. & McCarthy, J. D. (2004) *Mobile Users' Needs and Expectations of Future Multimedia Services. Proceedings of WWRF12*, 10-12 Nov 2004
5. Knoche, H. (2005) *A User-centred Mobile Television Consumption Paradigm.* Proceedings of *Human Centred Technology Workshop*, 28-29 June, Brighton, UK
6. Knoche, H., McCarthy, J. D. (2005) *Good News for Mobile TV.* Proceedings of *WWRF14*, 7-8 July 2005, San Diego, CA, USA.
7. May, H. & Hearn, G. (2005) *The Mobile Phone as Media.* International Journal of Cultural Studies. Vol 8(2), pp. 195-211.

8. McQuail, D. (1994) Mass Communication Theory. An Introduction. Third Edition. London:Sage.
9. Mäki, J. (2005) *Finnish Mobile TV Pilot, Results.* http://www.finnishmobiletv.com/press/Final_RI_Press_300805_english.pdf
10. Picard, R.G. (2005) *Mobile Telephony and Broadcasting: Are They Compatible for Consumers.* International Journal of Mobile Communications, Vo. 3.No. 1.
11. Repo, P., Hyvönen, K., Pantzar, M., Timonen, P. Mobiili Video (*Mobile video*). Helsinki: Kuluttajatutkimuskeskus, julkaisuja, 2003.
12. Siemens Communications Inc. (2006) Survey: US and World demand for wireless applications.
13. Södergard, C. (ed.) (2003) Mobile Television – Technology and User Experiences. Report on the Mobile-TV project. VTT Information technology. §

Semantic Modelling Using TV-Anytime Genre Metadata

Andrius Butkus and Michael Petersen

Technical University of Denmark,
Center for Information and Communication Technologies,
Informatics and Mathematical Modelling,
Building 371, DK-2800 Lyngby, Denmark
{ab,mkp}@imm.dtu.dk
http://www.cict.dtu.dk

Abstract. The large amounts of TV, radio, games, music tracks or other IP based content becoming available in DVB-H mobile digital broadcast, offering more than 50 channels when adapted to the screen size of a handheld device, requires that the selection of media can be personalized according to user preferences. This paper presents an approach to model user preferences that could be used as a fundament for filtering content listed in the ESG electronic service guide, based on the TVA *TV-Anytime* metadata associated with the consumed content. The semantic modeling capabilities are assessed based on examples of BBC program listings using TVA classification schema vocabularies. Similarites between programs are identified using attributes from different knowledge domains, and the potential for increasing similarity knowledge through second level associations between terms belonging to separate TVA domain-specific vocabularies is demonstrated.

Keywords: personalization, user modeling, TV-Anytime, item similarity.

1 Introduction

The large amounts of TV, radio, games, music tracks or other IP based content becoming available in DVB-H mobile digital broadcast, offering more than 50 channels when adapted to the screen size of a handheld device, requires that the selection of media can be personalized according to user preferences. The TV-Anytime metadata architecture has been chosen as standard in DVB-H for description of content in the ESG electronic service guide [1], which similarly provides possibilities for user interaction or submitting preferences utilizing the 3G channel as return path. This paper presents an approach to build implicit user profiles based on the metadata associated with the consumed content by combining attributes from multiple TVA *TV-Anytime* controlled term vocabularies in parallel [2]. The data models forming the fundament for the TVA metadata rely on describing media, preferences or the usage environment based on predefined classification schema attributes for classifying e.g. the specific genre of a piece of content in terms of its category, format, atmosphere or intended audience. As the semantic description can

P. Cesar et al. (Eds.): EuroITV 2007, LNCS 4471, pp. 226–234, 2007.

be extended to capture different media features by combining attributes from different TVA knowledge domains, this paper will in the subsequent sections:

- Assess the semantic modelling capabilities of TVA classification schema attributes based on BBC program information sample data.
- Identify partial similarity between programs based on TVA genre attributes from different knowledge domains.
- Demonstrate the potential for increasing similarity knowledge through second level associations between terms belonging to separate TVA domain-specific vocabularies.

2 Related Work

Current research within personalization related to recommender systems often combine content based and collaborative filtering models as well as statistical knowledge discovery techniques. Whereas content-based filtering uses specific features of the media to produce suggestions for other items of a similar genre or starring the same actor, collaborative filtering recommends other items based on the preferences of users who have requested the same media using correlation or vector similarity. Systems providing suggestions of movies like the CinemaScreen film recommender agent [3] combines collaborative with content based filtering. It takes into consideration actors, directors or genres that have previously appeared in collaborative filtering results and thus uses the content similarity for recommendation of new items that have not yet been rated by other users. To further improve recommendations and compensate for a lack of overlap in items rated by different users, case-based reasoning [4] apply data mining of profiles to retrieve additional similarity knowledge by extracting frequently co-occurring items and define association rules between pieces of content that appear to share certain characteristics.

Whereas these techniques in hybrid combinations can be used to retrieve similarity knowledge of items and users, a perhaps even more critical aspect is the selection of the features, which characterize the content and thus serve as a fundament for defining similarity. In the TVA metadata architecture these features are controlled terms selected from domain specific vocabularies listed in classification schemas. In the *iFanzy* recommender system the proposed TVA features are implemented to define item similarity based on a set of preferred channels, as well as being used to build collaborative filtering based on usage history to match the user to a stereotype group of other users with the same interests and viewing behavior [5]. In another content-based approach the TVA metadata attributes have been assembled in a hierarchical user model mirroring a taxonomy of TV program genres reflecting the features of the consumed media [6]. As less emphasis seems to have been directed towards how the features may complement eachother, the aim of this paper is to assess the potential for increasing item similarity knowledge by implementing multiple TVA domain specific attributes in parallel and thus extend the semantic dimensionality beyond traditional content genre hierarchies.

3 Semantic Modelling

Similar to the original MPEG-7 concept, the TVA Phase 1 classification schemas are indexing tools using controlled terms for describing a particular aspect of the metadata associated with the content. If generating implicit user preferences based on the media that is being consumed, the TVA terms may thus be implemented to classify the content Genre along several dimensions simultaneously based on attributes belonging to separate domain-specific vocabularies like:

Origination e.g. cinema, studio, on location
Atmosphere e.g. crazy, exciting, sad, insightful, heart-warming, analytical
Format e.g. documentary, cartoon, play, hosted show, quiz contest, DJ, structured
IntendedAudience e.g. adults, single, children 0-3, professionals
Content e.g. news, finance, soap, fascism, poetry, grunge, sports
Intention e.g. pure entertainment, inform, advice, enrichment, education.

The broadcaster BBC has since 2005 made their digital TV and radio program listings available in TVA format [7]. Implementing a subset of the TVA metadata architecture the BBC program information is mainly constructed around a description of Title, free text Synopsis, Keyword listings and structured Genre information combining terms from the Intention, Format, Content, IntendedAudience and Atmosphere vocabularies.

Which vocabularies and how frequently they are used to generate the TVA Genre information varies according to the needs of the channel for adequately describing its content. All channels rely primarily on the Content taxonomy to categorize the Genre within sub categories like e.g. soap opera, game show or daily news. Such subcategory terms alone would often in conventional recommender systems constitute what makes up the concept of a Genre description, whereas in the TVA architecture this type of Content categorization is only one among several aspects. Programs on the channels CBBC and Cbeebies to a large extent implement IntendedAudience terms to define that the described Content categories are meant for different age groups of children. Channels like BBC Four, News 24 and Parliament differentiate their Content categorizations by adding terms from the Format vocabulary, providing labels like documentary, cartoon or interview/debate/talkshow in order to simultaneously describe the internal structure of the Genre.

The BBC main channels One, Two and Three, which offer a high diversity of programs with a mixed schedule of current affairs, drama and entertainment, in addition to the above classification schemas also include attributes from the Atmosphere vocabulary like heart-warming, crazy or insightful to capture emotional aspects which go across the conventional Genre catagorization of Content.

Together the attributes from the Intention, Content and TVA knowledge domains provide taxonomies of terms, consisting of sub category hierarchies up to four levels deep. As such the terms are mainly nouns, which narrow down classification to specific types of Content or sum up the structure of a media item in

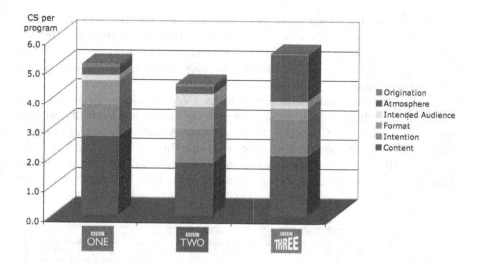

Fig. 1. Usage of TVA classification schemas for Genre description in BBC One, Two and Three program information over a twoweek period

regards to its Format. In essence the terms make up a top-down hierarchy for mapping numerous Genre features onto a small set of equivalence terms defined in the TVA classification schemas.

In contrast the attributes from the Atmosphere vocabulary are mainly adjectives capable of expressing associations, which instead of a hierarchy can be seen as spatially distributed. The distribution of the Atmosphere terms in itself might be more or less dense in regards to the number of adjectives available for describing the perceived responses when consuming the Content. Some of these terms define axes of opposites like gripping and laid back, or happy contrasted with heart-rending. The axes may intersect with planes of terms having an almost linear progression like intriguing, astonishing and stunning to emulate how compelling something is, or in the case of gutsy, powerful, gritty, irreverent and confrontational define degrees of radicalism. Yet other terms may appear isolated as dense sets of nuanced attributes like humorous, fun, satirical, silly, wacky or crazy capable of emphasizing specific aspects within the Atmosphere.

4 Item Similarity

Related to the aspects of entropy in information theory [8] a partitioning of items according to features reduces the data to a smaller number of significant characteristics and thus improves the effectiveness when predicting what media items to present in a personalized selection produced by a recommender system [9]. Seen in this light the TVA classification schemas provide a standardized selection of terms representing significant features of media items. So when considering information entropy in relation to probabilities associated with selecting two similar programs among the available items, we might assume close to zero entropy if knowing that features fully describing two chosen items are identical. If knowing that not all of the features describing two items are identical we might assume only partial similarity with a corresponding increase in entropy.

Assuming that metadata attributes from the TVA classification schemas could provide sufficiently significant features for defining Genre item similarity, we have analyzed 2 weeks of BBC program description data. Assessing the average usage of different TVA vocabularies in BBC One, Two and Three (Fig.1) we first extracted data from BBC Three as it appeared to have roughly equal amounts of metadata attributes describing the Genre using controlled terms from both the Content and the Atmosphere knowledge domains (Fig.2).

BBC THREE	PR	CONTENT	INTENTION	FORMAT	INTENDED AUDIENCE	ATMOSPHERE	ORIGINATION	SUM
MONDAY 12	15	2.4	1.5	0.5	0.3	2.5	0.0	7.2
TUESDAY 13	16	1.9	1.3	0.4	0.2	1.1	0.0	4.9
WEDNESDAY 14	11	2.0	1.3	0.5	0.1	0.6	0.1	4.5
THURSDAY 15	15	2.0	1.2	0.3	0.3	1.7	0.0	5.5
FRIDAY 16	17	2.1	1.2	0.4	0.2	2.0	0.0	5.9
SATURDAY 17	17	2.0	1.1	0.1	0.2	1.2	0.1	4.7
SUNDAY 18	14	1.9	1.2	0.3	0.3	2.0	0.0	5.7
MONDAY 19	15	2.3	1.5	0.5	0.3	2.0	0.0	6.5
TUESDAY 20	17	1.9	1.2	0.3	0.2	1.1	0.0	4.7
WEDNESDAY 21	12	2.0	1.3	0.3	0.1	0.6	0.1	4.4
THURSDAY 22	14	2.3	1.6	0.4	0.4	2.3	0.0	6.9
FRIDAY 23	17	2.1	1.3	0.4	0.3	2.4	0.0	6.5
SATURDAY 24	16	2.1	1.1	0.2	0.3	1.8	0.1	5.4
SUNDAY 25	15	1.8	1.1	0.3	0.3	1.9	0.0	5.3
AVERAGE		2.0	1.3	0.3	0.2	1.6	0.0	5.5

Fig. 2. The usage of TVA Classification Schemas for Genre description in the BBC Three program information

Working from the hypothesis that the Content and Atmosphere vocabularies could be orthogonal we wished to analyze whether it would be be feasible to retrieve additional item similarity between programs by combining attributes from the two vocabularies. These programs would not necessarily be close in terms of Content categorization but might still be relevant for recommendation due to their overlap in Atmosphere. We therefore first analyzed to what degree the BBC Three programs could be seen as similar based on whether they would share one or more Content classification metadata attributes, and following whether also taking their Atmosphere descriptions into consideration would increase the number of perceived similar media items.

After that we extracted data from the BBC Two program information, which from the distribution of classification schemas seemed to suggest that the Atmosphere vocabulary was much less used when describing the Genre and that we consequently would expect little effect in terms of identifying additional item similarity. We here similarly first looked for overlaps between programs sharing on one or more Content classification terms, and following whether including Atmosphere would extend the selection with additional perceived similar items.

BBC TWO	PR	CONTENT	INTENTION	FORMAT	INTENDED AUDIENCE	ATMOSPHERE	ORIGINATION	SUM
MONDAY 12	40	1.9	1.1	0.8	0.4	0.4	0.1	4.5
TUESDAY 13	40	1.8	1.2	0.7	0.5	0.3	0.1	4.6
WEDNESDAY 14	39	1.9	1.2	0.8	0.5	0.3	0.0	4.8
THURSDAY 15	37	1.9	1.2	0.8	0.5	0.3	0.0	4.8
FRIDAY 16	38	1.9	1.3	0.9	0.5	0.4	0.1	5.0
SATURDAY 17	35	1.7	1.2	0.7	0.4	0.1	0.1	4.2
SUNDAY 18	25	1.6	0.9	0.4	0.2	0.0	0.2	3.3
MONDAY 19	42	1.9	1.2	0.7	0.4	0.3	0.0	4.6
TUESDAY 20	40	1.9	1.2	0.7	0.4	0.3	0.0	4.5
WEDNESDAY 21	38	2.1	1.1	0.7	0.4	0.3	0.0	4.7
THURSDAY 22	38	2.0	1.1	0.8	0.4	0.3	0.0	4.7
FRIDAY 23	40	2.0	1.3	0.8	0.5	0.5	0.0	4.9
SATURDAY 24	33	1.8	1.2	0.7	0.5	0.1	0.1	4.3
SUNDAY 25	26	1.5	0.9	0.4	0.2	0.0	0.2	3.3
AVERAGE		1.8	1.2	0.7	0.4	0.2	0.1	4.5

Fig. 3. The usage of TVA Classification Schemas for Genre description in the BBC Two program information

5   Results

Analyzing Genre item similarity in the BBC Three program information based on the Content attributes only, highlights some of the challenges content providers are facing when indexing media in a hierarchal structure. No less than 16 out of 28 programs overlap on the very top level of the taxonomy by being identically labeled amusement/entertainment. One level deeper in the Content taxonomy 9 out of the 16 programs are defined as comedy using a second attribute, while 4 and 3 programs are labeled as non fiction/information and general light drama respectively. The usage of Content terms is thus mainly concentrated within the upper layers of the taxonomy resulting in a relatively general classification. Fewer programs are defined based on the lower more detailed levels of the Content taxonomy resulting in very little overlap between items that are more accurately defined in terms of their Genre.

Secondly when analyzing the BBC Three program information on a program level and not just considering an average usage of classification schemas on a channel basis, it becomes evident that the Atmosphere terms are in reality only used for Genre description in 4 out of 28 programs, which can also be seen from the fluctuating distribution over the two weeks period (Fig.4). In this case among 2 out of the 4 programs the Atmosphere vocabulary terms can be seen as axes consisting of the terms humorous, irreverent, satirical and silly. Yet another program is defined along an axis of the terms gripping, gritty and gutsy. When associated with the actual programs in the BBC Three program information data this additional information does not extend the item similarity. These characteristics are already captured in the Genre description based on the Content classification, and as a result the number of identified similar programs is not increased when analyzing two weeks of BBC Three program information.

When going through the same steps of extracting items sharing one or more TVA attributes, instead analyzing BBC Two program information, a different pattern emerges. The use of attributes from the Atmosphere vocabulary is much less pronounced but more evenly distributed across 9 different types of programs.

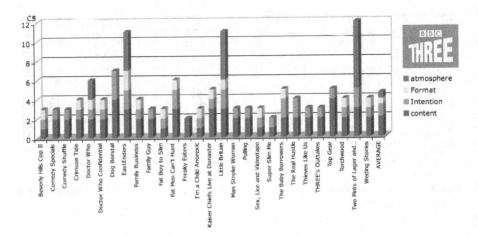

Fig. 4. Usage of TVA `Atmosphere` terms for Genre description in BBC Three program information related to specific programs during a twoweeks perio

Taking the auction show "Flog it!" as an example it would based on `Content` classification alone overlap with 33 other programs labeled as `amusement/ entertainment`, while its more descriptive `fine arts` label from the lower levels of the classification taxonomy would not be shared by any other programs. Due to the elements of `consumer advise` and `quiz/contest` in the program it will further overlap with 2 and 6 other programs respectively within these more defined `Content` taxonomy sub-categories.

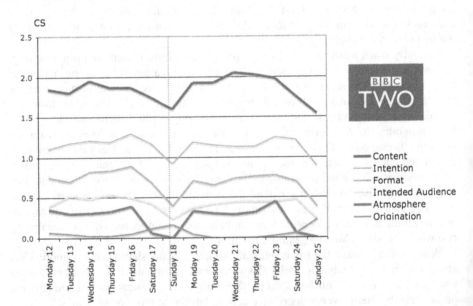

Fig. 5. Distribution of TVA `Atmosphere` terms for Genre description in BBC Two

Using attributes from the Atmosphere vocabulary "Flog it!" is also described in the program information as analytical, eclectic, insightful and astonishing. When filtering on the Atmosphere attributes it becomes apparent that this type of characterization makes the approch of the program rather than its fine arts subject stand out as the most significant feature. As a result one or two of these attributes characterizing "Flog it!" would be shared by 5 other programs, which are not closely related within the Content classification taxonomy. In this case it overlaps with programs defined by the following Atmosphere terms:

"Newsnight" - analytical, insightful, serious
"Newsnight Review" - analytical
"Gardeners World" - insightful, practical
"Escape to the Country" - analytical, practical
"TOTP2" - eclectic, rousing

None of these programs would be identified as similar to "Flog it!" if only taking Content classification into consideration when describing the Genre. If increasing our requirements when using Content classification and demanding that programs share at least 2 attributes based on differentiated terms indexed three levels down in the Content taxonomy, "Flog it!" would be identified as similar to only 8 programs. Adding terms from the Atmosphere vocabulary when analyzing item similarity of the BBC Two sample data would add 5 more programs, which could be considered relevant for recommendation when filtering media.

6 Conclusions

Though only very small samples of program information from the BBC channels Two and Three program information were analyzed, a number of issues related to retrieving item similarity between programs have been identified. Using only Content categorization as a basis for describing Genre will tend to identify similar items, which belong to closely related categories. One might argue that the terms belonging to the very attribute top levels of the Content taxonomy provide a too general categorization in order to efficiently identify similar program unless coupled with additional attributes from the more differentiated lower levels. At the same time this results in a scarcity of data due to lack of overlap between highly differentiated sub-categories of Content.

The Atmosphere attributes in the BBC Three sample data were associated with very few programs and the terms did not facillitate to further identify similar programs. Obviously the data sets were small but the results also highlight that the effectiveness of the Atmosphere attributes would depend on whether these terms are orthogonal to the description already captured by the Content classification. In the case of the analyzed program information from BBC Two the Atmosphere attributes were more evenly distributed among programs, and the potential for increasing item similarity between programs by combining the top-down Content classification approach with associative Atmosphere attribute terms was demonstrated.

References

1. DVB-H Mobile TV Implementation Guidelines: Nokia Profile of the Electronic Service Guide Datamodel for IP datacast over DVB, Release 1.5 (2006)
2. ETSI TS 102 822-3-1: "TV-Anytime; Part 3: Metadata; 1 Sub-part 1: Part 1 - Metadata schemas" (2006)
3. Salter and Antonopoulos: "CinemaScreen Recommender Agent: Combining Collaborative and Content-Based Filtering" vol.21 Issue 1 pp 35-41, IEEE Intelligent Systems, 2006
4. Wilson, Smyth & O'Sullivan: "Sparsity reduction in collaborative recommendation: A case-based approach", International Journal of Pattern Recognition, Vol.17, No.5, 2003
5. Akkermans, Aroyo and Bellekens: "iFanzy: Personalised filtering using semantically enriched TV-Anytime content", proceedings of ESWC, 2006
6. Pogacnik, Tasic, Meza and Kosir: "Personal content recommender based on a hierarchical user model for the selection of TV programmes" Vol.15, Issue 5, p.425-457 User Modeling and User-Adapted interaction, 2005
7. BBC Feeds & APIs, http://backstage.bbc.co.uk
8. Shannon: "Mathematical Theory of Communication", Bell System Technical Journal, vol.27, p.379-423, 623-653, July, October, 1948
9. Sung Ho Ha: "Digital content recommender on the internet", vol. 21 Issue 2 p.70-77, IEEE Intelligent Systems, 2006

Author Index

Akkermans, Paul   156
Alm, Norman   126
Aroyo, Lora   156

Beck, Elke   66, 146
Bellekens, Pieter   156
Bergh, Jan Van den   21
Bernhaupt, Regina   66, 146
Bhatnagar, Shalabh   175
Bjorkman, Martin   156
Bruynooghe, Bert   21
Bulterman, Dick C.A.   11
Butkus, Andrius   226

Cesar, Pablo   11
Chipchase, Jan   195
Coninx, Karin   21
Cook, Jonathan J.   96
Cruz-Lara, Samuel   11
Cui, Yanqing   195

Darnell, Michael J.   47
de Hesselle, Huub   185
de Ridder, Huib   136
Ducret, Julien   11

Fokker, Jenneke   136

García, Igor   107
Gopal, Lakshmi   175
Griffiths, Richard N.   76

Haffner, Christoph   37
Hand, Stacey   57
Handekyn, Koen   21
Harboe, Gunnar   116
Hemmeryckx-Deleersnijder, Bart   1
Houben, Geert-Jan   156
Hsu, Shang H.   166
Hübel, Anne-Katrin   205
Huypens, Steven   21

Iatrino, Arianna   31

Jung, Younghee   195

Kaptein, Annelies   156
Kegel, Ian   96

Lee, Chia-Hoang   166
Lee, Chun-Chia   166
Leurdijk, Andra   86
Lin, Hsin-Chieh   166

Mäkinen, Maarit   215
Massey, Noel   116
Mayer, Harald   96
Meesters, Lydia   185
Metcalf, Crysta   116
Modeo, Sonia   31
Moons, Jan   21

Noppari, Elina   215

Obrenovic, Zeljko   11
Obrist, Marianna   66, 146
Oksman, Virpi   215
Ollikainen, Ville   215
Ortiz, Amalia   107
Oyarzun, David   107

Petersen, Michael   226
Pouwelse, Johan   136

Reßin, Malte   37
Rice, Mark   126
Romano, Guy   116

Springett, Mark V.   76

Tammela, Antti   215
Theilmann, Johannes   205
Theilmann, Ulrich   205
Thomas, Maureen   96
Thorne, Jeremy M.   1
Tscheligi, Manfred   66, 146

Ugarte, Alex   107
Ursu, Marian F.   96

Van den Ende, Nele   185
Varan, Duane   57

Varatharajan, Sridhar   175
Velusamy, Sudha   175

Weiss, Astrid   146
Wen, Ming-Hui   166
Westendorp, Piet   136

Wheatley, David   116
Williams, Doug   96
Wyver, John   96

Zimmer, Robert   96
Zsombori, Vilmos   96

Lecture Notes in Computer Science

For information about Vols. 1–4372

please contact your bookseller or Springer

Vol. 4510: P. Van Hentenryck, L. Wolsey (Eds.), Integration of AI and OR Techniques in Constraint Programming for Combinatorial Optimization Problems. X, 391 pages. 2007.

Vol. 4486: M. Bernardo, J. Hillston (Eds.), Formal Methods for Performance Evaluation. VII, 469 pages. 2007.

Vol. 4483: C. Baral, G. Brewka, J. Schlipf (Eds.), Logic Programming and Nonmonotonic Reasoning. IX, 327 pages. 2007. (Sublibrary LNAI).

Vol. 4482: A. An, J. Stefanowski, S. Ramanna, C.J. Butz, W. Pedrycz, G. Wang (Eds.), Rough Sets, Fuzzy Sets, Data Mining and Granular Computing. XIV, 585 pages. 2007. (Sublibrary LNAI).

Vol. 4481: J.T. Yao, P. Lingras, W.-Z. Wu, M. Szczuka, N.J. Cercone, D. Ślęzak (Eds.), Rough Sets and Knowledge Technology. XIV, 576 pages. 2007. (Sublibrary LNAI).

Vol. 4480: A. LaMarca, M. Langheinrich, K.N. Truong (Eds.), Pervasive Computing. XIII, 369 pages. 2007.

Vol. 4472: M. Haindl, J. Kittler, F. Roli (Eds.), Multiple Classifier Systems. XI, 524 pages. 2007.

Vol. 4471: P. Cesar, K. Chorianopoulos, J.F. Jensen (Eds.), Interactive TV: A Shared Experience. XIII, 236 pages. 2007.

Vol. 4470: Q. Wang, D. Pfahl, D.M. Raffo (Eds.), Software Process Change – Meeting the Challenge. XI, 346 pages. 2007.

Vol. 4464: E. Dawson, D.S. Wong (Eds.), Information Security Practice and Experience. XIII, 361 pages. 2007.

Vol. 4463: I. Măndoiu, A. Zelikovsky (Eds.), Bioinformatics Research and Applications. XV, 653 pages. 2007. (Sublibrary LNBI).

Vol. 4462: D. Sauveron, K. Markantonakis, A. Bilas, J.-J. Quisquater (Eds.), Information Security Theory and Practices. XII, 255 pages. 2007.

Vol. 4459: C. Cérin, K.-C. Li (Eds.), Advances in Grid and Pervasive Computing. XVI, 759 pages. 2007.

Vol. 4453: T. Speed, H. Huang (Eds.), Research in Computational Molecular Biology. XVI, 550 pages. 2007. (Sublibrary LNBI).

Vol. 4452: M. Fasli, O. Shehory (Eds.), Agent-Mediated Electronic Commerce. VIII, 249 pages. 2007. (Sublibrary LNAI).

Vol. 4450: T. Okamoto, X. Wang (Eds.), Public Key Cryptography – PKC 2007. XIII, 491 pages. 2007.

Vol. 4448: M. Giacobini et al. (Ed.), Applications of Evolutionary Computing. XXIII, 755 pages. 2007.

Vol. 4447: E. Marchiori, J.H. Moore, J.C. Rajapakse (Eds.), Evolutionary Computation,Machine Learning and Data Mining in Bioinformatics. XI, 302 pages. 2007.

Vol. 4446: C. Cotta, J. van Hemert (Eds.), Evolutionary Computation in Combinatorial Optimization. XII, 241 pages. 2007.

Vol. 4445: M. Ebner, M. O'Neill, A. Ekárt, L. Vanneschi, A.I. Esparcia-Alcázar (Eds.), Genetic Programming. XI, 382 pages. 2007.

Vol. 4444: T. Reps, M. Sagiv, J. Bauer (Eds.), Program Analysis and Compilation, Theory and Practice. X, 361 pages. 2007.

Vol. 4443: R. Kotagiri, P.R. Krishna, M. Mohania, E. Nantajeewarawat (Eds.), Advances in Databases: Concepts, Systems and Applications. XXI, 1126 pages. 2007.

Vol. 4440: B. Liblit, Cooperative Bug Isolation. XV, 101 pages. 2007.

Vol. 4439: W. Abramowicz (Ed.), Business Information Systems. XV, 654 pages. 2007.

Vol. 4438: L. Maicher, A. Sigel, L.M. Garshol (Eds.), Leveraging the Semantics of Topic Maps. X, 257 pages. 2007. (Sublibrary LNAI).

Vol. 4433: E. Şahin, W.M. Spears, A.F.T. Winfield (Eds.), Swarm Robotics. XII, 221 pages. 2007.

Vol. 4432: B. Beliczynski, A. Dzielinski, M. Iwanowski, B. Ribeiro (Eds.), Adaptive and Natural Computing Algorithms, Part II. XXVI, 761 pages. 2007.

Vol. 4431: B. Beliczynski, A. Dzielinski, M. Iwanowski, B. Ribeiro (Eds.), Adaptive and Natural Computing Algorithms, Part I. XXV, 851 pages. 2007.

Vol. 4430: C.C. Yang, D. Zeng, M. Chau, K. Chang, Q. Yang, X. Cheng, J. Wang, F.-Y. Wang, H. Chen (Eds.), Intelligence and Security Informatics. XII, 330 pages. 2007.

Vol. 4429: R. Lu, J.H. Siekmann, C. Ullrich (Eds.), Cognitive Systems. X, 161 pages. 2007. (Sublibrary LNAI).

Vol. 4427: S. Uhlig, K. Papagiannaki, O. Bonaventure (Eds.), Passive and Active Network Measurement. XI, 274 pages. 2007.

Vol. 4426: Z.-H. Zhou, H. Li, Q. Yang (Eds.), Advances in Knowledge Discovery and Data Mining. XXV, 1161 pages. 2007. (Sublibrary LNAI).

Vol. 4425: G. Amati, C. Carpineto, G. Romano (Eds.), Advances in Information Retrieval. XIX, 759 pages. 2007.

Vol. 4424: O. Grumberg, M. Huth (Eds.), Tools and Algorithms for the Construction and Analysis of Systems. XX, 738 pages. 2007.

Vol. 4423. H. Seidl (Ed.), Foundations of Software Science and Computational Structures. XVI, 379 pages. 2007.

Vol. 4422: M.B. Dwyer, A. Lopes (Eds.), Fundamental Approaches to Software Engineering. XV, 440 pages. 2007.

Vol. 4421: R. De Nicola (Ed.), Programming Languages and Systems. XVII, 538 pages. 2007.

Vol. 4420: S. Krishnamurthi, M. Odersky (Eds.), Compiler Construction. XIV, 233 pages. 2007.

Vol. 4419: P.C. Diniz, E. Marques, K. Bertels, M.M. Fernandes, J.M.P. Cardoso (Eds.), Reconfigurable Computing: Architectures, Tools and Applications. XIV, 391 pages. 2007.

Vol. 4418: A. Gagalowicz, W. Philips (Eds.), Computer Vision/Computer Graphics Collaboration Techniques. XV, 620 pages. 2007.

Vol. 4416: A. Bemporad, A. Bicchi, G. Buttazzo (Eds.), Hybrid Systems: Computation and Control. XVII, 797 pages. 2007.

Vol. 4415: P. Lukowicz, L. Thiele, G. Tröster (Eds.), Architecture of Computing Systems - ARCS 2007. X, 297 pages. 2007.

Vol. 4414: S. Hochreiter, R. Wagner (Eds.), Bioinformatics Research and Development. XVI, 482 pages. 2007. (Sublibrary LNBI).

Vol. 4412: F. Stajano, H.J. Kim, J.-S. Chae, S.-D. Kim (Eds.), Ubiquitous Convergence Technology. XI, 302 pages. 2007.

Vol. 4411: R.H. Bordini, M. Dastani, J. Dix, A.E.F. Seghrouchni (Eds.), Programming Multi-Agent Systems. XIV, 249 pages. 2007. (Sublibrary LNAI).

Vol. 4410: A. Branco (Ed.), Anaphora: Analysis, Algorithms and Applications. X, 191 pages. 2007. (Sublibrary LNAI).

Vol. 4409: J.L. Fiadeiro, P.-Y. Schobbens (Eds.), Recent Trends in Algebraic Development Techniques. VII, 171 pages. 2007.

Vol. 4407: G. Puebla (Ed.), Logic-Based Program Synthesis and Transformation. VIII, 237 pages. 2007.

Vol. 4406: W. De Meuter (Ed.), Advances in Smalltalk. VII, 157 pages. 2007.

Vol. 4405: L. Padgham, F. Zambonelli (Eds.), Agent-Oriented Software Engineering VII. XII, 225 pages. 2007.

Vol. 4403: S. Obayashi, K. Deb, C. Poloni, T. Hiroyasu, T. Murata (Eds.), Evolutionary Multi-Criterion Optimization. XIX, 954 pages. 2007.

Vol. 4401: N. Guelfi, D. Buchs (Eds.), Rapid Integration of Software Engineering Techniques. IX, 177 pages. 2007.

Vol. 4400: J.F. Peters, A. Skowron, V.W. Marek, E. Orłowska, R. Słowiński, W. Ziarko (Eds.), Transactions on Rough Sets VII, Part II. X, 381 pages. 2007.

Vol. 4399: T. Kovacs, X. Llorà, K. Takadama, P.L. Lanzi, W. Stolzmann, S.W. Wilson (Eds.), Learning Classifier Systems. XII, 345 pages. 2007. (Sublibrary LNAI).

Vol. 4398: S. Marchand-Maillet, E. Bruno, A. Nürnberger, M. Detyniecki (Eds.), Adaptive Multimedia Retrieval: User, Context, and Feedback. XI, 269 pages. 2007.

Vol. 4397: C. Stephanidis, M. Pieper (Eds.), Universal Access in Ambient Intelligence Environments. XV, 467 pages. 2007.

Vol. 4396: J. García-Vidal, L. Cerdà-Alabern (Eds.), Wireless Systems and Mobility in Next Generation Internet. IX, 271 pages. 2007.

Vol. 4395: M. Daydé, J.M.L.M. Palma, Á.L.G.A. Coutinho, E. Pacitti, J.C. Lopes (Eds.), High Performance Computing for Computational Science - VECPAR 2006. XXIV, 721 pages. 2007.

Vol. 4394: A. Gelbukh (Ed.), Computational Linguistics and Intelligent Text Processing. XVI, 648 pages. 2007.

Vol. 4393: W. Thomas, P. Weil (Eds.), STACS 2007. XVIII, 708 pages. 2007.

Vol. 4392: S.P. Vadhan (Ed.), Theory of Cryptography. XI, 595 pages. 2007.

Vol. 4391: Y. Stylianou, M. Faundez-Zanuy, A. Esposito (Eds.), Progress in Nonlinear Speech Processing. XII, 269 pages. 2007.

Vol. 4390: S.O. Kuznetsov, S. Schmidt (Eds.), Formal Concept Analysis. X, 329 pages. 2007. (Sublibrary LNAI).

Vol. 4389: D. Weyns, H.V.D. Parunak, F. Michel (Eds.), Environments for Multi-Agent Systems III. X, 273 pages. 2007. (Sublibrary LNAI).

Vol. 4385: K. Coninx, K. Luyten, K.A. Schneider (Eds.), Task Models and Diagrams for Users Interface Design. XI, 355 pages. 2007.

Vol. 4384: T. Washio, K. Satoh, H. Takeda, A. Inokuchi (Eds.), New Frontiers in Artificial Intelligence. IX, 401 pages. 2007. (Sublibrary LNAI).

Vol. 4383: E. Bin, A. Ziv, S. Ur (Eds.), Hardware and Software, Verification and Testing. XII, 235 pages. 2007.

Vol. 4381: J. Akiyama, W.Y.C. Chen, M. Kano, X. Li, Q. Yu (Eds.), Discrete Geometry, Combinatorics and Graph Theory. XI, 289 pages. 2007.

Vol. 4380: S. Spaccapietra, P. Atzeni, F. Fages, M.-S. Hacid, M. Kifer, J. Mylopoulos, B. Pernici, P. Shvaiko, J. Trujillo, I. Zaihrayeu (Eds.), Journal on Data Semantics VIII. XV, 219 pages. 2007.

Vol. 4379: M. Südholt, C. Consel (Eds.), Object-Oriented Technology. VIII, 157 pages. 2007.

Vol. 4378: I. Virbitskaite, A. Voronkov (Eds.), Perspectives of Systems Informatics. XIV, 496 pages. 2007.

Vol. 4377: M. Abe (Ed.), Topics in Cryptology – CT-RSA 2007. XI, 403 pages. 2006.

Vol. 4376: E. Frachtenberg, U. Schwiegelshohn (Eds.), Job Scheduling Strategies for Parallel Processing. VII, 257 pages. 2007.

Vol. 4374: J.F. Peters, A. Skowron, I. Düntsch, J. Grzymała-Busse, E. Orłowska, L. Polkowski (Eds.), Transactions on Rough Sets VI, Part I. XII, 499 pages. 2007.

Vol. 4373: K. Langendoen, T. Voigt (Eds.), Wireless Sensor Networks. XIII, 358 pages. 2007.